Embedded Systems with .NET nanoFramework

Practical, Hands-On C# for Microcontrollers: Building Resource-Constrained IoT Devices from Peripherals to CloudMaster

José Simões

Apress®

Embedded Systems with .NET nanoFramework: Practical, Hands-On C# for Microcontrollers: Building Resource-Constrained IoT Devices from Peripherals to CloudMaster

José Simões
Leiria, Portugal

ISBN-13 (pbk): 979-8-8688-2095-3
ISBN-13 (electronic): 979-8-8688-2096-0
https://doi.org/10.1007/979-8-8688-2096-0

Managing Director, Apress Media LLC: Welmoed Spahr
Acquisitions Editor: Ryan Byrnes
Coordinating Editor: Gryffin Winkler

Cover image by Unsplash.com

Distributed to the book trade worldwide by Springer Science+Business Media New York, 1 New York Plaza, New York, NY 10004. Phone 1-800-SPRINGER, fax (201) 348-4505, e-mail orders-ny@springer-sbm.com, or visit www.springeronline.com. Apress Media, LLC is a Delaware LLC and the sole member (owner) is Springer Science + Business Media Finance Inc (SSBM Finance Inc). SSBM Finance Inc is a **Delaware** corporation.

For information on translations, please e-mail booktranslations@springernature.com; for reprint, paperback, or audio rights, please e-mail bookpermissions@springernature.com.

Apress titles may be purchased in bulk for academic, corporate, or promotional use. eBook versions and licenses are also available for most titles. For more information, reference our Print and eBook Bulk Sales web page at http://www.apress.com/bulk-sales.

Any source code or other supplementary material referenced by the author in this book is available to readers on GitHub (https://github.com/Apress). For more detailed information, please visit https://www.apress.com/gp/services/source-code.

If disposing of this product, please recycle the paper

To the nanoFramework community, particularly the Core Team. The project wouldn't be where it is today without the great contributions from everyone involved.

Table of Contents

About the Author

José Simões is the CEO of Eclo Solutions, a software consulting company in Leiria, Portugal. He is the founder and core team lead of .NET nanoFramework, an open-source project that allows programming in C# for microcontrollers. He was awarded Microsoft MVP five times for his work on Internet of Things (IoT) and developer technologies. He has shipped projects across embedded firmware, hardware design, and cloud-connected products, with a toolbox that includes .NET and Azure technologies alongside C, C++, microcontrollers, and electronics.

About the Technical Reviewer

Fabio Claudio Ferracchiati is a senior consultant and senior analyst/developer specializing in Microsoft technologies. He currently works at Telecom Italia (`www.telecomitalia.it`). Fabio holds several Microsoft certifications, including Microsoft Certified Solutions Developer (MCSD) for .NET, Microsoft Certified Application Developer (MCAD) for .NET, and Microsoft Certified Professional (MCP). He is also a prolific author and technical reviewer. Over the past decade, he has contributed numerous articles to both Italian and international technology magazines and has coauthored more than 10 books covering a wide range of computing topics.

Acknowledgments

I am grateful to many individuals for their support regarding this book and the .NET nanoFramework project.

I would like to thank Apress for inviting me to write this book and for providing the opportunity to spread the word about .NET nanoFramework.

Special thanks to Ryan Byrnes for initiating contact, guiding me throughout the process, consistently offering help, and being very patient with me. I also appreciate Nirmal Selvaraj, the production editor, for effectively coordinating all aspects and ensuring seamless execution. Thanks are due to Fabio Claudio Ferracchiati, the technical reviewer, who brilliantly pointed out inconsistencies, highlighted areas for improvement, and identified the inevitable bugs in code samples.

Acknowledgment is also due to Zan Gligorov, CEO at OrgPal, a pioneer in adopting .NET nanoFramework in production and a long-time supporter of the project. His generous provision of hardware used in several chapters allowed enriched learning experiences and insights from the real-world industry, and his assistance in reviewing the content improved the quality of this work and was always an inspiration.

I recognize Laurent Ellerbach, principal software engineering manager at Microsoft. He is a brilliant mind and a key member of the nanoFramework core team. He was always there to assist, discuss the next bold idea, or help one to get unstuck on a coding challenge. Overall, he is an invaluable contributor to the success of nanoFramework and reviewed several chapters and provided great feedback, particularly the chapter about MCP.

Additionally, Sander van de Velde, principal IoT architect at SDG Group and fellow IoT MVP, brought exceptional knowledge and enthusiasm to this book with insightful suggestions and practical improvements. He kindly and promptly reviewed all chapters, delivering valuable feedback from a reader's perspective.

I am very grateful to several members of the nanoFramework community and core team for their encouragement and support. You'll forgive me that I won't mention names to avoid unintentionally omitting anyone. When you read this, you'll know this is meant for you. As I keep saying: every contribution—whether it's sharing a helpful tip, answering a question, writing a library, or simply welcoming someone new, is valuable and makes a difference.

Finally, my deepest appreciation goes to my lovely wife Lau, who is always beside me every step of the way. She has been unwaveringly supportive and patient with the (immense!) amount of time I keep dedicating to these matters, always encouraging me and celebrating every milestone with me. To my eldest son, Diogo, for his encouragement from the very beginning to write this book. To my youngest son, Francisco, whose quiet presence beside me on the couch made long nights of writing and coding feel less lonely. And to my parents, for serving as enduring inspiration and role models.

Introduction

When I think about .NET nanoFramework, I am often reminded that we are standing on the shoulders of giants. It was a bold and impressive engineering feat to create .NET running on resource-constrained microcontrollers back in 2001. Not only was the concept innovative, but the attention to detail in the codebase is still evident today. Many parts of that original code are still in use or have evolved into what we rely on now. Today we have the luxury of a couple of megabytes of flash and some generous kilobytes of RAM, whereas in 2001, developers had to work with only a few hundred kilobytes of flash and minimal RAM.

We have come a long way since those days. However, the concept remains valid and is still perfectly adequate for many industry applications, educational scenarios, and even maker or hobbyist projects. Despite a growing range of increasingly cheap (and powerful, computation-wise) hardware platforms, we don't always need 8 cores and 16 gigabytes (GB) of RAM to tackle all the embedded or IoT projects that come to us. In addition, for most of those hardware platforms, we always need to start from the ground up, configuring a lot of stuff before we can actually code something useful. For example, setting up a Raspberry Pi for a simple sensor project often requires configuring the operating system, installing libraries, and troubleshooting issues before any coding can begin. And, when reaching that stage, making significant changes is not always easy. Additionally, transitioning to another platform due to changing requirements can be challenging and time-consuming.

The .NET nanoFramework proposal is to abstract all the complicated and low-level details that need to be mastered for any average embedded systems project and let the developer (and the team) focus on the task at hand. A proof of concept for any medium to averagely complex device is perfectly doable from just hours to a few working days, depending on the complexity. For example, setting up an ESP32 module on a breadboard connected to a BME280 sensor, sampling temperature, barometric pressure, and humidity and sending those readings to a cloud service shouldn't take you more than a couple of hours, without having to get familiar with the fine details of a new microcontroller series and digest the product manual. After a few weeks into the project, the customer changes the requirements or even the specs, which dictates a completely different platform. No problem, .NET nanoFramework makes this transition seamless. Most likely 95% of your code doesn't have to be rewritten. At most, you'll have to adjust small portions that are platform specific. This approach greatly enhances productivity and efficiency.

This is a disruptive approach to the common embedded systems development, usually based in C and C++. It brings the advantages of a managed language (C#) to the embedded world, along with the benefits of the .NET ecosystem. Any average .NET developer can all of a sudden become proficient with these matters. Developers don't need an electronics degree to understand what they are doing. Providing training on basic concepts is often all they need to get their mind into the matter and start being productive. The platform offers top-notch coding tools and enables code reuse from project to project and even different platforms. A bunch of libraries distributed as NuGet packages are ready to just "add a reference to." You get a unique debugging experience running correctly on the real device with a simple USB cable. You get real breakpoints, control execution flow, inspect, and watch and set variables. You also get unit test tools and virtual devices that allow testing code without physical hardware, speeding up the development cycles and reducing costs. Not to mention you get top-notch CI/CD tools and scripts. It is also multivendor and multiplatform. The list could go on and on.

It is worth pointing out that .NET nanoFramework doesn't present itself as the holy grail of embedded development and doesn't claim or pretend to replace the current technological offer available in the industry. If you want to use the infamous LED blinking test for performance comparison, you won't be impressed. But then again, if you want to toggle a GPIO, you don't need a microcontroller to do that, right? .NET nanoFramework excels when projects require more complex logic or integration with higher-level programming concepts. At the end of day, it lowers the complexity bar, thus decreasing the level of specialization requirements for developers and broadening its usage.

Beyond the individual developer, .NET nanoFramework also offers significant benefits for organizations and teams. It allows, for example, small to midsize OEM companies that traditionally outsource these projects to start having their own development team in house. Regardless of any project size or complexity, this decreases the development cycle count and overall development time, thus decreasing the time to market (and development costs). It also makes maintenance and support for shipped products much easier. Even for large teams, this empowers them to collect experience and pile up building blocks that can be reused repeatedly on new projects. This can make them more agile and capable of handling complex projects in a more efficient way and quickly delivering them. It also suits pretty much every use case. For example, it streamlines the development of industrial automation systems, enhances remote monitoring with IoT sensors in agriculture, provides complex industrial controllers, and upgrades a vending machine to the next generation with new features. Just pick your use case.

Adding to all this, C# is an excellent language for learning to code, making it a great choice for educational paths. Therefore, nanoFramework is perfectly suited for aspiring developers, regardless of their current skill level or the complexity of the course they choose.

Even for the hobbyist/maker tackling the occasional sprinkler project in their garage, nanoFramework offers a smooth path to accomplish a lot with few resources.

Additionally, .NET nanoFramework is architectured in such a way that developers and companies can choose the most suitable entry point for their needs. If you are starting a new project, you can simply select the traditional Project > New menu and begin coding right away. However, if you are developing a complex industrial solution, you have the flexibility to access lower layers and easily adapt the framework to that new hardware or platform.

This book covers everything from the architecture and build system to abstraction layers, culminating in the C# libraries that expose APIs for common embedded system building blocks. In the middle of the book, we'll delve into architecture and coding a complete embedded system with a real-world usage scenario. This book includes notes and key points on practical aspects of embedded systems projects. Networking and connectivity have their own chapter, where you'll discover the full range of nanoFramework features, from the widely used TCP/IP sockets and HTTP client to advanced options like MQTT and LoRa for IoT applications. And, as we move to the end of the book, we'll go through advanced coding topics, raising the bar on quality by leveraging unit and integration tests. To wrap up, AI is all around us, so there is a final chapter dedicated to the Machine Communication Protocol (MCP). We'll dive into this new technology and learn how to connect your .NET nanoFramework device to the *Intelligent* Internet of Things (IIoT).

This book is designed for developers, engineering managers, and SMB owners alike, providing practical advice, real examples, and insights into how nanoFramework can help your team work more efficiently and deliver high-quality projects quickly.

I am confident you will find valuable insights and practical guidance throughout this book!

CHAPTER 1

Origins and Initial Concept

In this initial chapter we'll take a brief look at the origins of .NET nanoFramework, how it started, the motivations behind it, and the initial vision that drove the founders.

Going Back in Time

.NET nanoFramework is a spin-off of Microsoft's .NET Micro Framework (.NETMF for friends). It's worth taking a moment to understand the original work and what motivated it.

All this started at Microsoft Research with the Smart Personal Object Technology (SPOT) project. In 2001, David Massarenti developed a proof-of-concept of a shrunken EMCA-compliant CLR, called the TinyCLR. This happened pretty much in line with the last stage of development of the "full" .NET, of which v1.0 was released in 2002.

.NETMF v1.0 was presented officially by Collin Miller at the 2006 Mobile and Embedded Developers Conference (in Boston) running on a Sumo robot. From there on, there were several releases: v2.0 in 2007, v3.0 in late 2008, and v4.0 by the end of 2009.

At that time, Microsoft released the source code to the developer community (through CodePlex) as free and open-source software. In March 2015, the code repository moved to GitHub, and the last official release, v4.4, dates from October 2015.

What Was the Need?

.NETMF—the predecessor of .NET nanoFramework—was a small and efficient .NET runtime capable of running managed code on resource-constrained devices.

J. Simões, *Embedded Systems with .NET nanoFramework*, https://doi.org/10.1007/979-8-8688-2096-0_1

This allowed Microsoft to deliver the vision of ".NET runs everywhere" as Windows CE and .NET Compact Framework were too big to fit on such small devices. Yet, the development workflow was (and keeps being) the same as any other .NET project.

Developers write their applications using Visual Studio, make use of NuGet packages, deploy them, and start a debug session by simply pressing F5. This provides a tremendous debugging experience, allowing developers to set breakpoints, inspect variables, and step through code just as they would with any other .NET application.

This seamless integration with Visual Studio makes the development process more efficient and accessible, even for those who may not have extensive experience with embedded systems.

Because of the Hardware Abstraction Layer (HAL) and Platform Abstraction Layer (PAL), which we will discuss in detail in the next chapter, the hardware intricacies are abstracted. Peripherals are presented as objects and expose a coherent, intelligible, and easy-to-understand API and properties.

This abstraction allows developers to focus on the application logic rather than the underlying hardware details. For example, instead of dealing with low-level register configurations, developers can interact with peripherals like GPIO, I^2C, and SPI through high-level APIs. This not only simplifies the development process but also makes the code more portable across different hardware platforms.

In the next chapters, we'll dive deeper into other details of this approach to embedded systems development. We will explore topics such as memory management, real-time constraints, and power consumption, which are critical considerations for embedded systems.

Additionally, we will discuss the various tools and libraries available for .NET nanoFramework, including how to leverage them to build robust and efficient connected (or stand-alone) applications. By understanding these aspects, developers can make informed decisions and effectively utilize .NET nanoFramework for their embedded projects.

Traditional Embedded Development

The traditional approach for an embedded system project was (and still is for a vast majority of projects) to write it using C, C++, and assembly. This method is challenging because it requires a significant amount of expertise in low-level programming languages and hardware-specific knowledge.

Developers need to understand the intricacies of memory management, interrupt handling, and real-time constraints, which calls for a team of specialized developers. These developers are expensive and not abundant on the market, making it difficult for many companies to find the right talent.

Moreover, the tools and Integrated Development Environments (IDEs) used for embedded system development aren't easy to use. Each vendor tends to have their own set of tools, which can vary significantly in terms of functionality and user experience.

For example, one vendor might provide a comprehensive IDE with debugging capabilities, while another might offer only basic tools that require additional external hardware for debugging.

Each microcontroller series has a specific software development kit (SDK) and minutiae that developers need to learn and understand, adding to the complexity of the development process.

In what concerns hardware, the cost is absolutely variable. The price of hardware components can range from inexpensive to very costly, depending on the vendor and the complexity of the board.

If there is a readily available evaluation board for the target microcontroller, it can significantly reduce development time and cost. However, some projects may require custom hardware, which can be expensive to design and manufacture.

Additionally, some evaluation boards include debugging capabilities, while others require external hardware to connect the debugger interface. This variability in hardware costs and capabilities can make budgeting and planning for embedded system projects quite challenging.

Motivation and Driving Forces

With the release of .NETMF as open-source software, a community of developers started to gravitate toward the GitHub organization.

They started to submit pull requests, raise issues, and continue work on the project, driven by a couple of developers from the original Microsoft team. Despite that, to the outside world, there was no real team working on the project and no visible coordination, let alone willingness to embrace "outsiders" in the closed circle.

In August 2016, following several informal contacts with other community members, I led an initiative presenting the feedback from the community about the project governance, what didn't feel right, and providing pointers on what should be improved:

namely, the need to involve the community, set goals, and discuss the future of the project. It took the form of a GitHub issue and was named "Manifest for .NETMF (the current state and the future we want for it)."

In parallel with this public initiative, several other informal and not visible approaches were put underway to make things change for the better.

Despite all the conversations that generated from these initiatives, not much changed in the months following that initiative.

In November 2016, the matter was brought up again, and I made another attempt to point out what wasn't working on the project and urging the person in charge to let community people in and open the project. Once again, several developers stepped into the conversation, but in the end things remained at the same pace and style.

Based on the conviction that .NETMF was a truly unique approach to embedded systems development and that it would be a complete shame to let it remain in its current agony until it was nothing more than an abandoned repository, I decided to take the matter into my own hands.

From several years of using it in my daily job (and also for personal use in maker and hobby projects), opening and replying to issues in GitHub, and occasionally interacting with other developers, I was very much aware of the existing pain points plaguing the project and what limitations the current architecture imposed. Several months before that, I started working on several proofs-of-concept to deal with some of the identified problems.

All things considered, the decision to spin off .NET Micro Framework started to become very clear in my mind.

The Core Team

It's easy to understand that the amount of work involved in tackling all this was considerable! Add to that the will to gather different sensibilities, involve more developers, split work, and take advantage of peer support.

All this called for a team to undergo this effort. Therefore, I reached out to developers who publicly expressed their support for a shift in the project governance and who expressed their willingness to actively participate.

The initial team was composed of myself and (in alphabetic order) Peter Wessel, Robin Jones, and two other developers (who preferred to remain anonymous) who left the project after some time. Later, Adrian Soundy joined the team. Last but not the least, Laurent Ellerbach joined the .NET nanoFramework Core team.

Naming the Project

Naming is always a tough task! There are too many things to consider, like how to properly convey the idea behind it, how to (try) to be unique, and how to make people aware of the intention.

Despite being a spin-off of .NETMF, the project team wanted to keep its origins very clear, and no effort was made to mask where it came from, along with the intention of being the "next generation" and carrying the torch of the C# embedded development framework, not to mention the close connection to the .NET ecosystem where it necessarily belongs.

If the predecessor was micro, one of the goals was to make it possible to target even more constrained devices, so why not the next submultiple in the scale? That stuck, and so it become *nanoFramework* (all one word, starting with lowercase to emphasize the intent to target constrained devices).

Revamping the Build System and the Codebase

The weaknesses of .NETMF were clearly identified, and the choice to address them was made and prioritized. In addition, a few other tasks were added to the to-do list.

One of the basic ones was the build system. The existing system was completely based on MSBuild, which is great for Visual Studio and .NET but totally inadequate for embedded systems. Building .NETMF was a complete pain (there was even a joke about this, that the ones able accomplish it should be entitled to a medal), not to mention that extending it or changing it was a feat by itself.

The decision was made to split the monolithic build and make use of more appropriate tools for each component/tool.

Regarding the codebase, a serious cleanup was in order. There were parts clearly over-engineered, others begging for simplification, and others completely unused.

CLR and Firmware

For the CLR (the firmware to flash the microcontroller with), the decision was made to use the open-source ARM GCC toolchain.

This toolchain is pretty much a standard for embedded systems these days and is vastly supported by most, if not all, microcontroller manufacturers.

The ARM GCC toolchain provides a robust and efficient set of tools for compiling and debugging code, making it an ideal choice for developing firmware for microcontrollers. Its widespread acceptance and support ensure that developers can rely on a consistent and reliable toolchain.

The decision to use the ARM GCC toolchain was driven by several factors. First, it is open-source. Second, it is compatible with a wide range of microcontrollers ensuring the .NET nanoFramework can be deployed across various hardware platforms without requiring significant modifications to the codebase.

For the build system, CMake was the winner. CMake is a modern build system that is much easier to work with than the old `make` (which was initially considered) and has gained great momentum and acceptance in the embedded world.

CMake provides a powerful and flexible framework for managing build configurations, simplifying the process of setting up and maintaining build environments. Its modular and extensible design makes it easy to add support for new hardware and software components without requiring extensive modifications to the core framework.

Using CMake as the build system offers several advantages. First, it simplifies the build process by providing a standardized and well-documented framework for managing build configurations.

This reduces the time and effort required to set up and maintain build environments, making it easier for developers to work with different platforms and SDKs. Second, its flexibility and extensibility allow for better integration with external components and vendor SDKs, enabling developers to leverage existing libraries and tools provided by hardware vendors.

Class Libraries

For the class libraries, this was a no-brainer; the obvious choice was Visual Studio solutions and *msbuild*.

Breaking from the previous build and release strategy, it was decided to split the class libraries completely. This means that instead of a simultaneous release of all class libraries, each individual library has its own release cycle, which is independent of the others, except for the ones it references, of course. This approach allows for greater flexibility and agility in the development process.

Each library can be updated, tested, and released independently, ensuring that changes in one library do not impact the others. This modularity also makes it easier to manage dependencies and maintain the codebase.

As part of this work, the base class library was shrunk by extracting all the namespaces that didn't need to be there into their own libraries.

The end result was a much smaller `mscorlib`, which allowed the deployment in devices with less flash and RAM. This optimization is crucial for resource-constrained devices, as it reduces the memory footprint and improves performance. By separating the namespaces into individual libraries, developers can include only the necessary components in their projects, further minimizing resource usage.

Class libraries are distributed as NuGet packages, just like any other .NET library. Additionally, NuGet packages can be hosted on public or private repositories, providing flexibility in how libraries are shared and distributed.

Tools

The same goes for the various tools that are required by the project, namely, the metadata processor (more or this in the coming chapter), the Visual Studio extension, and other CLR tools that were added to the project's toolbox as the need for them was identified.

A Single Toolchain

It was decided that support for compilers other than GCC would be dropped.

The previous approach was to support various toolchains, which made the implementation and maintenance much harder without any tangible benefits. Supporting multiple toolchains required significant effort to ensure compatibility and consistency across different compilers. This also requires testing, debugging, and optimization for each toolchain, which consumes valuable resources and time.

By focusing on a single toolchain, specifically the GCC toolchain, the team could streamline the development process and reduce the complexity of maintaining the codebase. GCC is a widely accepted standard for embedded systems and is supported by most, if not all, microcontroller manufacturers.

This choice provided several advantages, including better performance, reliability, and ease of use.

Additionally, focusing on a single toolchain enabled optimization on the build system and improved the overall efficiency of the development process.

Multiple Platforms

One of the goals was to target multiple platforms to make .NET nanoFramework more attractive to the embedded systems world and allow for easier reuse of code from one project to the next.

This goal required significant changes in the existing architecture and build system to ensure compatibility and flexibility across various hardware platforms.

Using CMake as the build system already put it within reach for the average developer. It simplifies the process of setting up and maintaining build environments, making it easier for developers to work with different platforms and SDKs.

Great care was put into the build system to make it as easy as possible to port .NET nanoFramework to new platforms and new SDKs and to bring in external components and vendor SDKs.

This involved designing the build system to be modular and extensible, allowing developers to add support for new hardware and software components without requiring extensive modifications.

By providing a modern and self-documented build process, the team ensured that developers could quickly and efficiently adapt .NET nanoFramework to their specific needs.

The modularity of the build system also allows for better integration with external components and vendor SDKs. This means that developers can leverage existing libraries and tools provided by hardware vendors, reducing the time and effort required to develop and maintain custom solutions.

A Self-Contained CLR

Another goal was to be able to build the Common Language Runtime (CLR), the interface to the Hardware Abstraction Layer (HAL), and the Platform Abstraction Layer (PAL) completely agnostic of the hardware it was running on.

This was accomplished by rearranging and refactoring so it could be built as a C++ library. The goal was attained, and this portability remains as one of the key aspects of the architecture.

The same C++ code can be built by GCC and run on a microcontroller or be built by VC++ and run on 64-bit platforms. This flexibility is crucial for ensuring that nanoFramework can be deployed across a wide range of hardware platforms without requiring significant modifications to the codebase. By using a C++ library, the CLR can be compiled and executed on different architectures, making it highly portable and adaptable to various environments.

The latter is the one that is used on the virtual nanoCLR. The virtual nanoCLR is a simulation environment that allows developers to test and debug their applications on a virtual platform before deploying them to actual hardware.

This virtual environment provides a convenient and efficient way to validate the functionality of the application and identify any potential issues. By using the same C++ code for both the virtual and physical environments, developers can ensure consistency and reliability across different platforms.

This enhances the portability of .NET nanoFramework, allowing it to be used on a wide range of devices, from small microcontrollers to powerful 64-bit platforms (if needed). This flexibility makes .NET nanoFramework an attractive option for various embedded systems projects.

RTOS Is a Must-Have

Another architectural breaking change from .NETMF was the decision to rely on a real-time operating system (RTOS).

By leveraging the features offered by a typical RTOS, a lot of things could be improved and others made so much easier. Let's delve into some of these improvements in detail.

As a starting point, we have the Common Language Runtime (CLR) running on an RTOS thread and the Wire Protocol handler on another (more on this in the next section). This separation allows for better management of tasks and ensures that each component operates efficiently without interfering with the others. Unlike its predecessor, the similar features for task management were part of the CLR.

Of course, other RTOS features are also used, which we'll look into with more detail in the following chapter.

Because of this requirement for an RTOS, the CMake build system was written in such a way that there is a glue layer to the RTOS and the services it offers.

This glue layer provides a standardized interface for interacting with the RTOS, allowing developers to leverage its features without having to deal with the intricacies of the underlying implementation. This approach also allows for a relatively easy path to bring in support for new and different RTOSs, which honors the goal of openness of the project.

By abstracting the RTOS-specific details, nanoFramework can be ported to various hardware platforms and RTOSs, ensuring flexibility and scalability.

Overall, the decision to rely on an RTOS has significantly improved the architecture of nanoFramework.

By leveraging the features of an RTOS, the system can handle complex tasks more efficiently, provide better resource management, and ensure smooth and concurrent execution of threads. This architectural change has made nanoFramework more robust and adaptable, paving the way for its adoption in a wide range of embedded systems projects.

Wire Protocol

A key component is the Wire Protocol, which is responsible for communication with the outside world.

This protocol plays a crucial role in enabling seamless interaction between the nanoFramework devices and various tools, including the Visual Studio debugger. During a debug session, the Wire Protocol facilitates communication with the Visual Studio debugger, allowing developers to inspect and analyze their code running on the microcontroller. This interaction is essential for identifying and fixing issues, ensuring that the application runs smoothly on the target device.

In addition to debugging, the Wire Protocol is used by Visual Studio and other tools to query the device capabilities. This includes retrieving information about the hardware specifications, available peripherals, and supported features. The protocol also enables the deployment of managed applications to the nanoFramework devices.

This process involves transferring the compiled application code from the development environment to the target device, where it can be executed.

Furthermore, the Wire Protocol allows for various device management operations, such as rebooting the device. This is particularly useful during development and testing, as it provides a convenient way to restart the device and apply changes without manual intervention. The ability to perform these operations programmatically enhances the efficiency and flexibility of the development process.

The native code of the Wire Protocol component was completely rewritten in C to allow better reuse across different platforms.

This rewrite aimed to make the protocol more versatile and adaptable, enabling it to be easily integrated with various transport channels, such as UART, USB, or even network connections.

By using C, the protocol can be compiled and executed on a wide range of hardware platforms, ensuring compatibility and performance.

The choice of C also allows for low-level optimizations, making the protocol more efficient and responsive.

Visual Studio Extension

The Visual Studio extension was completely rewritten to make use of the more modern Visual Studio extensibility SDK and WPF visual style.

This update was aimed at enhancing the overall developer experience and usability, which were chief concerns throughout this work.

The modern SDK provides a more robust and flexible framework for developing extensions, allowing for better integration with Visual Studio and improved performance. The WPF visual style offers a more polished and user-friendly interface, making it easier for developers to navigate and use the extension.

The main interface with nanoFramework devices became the Device Explorer. This is a modern interface on which the main view presents the devices connected in a tree view style.

This allows developers to select each device individually, interact with them, and perform various operations. For example, developers can request device capabilities, reboot devices, store certificates, and configure network settings.

The tree view style provides a clear and organized way to manage multiple devices, making it easier to keep track of their status and perform necessary actions.

Another significant improvement was the implementation of automatic detection of nanoFramework devices as they are connected and disconnected from the computer. This feature streamlines the development process by eliminating the need for manual device management.

As soon as a nanoFramework device is connected to the computer, it is automatically detected and added to the Device Explorer. Similarly, when a device is disconnected, it is automatically removed from the list. This automatic detection feature saves time and effort, allowing developers to focus on writing and debugging their code.

A key component of the Visual Studio extension is the debugger, which allows debugging C# code running on the microcontroller.

The debugger provides a comprehensive set of tools for inspecting and analyzing code, including setting breakpoints, stepping through code, and inspecting variables. This allows developers to identify and fix issues quickly and efficiently, ensuring that their applications run smoothly on nanoFramework devices.

The debugger library is fully integrated with Visual Studio debugger, providing a seamless and familiar experience for developers who are already accustomed to using Visual Studio for their .NET projects.

Project System

The modern Visual Studio extensibility SDK included support for customized project systems. However, at the time, there were some shortcomings in the SDK that made it impossible to extend the default C# project (csproj) files to accommodate nanoFramework.

These limitations were primarily related to the way the SDK handled project configurations and dependencies, which were not compatible with the unique requirements of nanoFramework.

Because of these limitations, the team decided to create a specific project extension named *nfproj*. This extension was designed to be compatible and aligned with the so-called CSP "old-style" C# project system. The main difference between the *nfproj* and csproj systems is the extension itself, but *nfproj* retains all the functionalities and features of the traditional C# project system.

The *nfproj* project system is distributed along with the Visual Studio extension, which also offers project templates for executable, class libraries, and unit test projects. These templates provide a starting point for developers, making it easier to set up new projects and ensuring that they follow best practices.

The templates include predefined configurations and settings that are optimized for nanoFramework, reducing the time and effort required to configure projects manually.

CI-CD

Last, but not the least, comes the organization of the project, where the code is stored and the build and distribution of deliverables are handled.

Being an open-source project, GitHub was the clear choice as the home of the project. Everything was set up there with the appropriate repositories with all the bells and whistles. From day one, high concern was put on making developers' lives as easy as possible.

Automating the build and distribution of deliverables was also put in place from the beginning. Contributions and changes (even from the team members) followed the usual GitHub workflow: pull request, review, and merge.

This transparent and collaborative approach allows developers to stay informed about the project's progress and to contribute effectively. Build pipelines from Azure DevOps were added to automate the build of the firmware and the various class libraries. This helped to streamline the process and provide the basic checks for building for the various platforms and microcontroller series.

The approach chosen ensured that every change made to the codebase is automatically tested and deployed, reducing the risk of introducing bugs and improving the overall quality of the code delivered.

Upon merging to the working branch, the pipeline gets triggered again, the build happens, and deliverables are published to either nuget.org (for the class libraries) or to a public binary repository to distribute the firmware packages ready to flash the microcontroller.

Community Gathering Point

As a community-driven project, a gathering point was a must-have. Being an open-source project without any funding, a free and widely accessible tool was necessary.

Back then, associated with GitHub, Gitter was taking its first steps trying to become the *de facto* discussion platform for open-source projects. .NET nanoFramework jumped on the bandwagon, and the first community gathering point where developers could engage in discussions, ask for support, provide feedback, and interact with other developers started.

The choice of Gitter as the community platform was strategic. It allowed for real-time communication and collaboration, which was essential for the project's growth and development. Developers could easily join the conversation, share their ideas, and get immediate responses from other community members. This interactive environment fostered a sense of belonging and encouraged active participation.

Over time the community grew, and the discussions became more diverse and insightful. Regular contributors emerged, and their expertise helped shape the direction of the project. The collaborative nature of the platform ensured that everyone had a voice, and the collective knowledge of the community was leveraged to solve problems and innovate.

Soon after the community moved to Slack and thereafter, following restrictions and features being removed from the free version, another move happened to Discord, were it remains until this date.

Public Announcement

In those few months, frenetic activity took place on the GitHub organization, on Azure DevOps pipelines, and on the Core team members' working machines.

Everyone involved was giving their best and excited to take part in this. Code was written and rewritten, concepts were tested, and components and tools were evaluated to find out if they were the perfect fit for the task at hand.

Things were progressing in a very encouraging way, and by the end of January 2017, the team was confident that very soon, an initial version would be ready to be released to the public for initial widespread testing and feedback. A blog post was made with the announcement, and the word got out about .NET nanoFramework.

During this period, the team faced numerous challenges and obstacles. However, the collaborative spirit and dedication of the members ensured that these hurdles were overcome. The continuous exchange of ideas and feedback helped refine the project and address all the issues that arose. The use of various tools and platforms, such as GitHub and Azure DevOps, played a crucial role in streamlining the development process and maintaining organization.

The excitement and enthusiasm of the team were palpable, and this positive energy was reflected in the quality of the work produced. The project saw significant advancements in a short amount of time, thanks to the relentless efforts of everyone involved.

Project Timeline

The following timeline marks the project's most significant milestones:

- August 2016: Initial movement to spin-off .NETMF
- January 2017: Public announcement of .NET nanoFramework

- December 2017: Visual Studio extension with debugging capabilities
- September 2018: First target with network capabilities (TLS included) wired and wireless
- October 2018: v1.0 released
- April 2019: Support for Visual Studio 2019
- June 2019: Spotted the first commercial product running .NET nanoFramework
- September 2020: Joined the .NET Foundation
- February 2021: Unit test framework released
- August 2021: Azure SDK released
- February 2022: Library for websockets and SignalR
- June 2023: Support added for Azure RTOS (renamed to ThreadX)
- December 2024: 20 million NuGet package downloads
- May 2025: Support added for C# generics

Summary

In this chapter, we explored the origins of .NET nanoFramework.

We delved into the motivations behind its creation, the challenges faced, and the collaborative efforts that drove the project forward. From the early days of .NET Micro Framework to the spin-off that became .NET nanoFramework, we saw how Microsoft Research engineers created TinyCLR so that a robust and efficient framework for embedded systems was available, as well as how the community came together to give new life to the moribund .NETMF.

The journey was filled with excitement, dedication, and a strong sense of purpose, culminating in the public announcement of the initial version.

As we move to the next chapter, we'll dive deeper into the architecture of .NET nanoFramework. We'll explore the design principles, the modularity, and the various components that make up the framework.

Expect to learn about the Common Language Runtime (CLR), the Hardware Abstraction Layer (HAL), and the Platform Abstraction Layer (PAL), among other critical aspects.

This chapter will provide a comprehensive understanding of how .NET nanoFramework is structured and how it achieves its goals of flexibility, scalability, and efficiency.

Additional Information

The following are some URLs where you can find more information about several topics discussed in this chapter.

Press Release from Microsoft about the release of the first developer kit for .NETMF: `https://news.microsoft.com/source/2006/09/26/microsoft-releases-first-broad-beta-developer-kit-for-net-micro-framework/`

Archived GitHub for .NETMF: `https://github.com/netmf`

Archived MSDN documentation about .NETMF: `https://learn.microsoft.com/en-us/previous-versions/windows/embedded/cc533015(v=msdn.10)`

Blog post with the official announcement: `https://nanoframework.net/my-name-is-framework-nanoframework/`

CHAPTER 2

Architecture

This is the first technical chapter in which you'll get an overview of the architecture of .NET nanoFramework, including how the various components are organized, interact, and depend on each other.

Overview

One of the best ways to understand the .NET nanoFramework architecture is to use a layered approach, such as the one in Figure 2-1.

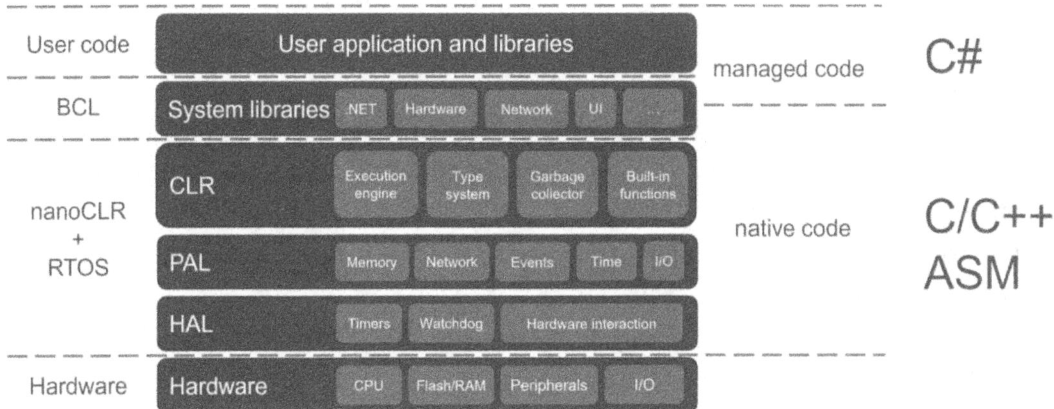

Figure 2-1. *Architecture of .NET nanoFramework*

User Code

At the top is the user code layer. This is code written by developers to implement the features specified in the project and accomplish the required tasks.

J. Simões, *Embedded Systems with .NET nanoFramework*, https://doi.org/10.1007/979-8-8688-2096-0_2

All the layers beneath provide the abstraction needed for a regular .NET C# developer to feel at home. Unless the task at hand requires one to go deep into the hardware details and have some domain-specific knowledge, nothing about the hardware or the platform surfaces and gets in the way of the developer.

All the intricacies and heavily complicated minutia typical of embedded systems like boot, memory, clocks, registers, and peripherals configuration, for example, are way deep in the stack and kept far from developers.

Class Libraries

The base class library (BCL), or core library, along with several other class libraries constitute the building blocks for all the .NET coding.

Much thought was put into having the API aligned as much as possible with the full .NET API. This is paramount not only to allow code reuse from desktop projects but to leverage all the available .NET documentation, samples, code patterns, blog posts, and other information available about .NET and C#.

There are available libraries for string manipulation, math, dependency injection, serialization, GPIOs, and communication with the usual embedded system buses like I^2C, SPI, and serial ports.

These provide networking services like sockets, UDP, TCP, Wi-Fi management, HTTP, WebSockets, SignalR, and connections to cloud providers like Amazon Web Services and various Azure services, namely, IoT Hub.

Libraries specific to each platform expose the specific services and features offered by the hardware or the low-level SDK.

To complete the package, the project offers a repository with a vast (and growing) collection of bindings, providing high-quality drivers for dozens of sensors, chips, displays, motor drivers, modems, communication modules, and utilities.

Most of these bindings are in sync with .NET IoT Core where counterparts exist. The bindings make it easier to write code that runs on different .NET flavors or that can be reused.

It comes as no surprise that all these libraries and bindings are distributed as NuGet packages through the nuget.org feed. They are searchable and readily available directly from Visual Studio Package Manager or NuGet CLI.

Several of these libraries besides the C# "visible" part (called *managed*) rely on their counterpart's native implementation. The glue between these two parts is called Interop, and we'll address this in more detail in one of the next sections.

There are several motives that call for a library to have both managed C# and a native counterpart (native code in C or C++). One of them is performance. Another is the need to access low-level configurations, hardware/platform-specific features, or the platform SDK for the peripherals like UART, SPI, I^2C, cryptography accelerators, or other low-level components like the network stack.

The takeaway is that unless it is a platform-specific API or feature that's available only on a specific platform, it will be abstracted and exposed through the same API. This is a major advantage for code reusability and portability.

Just imagine if you could code once and reuse that component or library on all your future projects that require a similar feature set?

Or in another common situation, you develop a proof of concept on a vendor evaluation board, the project gets approval from the customer, and development starts. At some point, the specifications change, more features are added, and you realize you need to move to a highly performant series.

With an old-style approach using C/C++, at that point, you most likely would need to ditch a good portion of the code and start over.

With .NET and nanoFramework, that is not necessary. The existing code will just work. None, or very few, adjustments will be required.

The nanoCLR

Moving down the architecture layers, we next find the nanoCLR. This is, by far, the most complex part of the stack. It comprises various components that we're going to analyze with more detail.

Type System

The type system is responsible for dealing with everything related to the objects available in the various C# assemblies loaded in the deployment region that will be used during the execution of the code.

Because .NET nanoFramework is a .NET platform, it has to comply with the ECMA-335 standard that specifies the Common Language Infrastructure (CLI), which it implements closely.

At boot time, the Portable Executable (PE) files containing the metadata information about the types, code, strings, attributes, and resources are loaded from memory and processed in what is called the *type resolution*.

We'll be looking in more detail at how these files are produced in Chapter 3. This metadata is essential for the nanoCLR to understand the structure and behavior of the code that's going to be executed.

During type resolution, the CLR processes the metadata to identify and resolve all the types that the application will use. This involves checking the types defined within the program itself, as well as those referenced from external libraries (both base class libraries and user code libraries).

During this stage, the type system ensures that all type references are valid and that the necessary assemblies are available. This is a strict requirement as having the necessary assemblies means that the expected assembly name and version are available, as different versions may have different APIs or implementations.

This step is critical for maintaining the integrity and correctness of the program's execution.

Because the PE files are generated from the data available in .NET assemblies, compatibility with the ECMA-335 standard is guaranteed. It is the adhesion to this standard that allows interoperability between different .NET languages and platforms and ensures that the same code can run on any .NET-compliant platform.

By adhering to this standard, the nanoCLR can provide a consistent execution environment that produces the same outcome across various implementations of .NET.

Execution Engine

Providing that the type resolution stage went smoothly, the execution engine is ready to take over. This is the next key component on this complex system.

It's responsible for, as the name suggests, executing code. More specifically, the intermediate language (IL) instructions are contained in the loaded assemblies.

Also part of its responsibilities is managing the various .NET threads that may exist on the application being run. This includes executing timer handlers, event handlers, and exceptions that are properly handled and executed.

Part of the execution strategy involves creating the primary thread, which will always exist regardless of any .NET threads being created or not by the running application.

Some interesting things are happening on this initial thread. All the static constructors in all assemblies are identified and executed, which happens during the instantiation of the class objects they belong to. At this time, static properties and everything related are instantiated and initialized. All this has to happen prior to the execution of the application start. Note that this deviates slightly from the .NET behavior. It's kind of a shortcut that is specific to the nanoFramework execution engine. Despite this, this behavior is compliant with ECMA-355 VI.E.2 paragraph 5.

Speaking of which, during the type resolution stage, a special marker in the meta data was located: the entry point. This is the well-known method `Main()` living in the class named `Program`. All .NET developers will recognize the following code snippet:

```
using System;
namespace MyNanoApp
{
    static class Program
    {
        static void Main(string[] args)
        {
            Console.WriteLine("Hello World from .NET nanoFramework!");
        }
    }
}
```

In case the entry point hasn't been identified during the type resolution stage, the execution engine will throw an exception as it doesn't know what code it should start to execute. This happens typically when one tries to execute a library or when only libraries were deployed.

.NET nanoFramework also supports the program structure in the format of top-level statements, which was introduced with C# 9.0. This structure was introduced to simplify the boilerplate code that was required to start a C# application.

As such, the following code snippet is also valid and will produce the same result:

```
using System;
Console.WriteLine("Hello World from .NET nanoFramework!");
```

Part of the execution engine is the interpreter. This component is responsible for interpreting the stream of intermediate language (IL) instructions that result from compiling .NET code.

It executes each individual instruction, dealing with everything required to execute it successfully. This means, depending on what the instruction requires and if it returns anything, taking the required number or arguments from the stack, processing them as needed, and, in case it's a call to an "native handler" for a managed library, finding the C++ library and function that has to be called.

Upon returning (if it was a call) or simply wrapping up the execution of that instruction, the stack is validated for consistency and execution to see if any exception was generated or thrown.

If that happens, the execution engine checks if the code was being executed inside a `try catch`, and if that was the case, it will call the exception handler and resume the code execution following it.

If there is no `try catch` wrapping the execution, execution of that thread is immediately interrupted, the exception will bubble up, and the general execution will be stopped.

Garbage Collector

The garbage collector (GC) is a fundamental component of any .NET execution environment, with nanoFramework being no exception.

It's responsible for automatic memory management. Its primary role is to reclaim memory occupied by objects that are no longer in use, thereby preventing memory leaks and optimizing the application's performance.

In nanoFramework, the GC is called in three situations: 1) by the API available for this purpose, 2) whenever the used memory reaches a certain threshold (defined at build time), and 3) when trying to create certain object types and there is not enough heap memory available.

This is somewhat similar to what happens on regular .NET systems, in which the GC operates based on memory thresholds. However, it does not implement the object generation management. More details will follow.

It is also because of the constrained nature of the systems that nanoFramework runs on and the fact that GC runs typically take a long time (compared to the other running tasks).

During the GC run, no IL instructions are executed, so it may be relevant for the system performance to conscientiously control when garbage collection runs. This way, it won't, for example, kick in during the execution of a critical section of the program, thus hindering the overall performance.

Put simply, the GC identifies objects that are no longer referenced by the application code and frees up the memory they occupy. It's using a mark-sweep algorithm.

The initial phase is the "mark" phase. In this phase, it performs a graph traversal—using an explicit mark stack and a depth-first search (DFS) like strategy—to compute the reachability graph of objects, marking them alive if they are reachable from the roots.

Once this marking phase completes, a sweeping phase then runs to reclaim the unmarked objects, freeing the memory they occupy.

The garbage collector is particularly important in managed languages like C# and sets it completely apart from unmanaged ones (like C and C++) because it abstracts away the complexities of manual memory management.

Developers do not need to explicitly allocate and deallocate memory, as the GC handles these tasks automatically. This reduces the likelihood of memory-related bugs, such as dangling pointers and buffer overflows, and allows developers to focus on writing high-level code without worrying about low-level memory operations.

As already mentioned in the first chapter, the GC is one of the many advantages of using a managed language like C# for embedded systems development. Any developer who has coded with C/C++ is very much aware of this and how closely this matter needs to be accounted for.

Along with the garbage collection, there is a secondary algorithm that's responsible for the heap relocation. Following the garbage collection, the heap is usually fragmented with "holes" in memory from the blocks that were freed.

This arrangement may be OK if the objects being created afterward keep fitting in the various free memory spaces available. Now, if a large object needs to be created, even if there is enough free memory, it may be scattered, and there is not enough contiguous memory to hold that object.

When this happens, a heap relocation is required. What this does is move objects around in order to group them and arrange for a contiguous block of free memory to become available. There is more to it than just moving objects around. Objects pointing to other objects will have those pointers updated accordingly, so this process is quite critical and sensitive.

Built-in Functions

Along with the CLR, there are several built-in functions auxiliary to the overall functioning of the system. Let's review them in detail.

Event Manager

This component is responsible for managing the various events that occur throughout the system.

These can be hardware events, like a network connection or disconnection, an I^2C transaction becoming complete, or a managed event that needs to be surfaced to the running application.

Part of these are the asynchronous completions and asynchronous continuations. These are linked lists that are used to store asynchronous events that, when they "time out," have their callbacks executed by the execution engine.

Debugger and Wire Protocol

Along with the Wire Protocol, the Debugger provides communication from the microcontroller to the external world.

It's responsible for key tasks such as receiving and updating the CLR and deployment region where the C# assemblies are stored, reporting device capabilities when queried, participating in the device discovery process, and connecting with the Visual Studio debugger library during a debug session to provide the various services required during this complex process.

Regarding the Wire Protocol, this is a proprietary protocol using a frame structure that offers robust communication with the outside world using a serial stream. This allows it to use the most commonly available channels in the embedded world, like serial ports or USB CDC.

Serialization

Serialization is baked in the CLR, because of the importance it can have on embedded systems world.

By providing a native serialization (and deserialization) component, it frees the developer from having to find a suitable library or even implement its own. This is a highly compact, performant, and reliable component that is able to handle all base types, user-defined classes, and types.

Because of its proprietary protocol, there is a companion library for the regular .NET that allows seamless interchange of data between platforms.

Storage Manager

This component handles all the tasks related with storage. This can be flash (almost omnipresent in most of the devices) either internal to the microcontroller or external connected chip, (E-)EPROM storage (usually external, SPI connected chip), RAM, and removable storage media, like USB flash drive and SD cards.

Thread Manager

Just like any .NET platform worthy of that name, support for threads is mandatory, and nanoFramework is no exception.

Do not mix up .NET threads with RTOS threads (also known as Tasks in some RTOS). Although similar in concept, they are different and have a different implementation.

Because .NET nanoFramework (usually) runs on a single core processor, there is no real parallel execution of multiple threads. There is a scheduler that allots a 20-millisecond time slice to each thread in a round-robin fashion.

If a thread is capable of running (meaning that is not blocked for any reason), it will be executed for 20 milliseconds after which the execution will go to the next "ready to run" thread. Be aware that the quantum time for thread switching is configurable at compile time by means of a configuration option (search for `c_TimeQuantum_Milliseconds` in the code base).

By default, a .NET program is started with a single thread, often called the *primary thread*. However, it can create additional threads to execute code in parallel or concurrently with the primary thread.

These threads are often called *worker threads*. .NET nanoFramework implements several of the threading APIs that allow an interesting usage of it.

A variation of .NET threads are the timers. These are special threads with limited functionality, so to speak. They consist of a timer handler that executes each time the timer expires.

A timer will have a configuration for the period in which its hander will be called and a way to start and stop it.

Watchdog

Similar to most embedded systems, the .NET platform has a watchdog. To offer robustness, this relies on the hardware implementation of each platform. It's configured and included by default in the build. It can optionally be disabled. By design, there is no API to configure or interact with it.

At key points in the code, the watchdog ensures that it performs as expected. If the execution goes wrong, it will time out, and the configured outcome occurs. Typically this is a system reset.

For platforms that expose this information, there is an API that allows querying the wake-up reason, which may provide an insight into this matter so the software can act upon it.

Hardware Peripherals

The various hardware peripherals in the microcontroller will be exposed by the corresponding C# API, allowing the developer to interact with the hardware.

The following are the most common ones available on most platforms. Keep in mind that not all of them will always be available, depending on what each microcontroller includes. As expected from any embedded systems framework, one will find the usual suspects here.

- General Purpose Input and Output (GPIO) will access the microcontroller pins and interact with the external world.
- Universal Asynchronous Receiver and Transmitter (UART), commonly referred to as the serial port, offers communication capabilities using one or more wires and, optionally, software or hardware flow control.
- Inter-integrated circuit communication (I^2C) will communicate with external devices. It operates on a master-slave architecture over a common bus.
- Serial Peripheral Interface (SPI) is another popular communication protocol. Again, it operates over a common bus, using a master-slave architecture, and allows communication with external devices.

- Analog Digital Converter (ADC) converts analog signals and quantize them in a digital value.
- Digital Analog Converter DAC) performs the opposite, i.e., converting a digital value into an analog signal.
- Network interfaces can be Wi-Fi or wired, usually Ethernet. They provide a connection to a local network and possibly to the Internet.
- Real-time clock (RTC) provides accurate time keeping and usually wake-up features that allow waking up the microcontroller from a sleep state after a set period of time.

Interoperability

Interoperability in .NET nanoFramework refers to the capability that allows managed code (C#) to interact directly with native code, typically written in C or C++.

This feature is crucial for scenarios where low-level hardware access, performance optimization, or use of existing native libraries is required—something that managed code alone may not efficiently support.

Interoperability is achieved through a mechanism called *Interop assemblies*. Developers can create custom native code modules and expose specific methods to the managed environment by defining corresponding C# declarations with special attributes.

These declarations are then matched with their native implementations during the build process. The result is a seamless bridge between the high-level managed world and the low-level native layer, enabling greater flexibility and control.

Interop is particularly valuable in embedded systems development, where accessing device registers, handling real-time constraints, or leveraging existing C libraries is often necessary.

By supporting interoperability, .NET nanoFramework balances developer productivity with the performance and precision that embedded applications demand.

This feature empowers developers to optimize critical code paths while still enjoying the safety and ease of .NET's managed environment for the rest of the application.

HAL and PAL

The Hardware Abstraction Layer (HAL) and Platform Abstraction Layer (PAL) are core architectural components that enable .NET nanoFramework to be portable, modular, and adaptable to different microcontroller platforms.

The HAL provides a consistent and standardized interface to low-level hardware features. These include peripherals such as GPIO, I^2C, SPI, UART, ADC, PWM, and system timers.

By abstracting direct hardware access, HAL allows the upper layers of the system—including the nanoCLR and user applications—to interact with the hardware without needing to know the exact implementation details of the underlying microcontroller. This abstraction promotes code reuse and simplifies portability across various device families.

On top of the HAL sits the PAL, which handles higher-level and more platform-specific services such as networking stack(s) (TCP/IP, Thread), file systems (e.g., FAT, littlefs), cryptographic functions, native threading, and memory management.

PAL implementations are specific to each hardware platform or RTOS, but the interface they expose to the nanoCLR remains consistent. This design ensures that developers can rely on familiar APIs, regardless of the underlying hardware.

A key role of both HAL and PAL is to serve as a bridge between the nanoCLR (equivalent to the .NET runtime) and the hardware-specific SDKs provided by microcontroller vendors. These SDKs—such as STM32Cube HAL for STMicroelectronics chips or the ESP-IDF for Espressif devices—offer low-level driver support and optimized access to the capabilities of each platform.

HAL and PAL effectively "glue" the nanoCLR to these SDKs, allowing nanoFramework to take advantage of platform-specific features while maintaining a consistent managed-code interface for developers.

The .NET nanoFramework build process and platform ports rely heavily on the underlying microcontroller SDK to perform the essential hardware setup required to bring the system to life. These SDKs provide the initialization code needed to configure clocks, memory, peripherals, and interrupt controllers—steps that are critical to ensure a successful boot sequence.

At power-up, the startup code included in the SDK is responsible for performing the low-level configuration specific to the target MCU. This includes setting up the system clock tree, enabling memory regions, and preparing peripherals that may be needed early in the boot process. .NET nanoFramework uses this initialization as a foundation to begin loading its runtime.

Once basic hardware setup is complete, the SDK is also used to initialize the RTOS. After the RTOS is initialized, the system proceeds to create and schedule the primary system threads:

- The CLR thread runs the nanoCLR—the .NET runtime responsible for executing managed C# applications.
- The Wire Protocol thread handles communication between the device and the development tools (e.g., deployment and debugging), typically over serial, USB, or network transports.

RTOS

.NET nanoFramework requires a Real-Time Operating System (RTOS). Multiple ones are currently supported, like ChibiOS, FreeRTOS, ThreadX, and TI-RTOS, providing flexibility to match different platform and application requirements or even a company preference for a brand or licensing options.

As already mentioned, at system startup two RTOS threads are launched: one with the CLR and another one with the handler for the Wire Protocol.

Depending on the code that is running, other threads can be launched at startup or as the code executes. For example, in targets that are network-enabled, one (or more) thread is launched to run the network stack. This ensures that network operations are handled independently and do not impact the performance of other tasks.

For time-consuming tasks, such as large SPI transactions to a display or servicing the serial port and storing data in a temporary buffer for processing, having these tasks run smoothly and concurrently is now up to the RTOS.

The RTOS manages the scheduling and execution of these threads, freeing the CLR from having to manage all that. This allows the CLR to focus on executing the application code without being burdened by the complexities of task management.

Besides threads, other common RTOS features are extensively used, like semaphores, which are used to manage access to shared resources, ensuring that multiple threads can operate without interfering with each other.

Inter-thread communication mechanisms, such as message queues and mailboxes, allow threads to exchange information efficiently. Interlocking mechanisms ensure that critical sections of code are executed atomically, preventing race conditions.

These features collectively enhance the reliability and performance of the system, which was one of the design decisions to add an RTOS as a requirement for nanoFramework.

Worth noting that another intentional design decision of decoupling the RTOS features from the CLR was made on purpose to allow ports to different RTOS. This brings a tremendous flexibility to the overall system and allows, for example, professional users to choose the one they prefer or that have better commercial or licensing options. It also makes it possible to (more) easily incorporate platforms that are locked to a specific RTOS, which was the case of ESP32 that uses a customized version of FreeRTOS.

Advantages of the Flexible Architecture

The layered architecture of .NET nanoFramework is one of its most powerful features, offering exceptional flexibility, modularity, and scalability for embedded systems development.

By clearly separating concerns across hardware, platform, and application layers, the framework allows developers and teams to engage at the level most relevant to their expertise and goals.

This approach enables specialized contributors to work independently, but more importantly, it allows entire teams to tailor their involvement according to project-specific needs.

Whether the task is adding support for a new microcontroller family, adapting the platform to a custom board design, integrating hardware-specific features, or simply reusing existing code and libraries in a managed application, each role can contribute without needing to understand or modify the entire system stack.

The flexible build system further reinforces this modularity, supporting conditional inclusion of components, customizable build configurations, and scalable project structures. This means hardware engineers can focus on low-level initialization and board bring-up, firmware developers can implement or modify native platform code, and application developers can stay entirely within the managed C# environment, all within the same cohesive platform.

Teams can evolve their use of the framework over time: starting with a reference platform to accelerate development and then extending or adapting lower layers as hardware requirements become more complex or specific. This makes .NET nanoFramework equally suitable for prototyping, product development, and long-term platform maintenance.

By enabling this level of targeted involvement and modular contribution, .NET nanoFramework empowers developers to build robust, portable, and maintainable embedded solutions, while minimizing overhead and maximizing team efficiency.

Summary

This chapter presented a comprehensive overview of the architecture of .NET nanoFramework, detailing how its modular and layered design supports a wide range of embedded development use cases.

At the application level, developers can write C# code using familiar .NET patterns and APIs, supported by a rich set of class libraries and device bindings delivered via NuGet.

A key architectural strength of .NET nanoFramework is its strong affinity with the broader .NET ecosystem.

Great effort has been made to align the available APIs with the full .NET platform, enabling code reuse across devices and projects, and leveraging the vast amount of existing .NET documentation, tooling, and community knowledge.

Furthermore, nanoFramework adheres to the ECMA-335 specification, which defines the Common Language Infrastructure (CLI). This compliance ensures compatibility with other .NET implementations and preserves the core behaviors and guarantees expected of a .NET runtime environment.

At the core of the platform is the nanoCLR, which includes the type system, execution engine, interpreter, garbage collector, and other supporting services like debugging, event handling, and serialization. These components work together to provide a managed runtime environment that is consistent, efficient, and secure.

Supporting this execution layer are the Hardware Abstraction Layer (HAL) and Platform Abstraction Layer (PAL), which isolate hardware specifics and interface with the SDK and RTOS to bring the system to life and maintain portability across MCU platforms.

The chapter also emphasized the platform's flexible architecture, which allows different developer roles—application developers, firmware engineers, and hardware specialists—to engage with the system at the appropriate level. This separation of concerns, along with the modular build system, supports targeted contributions, high code reusability, and easy adaptation to new hardware or project requirements.

In summary, .NET nanoFramework combines the power and familiarity of .NET with the performance and control needed for embedded systems, offering a scalable, standards-compliant platform for modern embedded development.

In the next chapter, we will dive into the build system and go through the details of configuring the build for a firmware image.

Additional Resources

The following are some URLs where you can find more information about several topics discussed in this chapter:

Official GitHub repository: `https://github.com/nanoframework/`

Archived GitHub for .NETMF: `https://github.com/netmf`

GitHub repository for Microsoft IoT Libraries: `https://github.com/dotnet/iot`

C# and .NET standards: `https://learn.microsoft.com/en-us/dotnet/fundamentals/standards`

C# program structure: `https://learn.microsoft.com/en-us/dotnet/csharp/fundamentals/program-structure/`

CHAPTER 3

The Build System

Building embedded firmware for a complex platform like .NET nanoFramework involves orchestrating many components—from real-time operating systems (RTOSs) to hardware abstraction layers—into a cohesive binary.

This chapter dives into the build system of .NET nanoFramework, explaining how it uses CMake and Ninja to target multiple architectures and RTOSs.

We'll first introduce CMake and Ninja for readers new to these tools, and then we'll explore the structure of the nanoFramework build system, including general configuration, RTOS integration, platform and target setup, and the use of CMake presets for managing builds.

Next, we'll provide guidance on extending the build system to support new platforms or boards.

Finally, we'll take a look at how to use developer containers for a smooth developer experience and how to orchestrate build pipelines in the cloud.

Note If your focus with .NET nanoFramework is on writing C# code and you are not planning to delve into firmware building matters, you can skip this chapter entirely. In that case, you can simply grab the ready-to-use firmware packages and flash your device with the appropriate one.

Build Tools: CMake and Ninja in a Nutshell

Traditional embedded projects often rely on IDE-specific or Makefile-based build processes. .NET nanoFramework instead adopts CMake, a cross-platform build generator, to streamline builds on all major OSs.

J. Simões, *Embedded Systems with .NET nanoFramework*, https://doi.org/10.1007/979-8-8688-2096-0_3

CMake is a popular, cross-platform build system generator. Instead of creating platform-specific Makefiles or project files directly, CMake uses a set of configuration scripts (`CMakeLists.txt`) and generates build instructions for your chosen environment and toolchain. This approach makes it easy to add or remove modules, toggle features on or off, and adapt to different operating systems or compilers.

The following are the key advantages of CMake:

- **Portability:** CMake decouples your build definitions from the host environment so you can compile on Windows, Linux, or macOS with minimal friction.
- **Modular structure:** `CMakeLists.txt` scripts can be broken into multiple files for clarity, making it easier to maintain large, complex projects.
- **Widespread adoption:** Many embedded toolchains and ecosystems now provide first-class CMake support or integrations, simplifying getting started on different hardware.

CMake allows the project to define the build in a high-level language (CMakeLists scripts), which can then generate platform-specific build files (Makefiles, Ninja build files, etc.). This approach reduces friction for developers.

By using CMake, nanoFramework can easily support different toolchains and environments and integrate with VS Code or Visual Studio (any edition, from the free Community one up to the full fledged Enterprise).

Along with CMake, the build system uses Ninja as the actual build executor (the "make" tool). Ninja is a build tool that focuses on speed. It processes instructions generated by CMake, taking advantage of parallel compilation and incremental builds to reduce the total build time. Compared to older tools like GNU Make, Ninja can handle large projects efficiently while providing helpful error reporting.

Here are some highlights:

- **Fast parallel builds:** Ninja spawns compiler jobs in parallel where possible, which is especially handy when you're managing multiple modules or library dependencies.
- **Simple syntax:** You rarely edit the Ninja file yourself—CMake generates it—but if you do, it's lightweight and easier to parse than many alternatives.

- **Incremental building:** Ninja quickly figures out what changed and rebuilds just that portion, saving time in your edit-compile-test loop.

In practice, CMake will generate Ninja build files, which Ninja then uses to compile source files in parallel and perform minimal rebuilds. This combination of CMake + Ninja provides a robust, cross-platform, and efficient build pipeline for nanoFramework firmware.

These are the key advantages of using CMake and Ninja:

- **Cross-platform consistency:** CMake abstracts away build platform differences. Developers on Windows, Linux, or macOS can all configure the build in the same way (in our case via CMake presets as we'll see) and let CMake generate appropriate build files for their system.
- **Out-of-source builds:** nanoFramework follows best practices suggested by CMake and encourages building in a separate build directory, which avoids cluttering the source tree with object files and also can be wiped easily. CMake makes this simple to manage.
- **Fast incremental builds:** Ninja excels at quickly determining what needs to be rebuilt. It is "designed for speed," which is valuable when dealing with large codebases and multiple targets.

In a nutshell, CMake provides the structure and configuration for the build, while Ninja provides the speed. With these tools introduced, let's examine how .NET nanoFramework organizes its build files and options.

Overview

The .NET nanoFramework firmware build is highly configurable to support different microcontroller platforms (architectures/RTOS combinations) and specific targets (boards). The build system is centered on a top-level CMake project that conditionally pulls in the right components based on build options.

The source code and everything pertaining to the build system lives in the GitHub repository: `https://github.com/nanoframework/nf-interpreter`.

Key build inputs include the following:

- **TARGET_BOARD:** The code name of the target board (or MCU) to build for (e.g., ST_NUCLEO64_F091RC, ESP32_REV3). This is a mandatory parameter that selects a specific hardware target.
- **RTOS:** The real-time operating system (or platform) to use (e.g., ChibiOS, FreeRTOS, ThreadX, TI-RTOS). This determines which OS abstraction and drivers are used. It's also a required parameter—the build won't proceed without an RTOS specified.
- **Toolchain and build type:** The compiler toolchain is usually inferred by CMake (for ARM Cores, the GNU Arm Embedded toolchain is used, for ESP32, the modified version of GCC) and the build. .NET nanoFramework build supports several CMake build types (`Debug`, `Release`, `MinSizeRel`, `RelWithDebInfo`) and validates the selection. A debug build will define the traditional DEBUG compiler definition (for conditional code) and include extra diagnostic information.

Regarding the build types, it is worth noting that the debug variants (`Debug` and `RelWithDebInfo`) are the ones on which a debug session can be started. This is useful if you intend to debug the interpreter or the CLR. The only variation is that the `RelWithDebInfo` flavor includes pretty much all the compiler and linker optimizations that the release builds have, except it includes debugger information.

When you invoke CMake for nanoFramework, you must supply at least the `TARGET_BOARD` and `RTOS` options (either via command-line `-D` options or, more conveniently, via a CMake preset as discussed later). The root CMake script (`nf-interpreter/CMakeLists.txt`) checks for these and will error out if they are missing or invalid, like this:

```
# in nf-interpreter/CMakeLists.txt
if(NOT TARGET_BOARD OR TARGET_BOARD STREQUAL "")
    message(FATAL_ERROR "Missing build option ‘TARGET_BOARD’.")
endif()
if(NOT RTOS OR RTOS STREQUAL "")
    message(FATAL_ERROR "Missing build option ‘RTOS’.")
endif()
```

Once CMake knows the target board and RTOS, it prints some banner information (project version, build type, etc.) and begins including the relevant subdirectories.

The source tree is organized under a top-level targets/folder, which contains one subfolder per supported platform and RTOS combination. For example, `targets/ChibiOS/` contains support for STM32 boards using the ChibiOS RTOS, `targets/FreeRTOS/` contains targets using FreeRTOS (such as NXP i.MX RT boards), `targets/AzureRTOS/` for ThreadX (formerly known by Azure RTOS) targets like Silicon Labs Giant Gecko, `targets/ESP32/` for ESP32 (which uses Espressif's FreeRTOS-based SDK, known as IDF), and so on.

There is an utility target at `targets/netcore`, which is a .NET CLI written in C# that uses .NET Interop to connect to a nanoCLR compiled as a VC++ library. This uses the same code as the other targets and uses Windows APIs for the RTOS equivalents. It's called the virtual device. It can be used just like any other hardware-based hardware, which, because of its CLI features, makes it very convenient to use. It's used by the Test Framework as the unit test runner, as an example of usage in CLI style.

CMake uses the RTOS name to select the platform directory. A helper converts the name to uppercase and defines an internal flag, e.g., setting `RTOS_CHIBIOS_CHECK=TRUE` or `RTOS_FREERTOS_CHECK=TRUE`. This allows the build scripts to easily branch logic depending on the RTOS. The root CMakeLists then includes the appropriate sub-builds.

In pseudo-code, the logic is as follows:

- If RTOS is FreeRTOS or ThreadX, go into the corresponding folder under `targets/` (these RTOS support multiple vendors, so their folder will in turn include subfolders for each vendor or board).
- Elseif RTOS is ESP32, perform ESP32-specific setup (based in the IDF *sdkconfig* file and options) and then include the `targets/ESP32` folder followed by the series subfolder. (ESP32 is treated specially because it uses Espressif's build system integration, as you'll see.)
- Otherwise (for any other RTOS like ChibiOS, TI_SimpleLink, etc.), include the RTOS folder and then include the board's folder within it.

In all cases, the build ultimately brings in two layers of CMake subdirectories: one for the platform (the RTOS and common code for that family of MCUs) and one for the target board (specific initialization and configuration for the exact board). Figure 3-1 illustrates this flow of control in the CMake build.

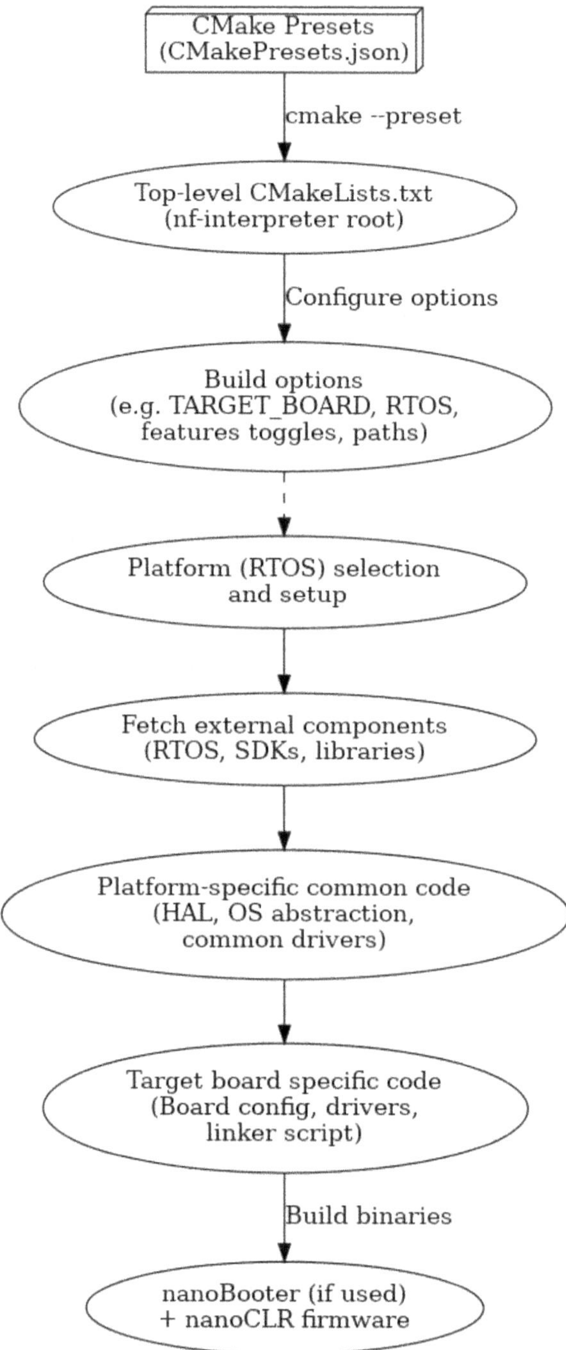

Figure 3-1. *.NET nanoFramework build system flow*

The top-level CMake also sets up some global settings, like the nanoFramework version number (from BUILD_VERSION) and names for the firmware outputs (nanoCLR for the runtime and nanoBooter for the tiny bootloader). By default, nanoBooter is only built for targets that use a separate secondary bootloader; many targets just build the nanoCLR image. The build system supports a "Release" vs. "Debug" distinction, where "Release" (or specifically an RTM build) can strip out debugging features for a smaller image.

CMake Presets for Common Configurations

To simplify build invocation, .NET nanoFramework takes advantage of *CMake presets*, a feature that allows predefined build configurations to be stored in JSON files. The repository provides a `CMakePresets.json` file with the preset entries for each reference target, and a template for a user-specific overrides file (CMakeUserPresets.TEMPLATE.json). Instead of manually typing `-DTARGET_BOARD=... -DRTOS=... -DCMAKE_BUILD_TYPE=...` each time, you can simply call CMake with a preset name. For example, to build the NUCLEO-F091RC board, the command line call would be:

```
cmake --preset ST_NUCLEO_F091RC
cmake --build --preset ST_NUCLEO_F091RC
```

This invokes the preset named `ST_NUCLEO_F091RC`, which encapsulates all the necessary settings (it will set `TARGET_BOARD=ST_NUCLEO64_F091RC, RTOS=ChibiOS`, select the appropriate toolchain, etc.). Presets dramatically reduce the chance of misconfiguring the build, since the official settings for each board have been adjusted, have been validated, and are checked in.

Under the hood, a preset for a board *inherits* from a platform/base preset and then sets the cache variables for that specific board. For instance, a preset might do this:

```
{
  "name": "ST_NUCLEO64_F091RC",
  "inherits": "STM32_ChibiOS",
  "cacheVariables": {
    "TARGET_BOARD": "ST_NUCLEO64_F091RC",
    "RTOS": "ChibiOS",
```

```
    "CHIBIOS_SOURCE_FOLDER": "",
    "NF_FEATURE_HAS_SDCARD": "OFF",
    ...
  }
}
```

This is a simplification, while the real `CMakePresets.json` is structured with multiple layers; e.g., a base preset for all `STM32/ChibiOS` boards might set common options like the toolchain path and `RTOS=ChibiOS`, and each board preset inherits those and then adds its specific board name and any feature flags. Using inheritance, the project avoids repeating large option sets. The benefit of CMake Presets is that everything gets updated and goes in sync, automagically between local builds and CI pipelines, since the same presets `json` is used everywhere.

Tip You can customize or extend presets by leveraging a `CMakeUserPresets.json` file. There is already a template for such a file in the `config/` folder. You should copy and rename it to remove "template" from the name. Then adjust it to your local setup and preferences.

For example, to experiment with a custom configuration, you can inherit an official preset and then override a few options (like disabling an optional feature). This mechanism makes it easy to tweak builds without modifying the main preset file.

In summary, CMake presets provide a convenient interface on top of the build system. Whether you invoke CMake from the command line or through an IDE, you'll usually pick a preset matching your board. Next, let's look at what happens once the build files are generated—specifically, how the CMake scripts pull in the appropriate code for the chosen RTOS and platform.

Platform (RTOS) Support and Integration

One of the strengths of .NET nanoFramework is its ability to run on multiple RTOSs. Currently, the firmware can be built on several platforms: ChibiOS, FreeRTOS, ThreadX (former Azure RTOS), TI SimpleLink (TI-RTOS), ESP32 FreeRTOS, as well as a special .NET Core build that performs as a virtual device (in a oversimplified description attempt, it runs the nanoCLR wrapped in a .NET Core app). Each platform has its own directory under `targets/` with the code and configurations needed to interface the nanoFramework CLR with that RTOS and hardware.

The CMake build system isolates platform-specific code nicely. After the top level, CMake adds the platform subdirectory (targets/<RTOS>). The build rules in that subdirectory take over to configure the HAL, RTOS kernel, and any vendor or third-party SDKs required. The key aspects of platform integration are described next.

Including RTOS Source or Libraries

For some RTOSs, the build will fetch or reference the RTOS source code itself. For example, for ChibiOS (used on STM32), the build can automatically download the ChibiOS source if you don't provide a local path by adding the build parameter:`DRTOS_SOURCE_FOLDER`. By default, the ChibiOS kernel (and its HAL drivers for STM32) is pulled from a GitHub mirror of the official Subversion repository. On subsequent builds, CMake checks for updates and merges them, caching the RTOS source in the build directory. If you prefer, you can clone ChibiOS yourself and pass `-DCHIBIOS_SOURCE_FOLDER="C:\path\to\ChibiOS"` to use a local copy, which avoids Internet downloads and gives you control over the exact version (you should check out the stable tag that nanoFramework expects). This mechanism is implemented using CMake's `FetchContent` module inside `targets/ChibiOS/CMakeLists.txt`.

Vendor SDK and HAL Integration

In addition to the RTOS kernel, microcontroller vendors often provide low-level drivers or SDKs (for peripherals, network stacks, etc.). The build system either downloads these or expects them to be available locally. For instance, FreeRTOS targets (like NXP i.MX RT boards) may require the NXP MCUXpresso SDK for device-specific drivers. In the targets/FreeRTOS/NXP folder, you'll find an `_include` and `_common` set of files that originate from NXP's SDK, as well as FreeRTOS configuration. Similarly, for TI SimpleLink, the `targets/TI_SimpleLink` directory contains the OS and driver code needed for TI CC32xx and CC13x devices (using TI-RTOS provided by TI). The nanoFramework build tries to automate as much as possible. For example, it can fetch common middleware like FatFS (file system) or lwIP (lightweight IP stack) when needed. In the ChibiOS build scripts, after fetching ChibiOS, it also use FetchContent on the ChibiOS-Contrib repository (which contains community board definitions and drivers), as well as FatFS and littlefs for file system support. This means that if your configuration enables the file system or networking features, the build will include those libraries automatically. The build caches these components so they aren't downloaded repeatedly on each build.

Common HAL and PAL Setup

Each platform directory usually defines a common HAL and PAL for the CLR to run. This includes things like startup code (reset vectors, etc.), interrupt handling, threading and timing based on the RTOS, and drivers for core peripherals (GPIO, SPI, I^{2}C, etc.) that the class libraries depend on. For example, the ChibiOS platform uses the ChibiOS HAL for most peripheral implementations. The build script for ChibiOS defines `HAL_USE_xxx_OPTION` CMake flags based on which nanoFramework API classes are enabled (e.g., if the `System.Device.Gpio` API is included, it sets `HAL_USE_GPIO_OPTION TRUE`). These flags then control which driver source files are compiled. In contrast, the ESP32 platform uses Espressif's IoT Development Framework (IDF) for HAL functions—if you enable the Network or Bluetooth API, the build will leverage IDF components for Wi-Fi, lwIP, BLE, etc., and it sets the corresponding flags (e.g., `HAL_USE_BLE_OPTION`) to either include or exclude those features.

RTOS Initialization

The `CMakeList.txt` file for each platform is responsible for ensuring the RTOS is correctly configured and started. For ThreadX (Azure RTOS) on the SiliconLabs Giant Gecko, for example, the `targets/AzureRTOS` CMakeLists will include ThreadX and NetX Duo (for networking) sources and set up the thread stack sizes, etc., appropriate for each target.

Platform-Specific Code Organization

In each platform folder, code may be further organized by vendor or MCU family. For example, under `targets/AzureRTOS/`, you will find subfolders like `ST/`, `SiliconLabs/`, `Nordic/`, etc., each containing board support files for that vendor using ThreadX RTOS.

Under targets/FreeRTOS/, there is an NXP/ subfolder for NXP i.MX RT boards (which use FreeRTOS). In targets/ChibiOS/, since ChibiOS is primarily used for STM32 targets in nanoFramework, most boards are directly under targets/ChibiOS/ without an extra vendor layer (the STM32-specific code is part of ChibiOS itself). Instead, ChibiOS organizes by MCU series: the CMake scripts determine the series (e.g., STM32F4xx versus STM32L4xx) from the board selection and include the appropriate ChibiOS port and driver sources. This is done by a series of includes like include(CHIBIOS_${TARGET_SERIES}_sources.cmake), which pull in a list of source files tailored to that MCU family and set up include paths for CMSIS and ChibiOS OS files.

In summary, the platform layer of the build abstracts the differences in RTOS and MCU vendor details. The top-level build passes control to the platform CMakeLists, which handles getting the RTOS and vendor SDK (either via download or using local files), configuring necessary compile definitions for that platform, and readying the environment for the specific target board to be added. By the time the platform CMake has finished, we have a set of source files and include paths specific to (for example) "STM32 with ChibiOS" or "ESP32 with ESP-IDF" or "NXP with FreeRTOS+MCUXpresso," etc. Next, and lastly on the build system tour, we'll shift our focus to the target board—the final piece that adds board-specific configuration to, finally, compile the firmware binaries.

Target-Specific Configuration (Board Support)

Within a given platform/RTOS, multiple boards or modules may be supported. The target board layer of the build includes any source code or settings unique to that board (or to the specific microcontroller variant on that board). Typically, each board has its own subdirectory named after the TARGET_BOARD identifier. For example, under targets/ChibiOS/ you might find ST_NUCLEO64_F091RC/, ST_NUCLEO144_F746ZG/, etc., each corresponding to an STM32 Nucleo development board; under targets/ESP32/ you find ESP32_DEVKITC or other module names; under targets/FreeRTOS/NXP/ you'll see NXP_MIMXRT1060_EVK/ for an NXP's eval board.

The responsibilities of the board-specific CMakeLists (and accompanying files) are described next.

Defining the Final Firmware Targets

Usually at the board level, the build defines the output executables (or binaries) for that board. For instance, it will create an executable target for `nanoCLR.elf` (the main firmware) and, if applicable, one for `nanoBooter.elf` (the bootloader). It then links all the object files accumulated from the platform and from the board-specific sources. The board CMakeLists might use CMake functions provided by the platform to simplify this. For example, in ESP32 targets, after including the common `targets/ESP32` directory, the build uses a helper function `nf_add_idf_as_library()` to bring in the precompiled ESP-IDF components, and then the board directory adds its specific code (like partition tables, etc.).

Board Initialization Code

Many boards require specific initialization—e.g., setting up clock sources, configuring external memory chips, etc. In ChibiOS, this is typically handled by a *board definition* consisting of a `board.h` and `board.c` files. The build system checks if the board's directory contains a custom `board.c/board.h` combination; if not, it falls back to a board definition from ChibiOS-Contrib or the ChibiOS source code. This gives flexibility. For widely used boards, the definitions may already exist upstream, but for custom boards you can supply your own. Similarly, for other platforms, you might have startup assembly files or linker scripts that are board-specific. The build system will include these from the board folder. For example, an NXP board might have a custom linker script (LD file) to accommodate its external RAM, and that file would reside in the board directory and be passed to the linker.

Memory and Device Configuration

The board layer often specifies memory regions and sizes (for the linker) and may toggle features like external QSPI flash, network interface types, etc., depending on the board's hardware. In the preset configuration for each board, there are cache variables controlling them. For instance, a board with an Ethernet port might set `ESP32_ETHERNET_SUPPORT=ON` (used in ESP32 build to include Ethernet drivers), or a board with a specific Wi-Fi module might set a particular `WIFI_DRIVER` option. The board's CMakeLists can read these and pull in the corresponding driver code. In targets under the ThreadX platform, if a board supports NetX Duo for networking, it might set `NF_FEATURE_USE_NETWORKING` and include the NetX IP initialization on startup.

Community Targets vs. Official Targets

The nanoFramework project maintains a separate Community Targets repository (included as a Git submodule in `targets-community/`) for target boards contributed by the community. The build system can search the `targets-community` directory if it doesn't find a board in the main `targets` folder. It marks an `IS_COMMUNITY_TARGET` flag in such cases. From a build perspective, community board support works the same way—the files just live in a different folder. When adding a new board, you might prototype it in the main repository and later move it to the community repo. The CMake logic ensures that regardless of whether a board's files are in `targets/<RTOS>/<Board>` or `targets-community/<RTOS>/<Board>`, they will be picked up and built appropriately.

By the end of including the board subdirectory, the build has compiled all the necessary source files and is ready to link the firmware. The output build artifacts are placed in the `build` directory. For example, you'll get `.elf` files, and CMake rules also convert those to HEX or BIN as needed. The deliverables typically include the nanoCLR firmware image (and optionally a nanoBooter image) in formats like HEX, BIN, or DFU depending on the board.

Example: ESP32 Build Specifics

To illustrate how platform and board layers come together, consider the ESP32 targets. The ESP32 uses a modified version of FreeRTOS provided by Espressif (the ESP-IDF). The build system treats `RTOS=ESP32` as a special case. When you select an ESP32 board (for example, ESP32_DEVKITC), the platform step (in `targets/ESP32/CMakeLists.txt`) does some extra configuration: it defines an `ESP32_USB_CDC` option (to allow USB CDC on certain ESP32 series), sets up base paths for the class libraries, and adjusts features like Bluetooth and Ethernet based on the build options. Notably, it checks if the Bluetooth or Thread networking APIs are enabled and sets `HAL_USE_BLE_OPTION` or `HAL_USE_THREAD_OPTION` accordingly, printing a message to confirm ("Support for Bluetooth enabled" or "disabled", etc.).

After configuring these options, the ESP32 platform code calls a function `nf_add_idf_as_library()`. This function (defined in the ESP32 CMake module) effectively brings in the precompiled ESP-IDF libraries for the ESP32. The Espressif toolchain and SDK must be installed (the documentation guides developers to run the ESP-IDF installer prior to building). The build will locate the ESP-IDF components and link against them, rather than compiling the RTOS from source. This is different from other platforms where the RTOS (ChibiOS, FreeRTOS) is compiled as part of the build; for ESP32, the OS and HAL are provided by the vendor as libraries.

Finally, the ESP32 board directory (e.g., `targets/ESP32/ESP32_DEVKITC`) might include a CMake fragment to specify the partition table or any board-specific initialization (though most of that is handled by IDF). Once built, the result is a firmware image that can be flashed with Espressif's tools (or the nanoFramework *nanoff* utility, which wraps these tools in a convenient .NET Core CLI). The important takeaway is that the build system was flexible enough to accommodate Espressif's build flow within CMake—a testament to the power of using CMake for multiplatform projects.

Adding New Platforms and Targets

One of the design goals of .NET nanoFramework is to make it easily expandable to other hardware platforms and RTOSs. If you want to port nanoFramework to a new platform (meaning a new RTOS or a new family of MCUs not yet supported) or add a new target board under an existing platform, the build system is ready to be extended. This section provides a high-level guide for doing so.

Adding a New Platform (RTOS or MCU Family)

Adding a new platform is the more involved case—it's akin to porting nanoFramework to a new RTOS or a new vendor SDK. You will need to create a new folder under `targets/` and provide the glue code for that platform. Follows a step-by-step outline.

Create the Platform Directory

Make a new directory under `targets/` named after your platform (for example, `targets/Zephyr` if you were porting to the Zephyr RTOS). Inside it, create the expected substructure. At minimum, you'll want the following:

- A `CMakeLists.txt` file for the platform.
- An `_include/` folder for any platform-specific header files, includes for HAL, etc.
- A `_common/` folder for common source files (e.g., implementations of nanoFramework PAL functions for this platform).

- You'll also need _nanoCLR/ and _nanoBooter/ subfolders (nanoBooter is required if the platform doesn't offer its own bootloader, like Espressif IDF does). These typically contain the sources or linking directives for building the CLR on that platform.
- Any other components your platform needs (for instance, a _lwIP/ or _FatFs/ if you integrate those, or vendor-specific subfolders if supporting multiple families under this RTOS).

Integrate External Dependencies

Include the RTOS selected to support the platform and/or SDK. The common approach is to use CMake's FetchContent or ExternalProject functions. You might mirror what's done for existing platforms:

- Write a Find<Name>.cmake module or use the platform CMakeLists to check for a *_SOURCE_FOLDER variable. For example, if porting to Zephyr, you would have an option ZEPHYR_SOURCE_FOLDER. If not set, your CMakeLists could attempt to clone a particular tag of Zephyr from GitHub. Alternatively, since Zephyr is complex and heavy, it may be preferable for a developer using it to have its local fork and just specify the path to it.
- Fetch or locate any vendor HAL libraries needed. For instance, if the new platform is a vendor's proprietary OS, you might need to include their SDK libraries in the build. You can add CMake commands to add those libraries (using add_library(... IMPORTED) or by compiling source).
- Make sure to add include directories for all external components so that the compiler can find headers.

Implement the HAL/PAL for nanoFramework

This is more about coding than build, but it is worth mentioning that you'll need to provide implementations for the nanoFramework's platform abstraction interfaces (for example, functions to initialize the hardware, timers for the managed Thread.Sleep, drivers for SPI and I²C transactions, etc.). These go into the source files in _common (if they are common to the different series or to CLR and booter) and other specific files for _nanoCLR/ and _nanoBooter/. The build system should compile these. If your platform can reuse some code from an existing one, consider copying and adapting. For example, much of the networking code might be reusable if the RTOS has a BSD socket API like lwIP offers.

Add the Platform to the Top-Level CMake Logic

Open the top-level CMakeLists.txt in the repository. There is a section where it checks RTOS and sets flags like RTOS_FREERTOS_CHECK and others that are common to other platforms or even specific for the one you're adding. Add a branch for your platform. The simplest way is to extend the conditionals:

- At the top, where it validates the RTOS name, ensure it recognizes your new platform string. The current logic looks like this:

```
if(IS_DIRECTORY ${CMAKE_SOURCE_DIR}/targets/${RTOS})
    string(TOUPPER ${RTOS} RTOS_UPPERCASE)
    set(RTOS_${RTOS_UPPERCASE}_CHECK TRUE)
else()
    message(FATAL_ERROR "'${RTOS}' is an invalid option
    for RTOS.")
endif()
```

This will automatically allow any folder name under targets to be a valid RTOS option. So, simply by creating targets/Zephyr, the build would accept -DRTOS=Zephyr. You might not even need to modify this part if your folder name matches the RTOS you pass.

However, later in the file, there is logic to handle certain RTOS in special ways (FreeRTOS and ThreadX are grouped, ESP32 is a special case, else for others). If your platform can be treated like "others" (i.e., just add the platform folder and then the board), you might not need a new block. But if you need custom handling (perhaps Zephyr requires running its own CMake like ThreadX, or maybe a special tool), you could add an elseif(RTOS_ZEPHYR_CHECK) section with custom commands. Otherwise, falling into the generic else is fine. It will do the following, which means it will include your platform and the board directory:

```
add_subdirectory(${CMAKE_CURRENT_SOURCE_DIR}/targets/Zephyr)
add_subdirectory(${TARGET_BASE_LOCATION})
```

Add a CMake Preset

This step is optional but highly recommended. To make developer's life easier, define a CMake preset for at least one board on the new platform (perhaps a reference board you are using to develop the port). You can copy an existing preset as a template. Set the `TARGET_BOARD` to your new board, set the RTOS to your new platform name, and set any relevant default options. This preset can be added to the main `CMakePresets.json` file (or just kept in your user presets during development). Having a preset will also let VS Code or CMake GUI pick up the new platform easily.

With these steps, the build system should be aware of the new platform. The bulk of the work is implementing the platform support (which is outside the scope of CMake), but the build files provide the structure to slot it in. In fact, community contributors have used this process to port nanoFramework to new environments.

Adding a New Target Board

Adding a new target (board) under an existing platform is a more common scenario—for instance, you have a new STM32 board that runs ChibiOS, or a new ESP32 series. The process is generally as follows.

Start with a Similar Board

Identify an existing board in the repository that is close to your target in terms of MCU and features. It helps if the same MCU (or at least the same series) is already supported, because you can reuse the startup files, linker script, and maybe board config with only minor changes. For example, if you're adding an STM32F413-based board, start with an STM32F411 Nucleo board as a *template*.

Create the Board Directory

Under `targets/<YourRTOS>/`, create a folder with the new `TARGET_BOARD` name. Copy the files from the similar board into it. Typical contents could be:

- `board.h`/`board.c` (for ChibiOS) or other board initialization code
- Linker script (`*.ld`) if this is not provided by the platform SDK, like with Espressif IDF

- A `CMakeLists.txt` file (some platforms have a simple CMakeLists in each board folder to list the source files or to define any board-specific compile definitions)
- Any config files (for example, ChibiOS boards may have a `mcuconf.h` and a `halconf.h` to configure the HAL features for that board's MCU)

Adjust Board Configuration

Go through the files and update the definitions to match your board's hardware:

- Pin definitions in `board.h`, like in ChibiOS (LED pins, USART used for debug, etc.).
- Clock setup (e.g., if your board uses a different crystal frequency or PLL settings, adjust those in `board.c` or equivalent).
- Memory sizes in the linker script (flash and RAM sizes for your MCU variant).
- If your board has peripherals that the reference didn't (or vice versa), you might need to enable/disable certain drivers. For instance, enable the FSMC driver if you have external SRAM, or disable/remove a GPIO port that doesn't exist in the MCU.
- Update the name in files/comments if needed (purely cosmetic but good practice).

CMake Integration

In many cases, you won't need to modify the platform CMakeLists at all for a new board. The platform scripts dynamically picks up all boards. For example, the ChibiOS CMakeLists scans for the board directory and either uses the custom board files or uses the default ones. Just ensure the `TARGET_BOARD` name you plan to use (e.g., `MY_NEW_BOARD`) matches your folder name exactly.

- If the board requires some special compile flag, you can add that in the board's CMakeLists or in the preset (for example, if your board needs `-DENABLE_EXTRAM`, you could add to the target CMakeLists).

- Double-check that the board's files are being included. When you run CMake, it should print a message that support for your board was found either in main or community targets and show the path. If it says "not available," then CMake didn't find your directory—possibly a naming mismatch or a case difference in the name if running in Linux.

Add Build Preset Entry

As with platforms, it's mandatory to add a preset for your new target board. Again, it's easier to reuse the one from the board you started with. In practice, copy an existing board's preset, change the name, and adjust any options (like if your board doesn't have external flash, turn off QUADSPI feature, etc.). Update the toolchain path if needed (or inherit from the same toolchain preset). This will allow you (and others) to build your firmware simply with `cmake --preset MY_NEW_BOARD`.

Build and Test

Generate the build and flash the firmware to your board. Often the first build will succeed if all paths and files are correct, but the firmware might not run until you fine-tune the clock or memory settings. Use a debugger or serial output to verify it boots. If it fails early, enable verbose build and ensure all expected source files (especially startup code) were linked. You can also compare map files or section sizes with the reference board to catch any anomalies.

If your new target is for a platform that requires external source code (say you add an NXP board and it needs a certain version of the NXP SDK), make sure to update documentation or scripts accordingly. However, in many cases (especially adding another STM32), the heavy lifting is already done by the existing platform code. It's mostly about providing the right board definition. Be extra careful with clock configurations and memory space addresses as a first step, because that's often where things go wrong if not set correctly for a new board.

Once your new board is running, you can contribute it back—either to the main repository if it's a widely useful board or to the Community Targets repository. The build system supports either location seamlessly, as discussed.

During this process of adding a new platform (or target board), the compiler will be your best friend. You basically have to follow the errors and address its complains, fix the errors, and repeat until you clear them all. It often starts with hundreds of them, and it will decrease as you make your progress. Very often the last ones are the trickier to solve. As commonly said: the last mile is the hardest.

It is worth noting that the CMake macros and functions in nanoFramework build system follow CMake recommendations (like module filenames starting with *Find*). they group logical units (e.g., macros and functions required for ChibiOS targets live in `binutils.ChibiOS.cmake` file), macros and function names usually start with the prefix `nf_` to clearly disambiguate from the CMake API, and so on.

Developer Containers

One of the easiest ways to set up the build environment for .NET nanoFramework is by using development containers. A development container is a preconfigured Docker-based environment for development that runs in isolation from your host machine.

The nanoFramework team provides official dev container images with the entire firmware build toolchain and all dependencies already installed. This means you don't have to manually set up compilers, SDKs, and other required tools on your machine. The container has everything ready to go, avoiding any need to "pollute" your host system with specialized build tools and also free you from a tedious and time-consuming task of going through docs, finding the right tool and version to install, and individually configuring everything.

These containers are fully maintained by the nanoFramework team and drastically reduce the setup burden for contributors and developers working on nanoFramework firmware projects.

Key benefits of using nanoFramework dev containers include the following:

- **All-in-one environment:** The container comes with all required compilers, SDKs, libraries, and scripts to build the nf-interpreter firmware. For example, it includes the appropriate GCC cross-compilers, CMake, and platform-specific SDKs (like Espressif's ESP-IDF for ESP32)—essentially "the toolchain and all required tools installed and ready to use." You can start building the firmware immediately without hunting down dependencies.

- **Isolation and cleanliness:** Because the development happens inside a Docker container, your host OS remains clean. The container is an isolated environment, so you don't need to install any exotic build tools locally. This isolation prevents version conflicts and the "it works on my machine" syndrome, since everyone uses the same environment.
- **Consistency across platforms:** Dev containers ensure a consistent setup whether you are on Windows, Linux, or macOS. As long as you can run Docker, you get the same build environment. (On Windows, it's recommended to use WSL2 for better performance, but the principle remains the same.) This consistency also extends to cloud environments like GitHub Codespaces; therefore, you'll get an identical setup there.
- **Up-to-date and maintained:** The container images are built and kept up-to-date by the .NET nanoFramework team. They are hosted on the nanoFramework's GitHub Packages registry, so you can pull the latest image knowing it includes the latest toolchain versions and fixes. In short, the team handles maintenance; you just use it.

The nanoFramework dev containers are available in multiple flavors to suit different needs. There is a general "all-platforms" container (supporting builds for all target platforms), and several platform-specific containers focusing on individual platforms or RTOSs. For example, the team provides separate images for ESP32 targets, ChibiOS (STM32) targets, TI SimpleLink targets, ThreadX targets, and so on. You can choose the all-in-one image if you work with many devices, or pick a slimmer platform-specific container if you care only about one platform. In either case, all these images are maintained by nanoFramework and offer the same convenience.

Using the dev container is straightforward. You can use them locally with Docker or even in the cloud via GitHub Codespaces, whichever you prefer. The `nf-interpreter` repository already contains configuration for dev containers (look for the `.devcontainer` folder at the repository root), so the setup is largely automated. For a local setup, make sure you have Docker installed (on Windows, having Docker through WSL2 is recommended) and Visual Studio Code with the Dev Containers extension (which has to be installed from the Marketplace). Then simply clone the `nf-interpreter` repo and open it in VS Code. VS Code will detect the dev container configuration and prompt you to reopen the folder inside the container. Once you confirm, it will pull/build the container image and drop you into a fully configured environment inside VS Code; no additional setup needed. For example:

```
# Clone the nf-interpreter repository
git clone https://github.com/nanoframework/nf-interpreter.git
cd nf-interpreter

# Open the folder in VS Code (Dev Containers extension will handle
the rest)
code .
```

After running the previous, Visual Studio Code will prompt you to reopen the project in a container. Select the .NET nanoFramework dev container configuration (for instance, the "nanoFramework (nf-interpreter)" container definition), and the environment will be built automatically. This process might take a few minutes on the first run (as the Docker image is downloaded and initialized), but after that you'll have a VS Code workspace running inside the container with everything set up. You can immediately compile the firmware or run CMake targets as if you had set up the entire toolchain on your machine. If you prefer not to install anything locally, you can achieve the same result on GitHub Codespaces. Just open the repository in a Codespace, and it will use the same dev container to give you a ready-to-go development environment in the cloud.

The big advantage of using the dev container approach is having a consistent, working build environment out of the box. You don't need to troubleshoot installation issues or configure paths. The container is preconfigured with known-good settings and simply works.

It would be out of scope for this content to provide a full walkthrough on the process of downloading the dev container. There is a comprehensive guide available in the official .NET nanoFramework documentation. The docs include step-by-step guides and troubleshooting tips, should you need them. Please find the URL to the doc in the "Additional Resources" section at the end of the chapter.

Building in the Cloud

The .NET nanoFramework project uses a cloud-based build system to compile firmware for all supported targets in an automated and consistent way. The official firmware builds run on Azure DevOps (AZDO) as YAML-defined pipelines, which are stored alongside the code in the nf-interpreter repository (for example, see the `azure-pipelines.yml` file in the repo root). Whenever code is pushed or a pull request is opened, Azure DevOps triggers the CI pipeline to build the firmware for multiple target boards. This ensures that any change is immediately validated against all platforms and that up-to-date firmware binaries are produced without manual intervention.

Figure 3-2 illustrates the high-level architecture of the cloud build pipeline. The code in the .NET nanoFramework GitHub repository triggers an Azure DevOps pipeline defined by a YAML configuration, which orchestrates multiple parallel jobs to build firmware for different target families. Each job uses predefined template steps (from the `nf-interpreter` repository and the `nf-tools` one) to set up the build environment and compile the firmware, finally producing firmware binaries that are collected as build artifacts and published to a public feed for consumption.

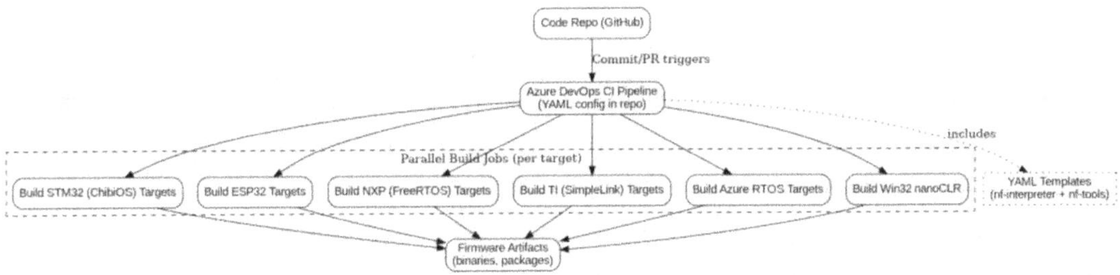

Figure 3-2. *Cloud-based CI pipeline for .NET nanoFramework firmware builds (Azure DevOps with parallel jobs and YAML templates)*

The pipeline configuration is defined *as code* in YAML and is split into reusable templates to avoid duplicating logic for each target. Rather than one huge script, the build process is broken down into modular YAML files under the `azure-pipelines-templates` folder in the `nf-interpreter` repo, as well as in the separate `nf-tools` repository. The main pipeline YAML references these template files to perform common tasks, for example, installing the ARM GCC toolchain, CMake, and Ninja build system, checking code formatting, running the build, and packaging the output. Each of those steps is defined in a template (e.g., `download-install-llvm.yml` or `check-code-style.yml`) that can be included wherever needed. This template-based approach promotes reuse and maintainability: if a build step needs to be updated (say, a new tool version or a fix in the build process), it can be changed in one template file, and all pipeline jobs will immediately use the updated logic. The pipeline even uses templates for final steps like packing the compiled binaries and publishing them to the nanoFramework's artifact feed hosted in CloudSmith (a cloud-based artifact distribution provider), ensuring that the output of each build is consistently packaged and made available.

In terms of structure, the Azure DevOps pipeline is organized into multiple jobs that run in parallel to build firmware for different platform families. For example, one job builds all STM32-based targets (using the ChibiOS HAL), and another handles ESP32 targets; additional jobs cover NXP boards (FreeRTOS), TI SimpleLink devices, ThreadX (Azure RTOS) based targets, and even the Win32 nanoCLR and .NET CLI application. Each job uses the shared YAML templates to set up its build environment (installing required compilers and tools) and then invokes the CMake build for each board in that family. Because these jobs run in parallel on the cloud, the system can build firmware for many targets relatively quickly. Once all the compilation jobs finish, the pipeline uses further templates to gather the firmware binaries, package them (for example, into NuGet packages or zip files), and publish them as build artifacts or push them to a package feed for distribution.

Developers can leverage this cloud build system for their own needs as well. Since the pipeline definitions and templates are part of the open-source repository, you can study and even copy them to set up builds for custom targets or personal projects. The YAML template files in `nf-interpreter` and `nf-tools` serve as a reference on how to configure various build steps. In fact, the `nf-interpreter` pipeline itself pulls in the `nf-tools` repository as a resource (templates) to reuse common build logic. By referencing the same templates, you can ensure your custom firmware builds follow the same proven steps as the official ones. For instance, if you were adding a new target, you could create a new job in a YAML pipeline that calls the existing build templates. This gives you a jump-start, since the templates handle things like setting up the compiler, invoking CMake with the right preset, and publishing the output.

The nanoFramework team actively maintains these pipeline templates so they are kept up-to-date with the latest tools and best practices. This active use by the core team (for every PR and release build) means the build system is continuously tested and improved, resulting in a very reliable setup that community developers can trust and adopt.

In addition to the Azure DevOps pipeline, the `nf-interpreter` repository also provides GitHub Actions workflows that support complete firmware builds. Under the `.github/workflows` directory you'll find workflow files that define build processes on GitHub's CI infrastructure. These workflows use Docker-based development containers to set up the build environment and then compile the firmware for various targets in a manner similar to the Azure DevOps pipeline. In particular, there is a `"smoke test"` workflow that builds a selection of firmware images using the dedicated dev container for each platform, ensuring that the entire toolchain can run on GitHub's runners as well.

While the primary CI is on Azure DevOps, these GitHub Actions are maintained in parallel by the nanoFramework team to be ready for automation or testing needs. They give developers an alternative way to automate builds or verify contributions (for example, in forked repositories or community-driven testing) using GitHub's infrastructure, all while following the same build steps defined by the official templates. In summary, whether via Azure DevOps or GitHub Actions, .NET nanoFramework's cloud build system provides a robust, reusable, and up-to-date solution for building firmware across a wide range of targets in an automated fashion.

Summary

In this chapter, we've delved into the build system of .NET nanoFramework, which uses CMake and Ninja to target multiple architectures and operating systems. It begins by introducing CMake and Ninja, explaining their advantages such as portability, modular structure, widespread adoption, and fast runs. The chapter then details the structure of the nanoFramework build system, including general configuration, RTOS integration, platform and target setup, and the use of CMake Presets for managing builds. Guidance is also provided on extending the build system to support new platforms and boards (targets).

We've seen how highly configurable the nanoFramework build system is in order to support different microcontroller platforms and specific targets. It uses a top-level CMake project that includes relevant components based on build options. Integration of RTOS and SDK, HAL and PAL configuration, RTOS initialization, and platform-specific code organization was covered.

Additionally, we went through target-specific configuration, including defining firmware targets, board initialization code, memory and device configuration, and support for community targets.

In the section about development containers you saw how these offer a convenient preconfigured environment for development. And in the final section we've went through the cloud-based build system using Azure DevOps pipelines and GitHub Actions to accomplish automated and consistent firmware compilation, required in professional projects.

In the next chapter, we'll discuss how nanoFramework integrates seamlessly into the .NET ecosystem and how the high-quality development tools available help developers to be productive and deliver.

Additional Resources

You can find more information about several topics discussed in this chapter at the following locations:

CMake: `https://cmake.org/`

CMake Presets: `https://cmake.org/cmake/help/v3.31/manual/cmake-presets.7.html/`

Ninja: `https://github.com/ninja-build/ninja/`

ChibiOS RTOS: `https://www.chibios.org/`

FreeRTOS: `https://www.freertos.org/`

Espressif IDF: `https://idf.espressif.com/`

ThreadX: `https://github.com/eclipse-threadx/threadx`

Official docs on how to build .NET nanoFramework: `https://docs.nanoframework.net/content/building/index.html`

CHAPTER 4

Being Part of the .NET Ecosystem

Without a doubt, .NET nanoFramework is part of the .NET ecosystem.

It plays a crucial role in realizing the .NET vision of “write, run, and build on multiple platforms,” specifically for resource-constrained platforms, such as microcontrollers. Although this is a broad and conceptual description that encompasses numerous technologies, some may argue that it is an oversimplification. Nevertheless, it effectively conveys the idea that one can write a piece of code or even a library that can operate on both a multicore high-end machine in the cloud or on a small microcontroller with only a few hundred kilobytes of RAM and flash memory (providing the same APIs are used). This capability is indeed significant. Only projects referencing the .NET nanoFramework Core Library can be loaded in devices running the nanoCLR.

This chapter delves deeply into what it means for nanoFramework to be part of the .NET ecosystem, exploring its tight integration with industry-standard tools, languages, packages, and learning resources. By leveraging this powerful ecosystem, developers can maximize productivity, accelerate project timelines, and enhance code portability across diverse platforms.

Visual Studio: The IDE

Visual Studio serves as the cornerstone of the .NET ecosystem, offering developers an intuitive and feature-rich environment designed to support the diverse stages of application development. For those working with .NET nanoFramework, there is a specialized extension for Visual Studio tailored to the unique challenges of embedded development, ensuring a streamlined and efficient workflow.

J. Simões, *Embedded Systems with .NET nanoFramework*, https://doi.org/10.1007/979-8-8688-2096-0_4

This extension enhances productivity by integrating tools that allow developers to seamlessly deploy their applications to microcontrollers. With just a few clicks, code can be transferred to connected devices, enabling rapid testing and iteration. Additionally, Visual Studio supports advanced debugging features, such as setting breakpoints, inspecting variables, and executing code step-by-step, allowing developers to identify and resolve issues with precision.

One standout feature of the Visual Studio extension for .NET nanoFramework is the Device Explorer. This tool simplifies the management of connected nanoFramework devices by automatically detecting hardware, managing firmware updates, and facilitating device interactions—all directly within the IDE. Developers can perform tasks ranging from flashing firmware to monitoring application data in real time, significantly reducing the complexity often associated with embedded system development.

Installing the Visual Studio Extension

Assuming that you already have Visual Studio in your system, make sure you have the ".NET desktop development" workload installed. If you don't have Visual Studio installed, you have to install it first. Go to `www.visualstudio.com/downloads` and get the installer.

There are versions of the extension available for Visual Studio 2019 and 2022. And the extension can be installed in any of the editions, from Community to Enterprise.

Once you have Visual Studio installed and working, open the Extension Manager and in the browser search box type **nanoFramework** (see Figure 4-1).

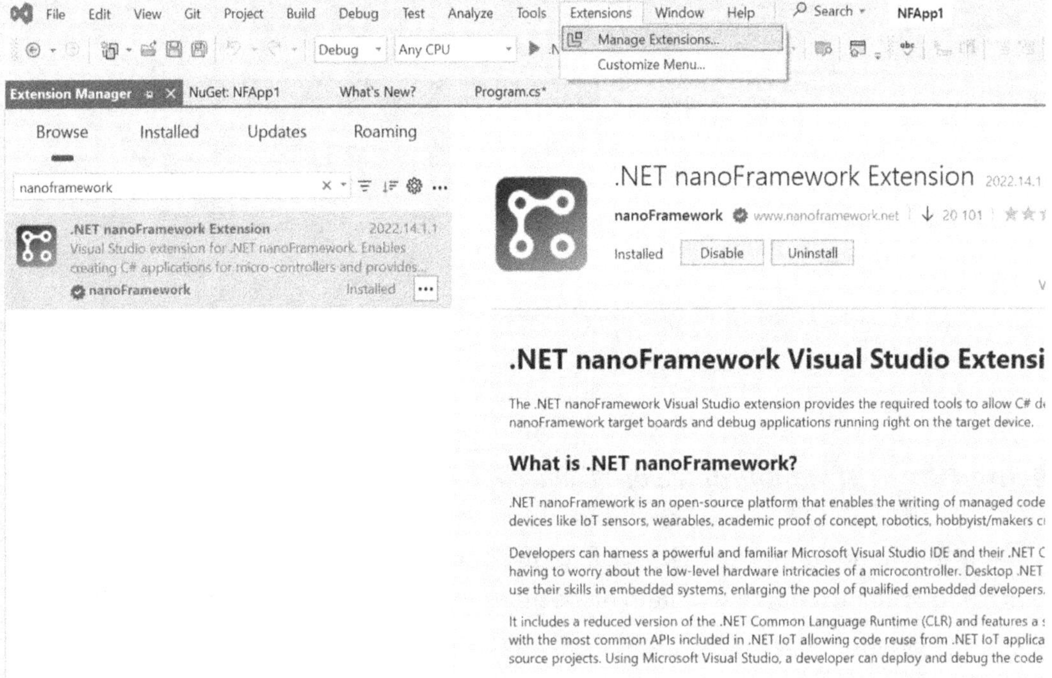

Figure 4-1. *Visual Studio Extension Manager*

When the nanoFramework extension shows up, click the Install button. A confirmation message will tell you that you need to close Visual Studio for the installation to start.

The install process is quite simple and requires only a couple of clicks to validate the install. Once you see a successful message, close the installer and re-open Visual Studio.

To activate the nanoFramework extension, navigate to View > Other Window and find Device Explorer (see Figure 4-2).

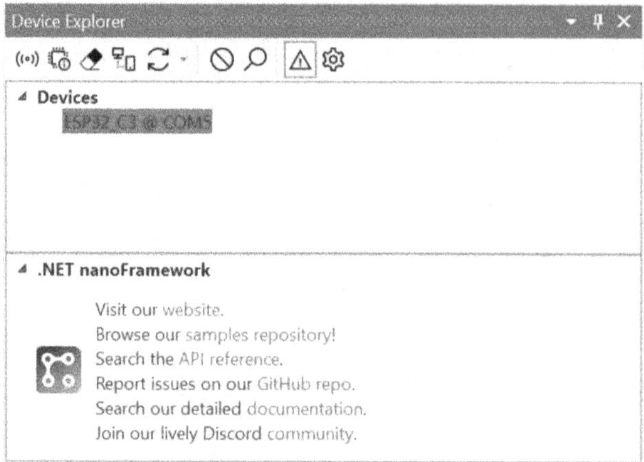

Figure 4-2. *.NET nanoFramework Device Explorer*

Now that nanoFramework Device Explorer was started, it will start searching (in the background) all the connected nano devices. As the discovered progresses, you'll see a progress message in the output pane, reporting what is happening.

Caution It is important to note that any other software accessing serial ports on your system can interfere with or even prevent the discovery process managed by the nanoFramework Device Explorer. To avoid conflicts, ensure that such software is either disabled or not actively using the serial ports during device detection and interaction. This precaution helps maintain a smooth workflow and guarantees reliable operation of the connected devices.

For each device that shows in the tree view, there are a number of operations you can perform, like query its capabilities, check if it is responsive, erase its deployment storage, send a reset command, or change network-related configurations.

Project Templates

The .NET nanoFramework extension for Visual Studio includes templates for the following project types:

- **Blank application:** This is for an application to be deployed into a nano device.
- **Class library:** This is a project with a library to be referenced in other projects.
- **Unit test:** This is a project with MSTest unit tests that can be run on a real or virtual device.

C#: A Powerful Object-Oriented Language

C# is a robust, modern, and versatile programming language central to the .NET platform. Its object-oriented capabilities, combined with powerful language features like generics, delegates, and LINQ, empower developers to write clean, maintainable, and reusable code.

When used with .NET nanoFramework, C# allows developers to benefit from automatic memory management, type safety, and structured exception handling, significantly reducing the complexity typically associated with embedded development. Additionally, ongoing enhancements to the language and runtime continually improve performance, security, and developer experience.

"Hello World" Application

We'll now create the customary "hello world" application as a nanoFramework C# application. Assuming you have the extension installed and immediately after launching Visual Studio, you're presented with the welcome screen on which you click "Create a new project" under the Get Started section on the right. Next you want to filter out the nanoFramework project, for which you type **nanoFramework** in the search box at the top. A list of the available project templates shows. Click in the Blank Application and the click Next. On the next page you enter the solution and project and select the location where all these will be saved.

The nanoFramework template has already boilerplate code that includes a call to `Debug.WriteLine()`, which outputs the string to the output pane after deploying it to a device.

```
using System.Diagnostics;
using System.Threading;

namespace NFApp1
{
    public class Program
    {
        public static void Main()
        {
            Debug.WriteLine("Hello from nanoFramework!");

            Thread.Sleep(Timeout.Infinite);
        }
    }
}
```

Let's look at this application briefly. A typical C# application structure involves the `Program.Main()` method. This method writes a debug message using `Debug.WriteLine()`, and then calls `Thread.Sleep(Timeout.Infinite)` to keep the application running indefinitely. This helps prevent the application from exiting and restarting, making start a debug session easier.

Project System

.NET nanoFramework C# projects use the CPS project system style. This is because of technical limitations of the Visual Studio Extensibility SDK. There are minor shortcomings because of these limitations, like not being able to use Package Reference or the modern dotnet CLI to create and build projects right from the command line. None of these limitations is anything major nor do they hinder developers' productivity.

A nanoFramework project file, identified by the `.nfproj` extension, is quite similar to C# `.csproj` files. The main differences are in the references, targets, and properties unique to nanoFramework. Because of this similarity, editing these files is straightforward. Additionally, there is extensive documentation available on MSBuild properties and various other aspects of project handling. This wealth of information makes it easy to tweak and perfect your nanoFramework projects, if the need arises.

Development Lifecycle: Coding to Debugging

The development lifecycle of a nanoFramework project closely mirrors typical .NET projects, providing developers with a consistent workflow.

Coding

Inside Visual Studio, developers write C# code leveraging powerful editor features and tools that are part of the IDE, not specific to nanoFramework. The most common ones are IntelliSense, refactoring, integrated Git support, or even GitHub Copilot. IntelliSense offers intelligent code completion, ensuring faster coding by predicting the developer's intentions and suggesting relevant classes, methods, and properties. Refactoring tools enable developers to efficiently restructure code without altering its external behavior, promoting code clarity and maintainability. Integrated Git support provides robust version control capabilities directly within the IDE, enabling easy collaboration and streamlined tracking of code changes. At the end of the day, you're coding in C#; therefore, all the integrated productivity features and helpers that are included in Visual Studio or any extensions that you have installed can help you to become more productive and efficient when writing code.

Building

Projects utilize the standard MSBuild system, maintaining consistency with other .NET applications and allowing straightforward integration with continuous integration (CI) pipelines.

MSBuild provides a flexible and extensible system to define and manage build processes, ensuring reproducible builds across various environments. Integration with CI tools such as Azure DevOps and GitHub Actions is straightforward, enabling automated and consistent builds, tests, and deployments.

Like with any other .NET C# solution, you can build (or rebuild) individual projects or the complete solution containing them. Likewise, you can add or remove projects and configure which ones are built along with the build type. Like with other C# projects, building in Release will remove unused code and will output smaller binaries. Note that building in Release will leave out all the data required to debug an application; therefore, even if you try to start a debug session of a Release build, it will be deployed in the device, but you won't be able to set breakpoint or control the execution.

Also, it's worth mentioning that the build process of nanoFramework projects uses Roslyn to compile and build, just like any other C# project. The difference is that following the regular build, it has an extra step, which is processing the IL file generated by Roslyn. This processing is carried out by a tool called the Metadata processor that, in a nutshell, stripes out all the nonessential data from the IL files and metadata, reduces the address jumps and calls to 32 bits, and simplifies enums, strings, and resources. The outcome of this process results in a PE file that is proprietary format, whose structure is very similar to standard C# IL metadata, just that in a condensed format.

Deployment

.NET nanoFramework provides streamlined deployment processes via the Visual Studio extension or command-line tools like `nanoff`, simplifying the flashing of firmware and managed applications. Within Visual Studio, deployment can be achieved with a single click, automatically transferring compiled binaries directly to connected devices. The `nanoff` command-line utility offers advanced users and automated scripts the ability to deploy and manage firmware efficiently, further supporting automation and integration into larger DevOps workflows.

Deployment from within Visual Studio can be accomplished by right-clicking the project to deploy in the Solution Explorer view or selecting the Build > Deploy Solutions menu. What does this do? If the project (and any other referenced projects) needs to be built, it will connect to the nano device selected in the Device Explorer view and deploy the application and all the required assemblies to the deployment storage.

Note that deploying a solution performs only that task: deploying all the required assemblies to the deployment storage. If you want the application to start running, you have to reset the device.

Another aspect to consider is that it is fundamental to select the "Start project" of a solution. Failing to do so will cause the build dependencies to be incorrect, and you may see unexpected build errors. Even worse (and usually cause of severe frustration) is the deployment of a solution that fails to start because of a misplaced entry point or even type resolution errors. Because of the nature of this issue, it may not be obvious at a first glance what could be the cause for the problem, which is why I'm highlighting it.

As the final step in the build process, the nanoFramework project system has an exclusive feature that packs a binary file that includes the complete deployment region (the PE file of the application and all the required assemblies). This binary file is stored in the output directory, has the name of the start project, and has a bin extension. It can be stored as a version backup or to flash in devices as part of a production or test workflow.

Debugging

Developers can seamlessly debug their code directly on the microcontroller, taking advantage of Visual Studio's powerful debugging features, including breakpoints, watches, and step-by-step execution.

Breakpoints allow developers to pause execution at critical points to inspect application states, while watches provide real-time visibility of variable values and expressions, facilitating detailed analysis of application behaviour.

Step-by-step execution enables developers to precisely control the debugging flow, assisting in isolating and correcting intricate logic errors and performance bottlenecks.

Advanced features like conditional breakpoints, expressions, hit count, and such are all available. Because of several technical reasons, namely, the need to deploy to the device storage, the Hot Reload feature is not available when debugging the .NET nanoFramework code.

Going back to the Hello World project, let's go through a typical debug session:

1. First, set a breakpoint at the code line of `Debug.WriteLine()`.
2. Check if the nano device that will be used for the debug session is selected in Device Explorer tree view.
3. Hit F5 or click the menu Debug > Start Debugging.
4. Observe the progress of the deployment stage where you'll see the details of the operation in the output pane and at the status bar.
5. Immediately after the deployment is completed and the debug session handshake stage occurs, you'll see the Visual Studio IDE interface change to the debug mode, and the first breakpoint will be hit.

At this point, the debug session is ongoing, and you can use all the available features at your disposal. We won't go into details on all those as it is beyond the scope of this content.

Before starting a debug session, if it happens that there is more than one nano device connected, make sure that the intended one is selected; otherwise, you'll end up deploying to the wrong device. Keep in mind that the deployment involves erasing the storage area and stopping the execution of any ongoing application. This can disrupt the operation of a running device.

The nanoFramework extension tries to be as developer friendly as possible. Another convenient feature that is there to assist developers is a pre-check of the required assemblies before the deployment actually takes place. What exactly is this? Put simply, the extension grabs a list of the assemblies that are going to be deployed to the nano device and compares the existence of support for it, and the required version is the one present on the device. If there is a mismatch somewhere, the deployment will abort with an explanation of whatever the mismatch I preventing the deployment to succeed.

To keep the debug session running smoothly, keep in mind the number of objects being presented. These include the *Locals* pane, the objects added to the Watch pane, and hovering a variable with the mouse cursor when the debugger is stopped. Each time a breakpoint is hit, the debugger queries the device execution engine for the content of all of these objects. As the number of these objects grows, so does the time the debugger takes to refresh their contents each time a session stops at a breakpoint or following a single-step move. Therefore, it's better to keep all those to the absolute minimum required.

NuGet Packages: Leveraging the .NET Ecosystem

NuGet packages are fundamental to .NET development, providing access to a vast collection of reusable libraries and tools. .NET nanoFramework fully embraces this mechanism, distributing class libraries, hardware bindings, and utility tools through NuGet and ensuring straightforward integration into any project.

Using NuGet, developers can easily incorporate drivers for sensors, displays, communication modules, and more, accelerating development and fostering reuse across projects. Besides consuming NuGet packages distributed through nuget.org, an organization can have their own internal or private repositories with the libraries developed internally as part of their components library.

For demonstration purposes, let's add a NuGet package to the Hello World project. There are several ways to accomplish this. Let's use the Visual Studio Package Manager interface:

1. In the Solution Explorer, right-click the project item and choose Manage NuGet Packages.
2. After the Package Manager window opens, switch the view to Browse.
3. In the search box, type **nanoframework runtime**.
4. You'll se a list of the available NuGet packages with those words on their name.
5. Select `nanoFramework.Runtime.Native` and click the Install button on the right side.
6. The package manager will then download it and add a reference to it in the project.

Now for the sake of this example, let's use an API from that namespace that outputs the device target name. Back in the `Main()` code, open a new line after the `Debug.WritLine()` one.

1. Start typing **SystemInfo**. You'll see IntelliSense offering to add a `using` entry for `nanoFramework.Runtime.Native`. Take it and now IntelliSense has context into that namespace.
2. Add a call to the `TargetName` property.
3. Wrap that inside another `Debug.WriteLine()` so that information is output.

You'll end up with something like this:

```
using nanoFramework.Runtime.Native;
using System.Diagnostics;
using System.Threading;

namespace NFApp1
{
    public class Program
    {
        public static void Main()
        {
            Debug.WriteLine("Hello from nanoFramework!");
```

```
            Debug.WriteLine($"Target name: {SystemInfo.TargetName}");

            Thread.Sleep(Timeout.Infinite);
        }
    }
}
```

Hit *F5* to start a new debug session. Deployment will happen followed by the debugger starting, and then you'll see the target name in the Output pane.

NuGet packages can depend on other packages. When that happens, the dependencies are declared in the package manifest, and Package Manager takes care of installing the required ones.

Note that in nanoFramework, because of a strict policy of type resolution, the dependencies have to be an exact version. Therefore, it's absolutely mandatory to respect the requested dependency version. Because of technical limitations of the platforms, it is not possible to declare assembly redirections.

Test Framework

You'll learn all about the Test Framework in Chapter 8. At this stage, we will provide a brief overview, as it is an essential component of the .NET toolbox.

The .NET nanoFramework Test Framework is a lightweight library designed to bring the familiar world of unit testing to resource-constrained devices. Inspired by larger frameworks like NUnit and MSTest, this framework lets you write and run tests directly on your device or in an emulator. Even though you're working with limited resources, you can still benefit from automated tests, just like in full-scale .NET development.

If you've worked with one of the previously mentioned test frameworks, you should already be familiar with how to use it.

It's pretty simple: you decorate the classes containing tests with the `[TestClass]` attribute and test methods with `[TestMethod]`. From there on, the framework takes care of running them.

The following are a couple of snippets from test classes taken from the nanoFramework JSON library:

```
using nanoFramework.TestFramework;

namespace nanoFramework.Json.Test
{
    [TestClass]
    public class JsonDeserializationArraysTests
    {
        const string IntArrayJson = "[405421362,1082483948,113170765
        4,345242860,1111968802]";

        [TestMethod]
        public void CanDeserializeIntArray()
        {
            var result = (int[])JsonConvert.DeserializeObject(IntArrayJson,
            typeof(int[]));

            Assert.AreEqual(result[0], 405421362);
            Assert.AreEqual(result[1], 1082483948);
            Assert.AreEqual(result[2], 1131707654);
            Assert.AreEqual(result[3], 345242860);
            Assert.AreEqual(result[4], 1111968802);
        }
    }

    [TestClass]
    public class IntConverterTests
    {
        [TestMethod]
        [DataRow("120", 120)]
        [DataRow("45", 45)]
        public void IntConverter_ToType_ShouldReturnValidData(string value,
        int expectedValue)
```

```
        {
            var converter = new Json.Converters.IntConverter();
            var convertedValue = (int)converter.ToType(value);

            Assert.AreEqual(expectedValue, convertedValue);
        }

    }
}
```

Running tests on .NET nanoFramework can be done either directly on a real device or using the nanoFramework virtual device. You can either use the Test Explorer in Visual Studio or use the `vstest` CLI.

The nanoFramework Test Framework is fully integrated with Visual Studio Test Explorer, and you can control test executions from there as well as navigating through the unit tests and running results. Figure 4-3 shows the Test Explorer after running a unit test for the JSON library.

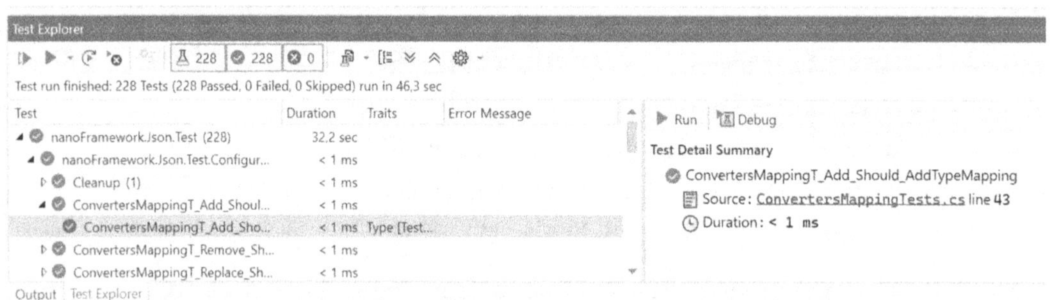

Figure 4-3. *Test Explorer after a test run*

Learning Resources: Empowering Developers

As a developer diving into the world of nanoFramework, you'll find yourself supported by a rich array of resources that cater to every learning style and level of expertise. Whether you're a beginner or an experienced coder working on embedded systems, the tools and communities available will guide you every step of the way.

nanoFramework GitHub Repository

The official nanoFramework GitHub repository is a treasure trove of information. Here, you'll find detailed code examples, active issue tracking, and opportunities to collaborate with other developers. Whether you're looking to contribute to the project or simply exploring its inner workings, GitHub acts as the central hub for staying updated on all things nanoFramework.

Community Forums: Sharing Knowledge and Building Connections

The saying "No developer is an island" rings especially true in the nanoFramework ecosystem. Platforms like Discord and GitHub Discussions offer dynamic spaces for developers to connect, troubleshoot, and share ideas. If you're stuck on a tricky issue or just looking to chat with like-minded individuals, these forums are your go-to destinations. Looking for an answer to a specific question? Stack Overflow is another fantastic platform where you can browse existing solutions or pose your own queries to the developer community.

Microsoft Learn and .NET Documentation

When it comes to mastering the .NET framework and its applications in embedded development, the Microsoft Learn platform and .NET documentation are invaluable. From tutorials on C# syntax to best practices for working with Visual Studio, these resources are designed to equip you with the knowledge you need to succeed. They are comprehensive, beginner-friendly, and continually updated to reflect the latest advancements in the .NET ecosystem.

Online Courses and Tutorials

For hands-on learners, there is a collection of samples curated by the nanoFramework Core Team covering pretty much all the areas and available APIs. There are also several sections about usage, tools, and development topics in the nanoFramework official documentation website. In addition, you can find tutorials and guides for the topics covered online.

A Community to Grow With

What sets nanoFramework apart is not just its technology but its vibrant and welcoming community. From GitHub repositories teeming with activity to forums buzzing with discussions, you're never alone in your development journey. The collective expertise and enthusiasm of this community make learning and innovating with nanoFramework an enjoyable and rewarding experience.

- **GitHub:** nanoFramework's official repositories offer code examples, issue tracking, and collaboration opportunities.
- **Community Forums:** Platforms like Discord and GitHub discussions provide robust community-driven support, guidance, and knowledge exchange.
- **Online Courses and Tutorials:** Numerous platforms offer detailed tutorials specifically geared toward mastering C#, Visual Studio, and embedded development with nanoFramework.

Summary

This chapter took you on an journey through the tools and features of .NET nanoFramework within the broader .NET ecosystem.

We began by installing the Visual Studio extension. With that in place, you saw how to create and debug a "Hello World" app to showcase the basics of C# in action.

Next, you navigated the world of NuGet packages, learning how to search for them, reference them in your projects, and utilize their APIs within your code. You also took a closer look at the nanoFramework test framework, discussing test class attributes and the processes involved in test execution.

Looking ahead, the next chapter will dive into a typical embedded system project. You'll examine the requirements and explore the various solutions available, continuing your hands-on exploration of .NET nanoFramework.

Additional Resources

You can find more information about several topics discussed in this chapter at the following locations:

Visual Studio download: `https://www.visualstudio.com/downloads`

nanoff CLI: `https://github.com/nanoframework/nanoFirmwareFlasher`

C# Guide: `https://learn.microsoft.com/en-us/dotnet/csharp/`

Visual Studio Getting Started: `https://visualstudio.microsoft.com/vs/getting-started/`

.NET nanoFramework official Samples: `https://github.com/nanoframework/samples`

NuGet packages: `https://www.nuget.org/packages`

MSTest: `https://learn.microsoft.com/en-us/dotnet/core/testing/unit-testing-csharp-with-mstest`

Visual Studio Test Platform: `https://github.com/microsoft/vstest`

CHAPTER 5

Interfacing with the Outside World

When your microcontroller needs to interact with the outside world, it uses its peripherals—things like GPIOs, UARTs, SPI and I²C buses, analog inputs, PWM outputs, and so on. In .NET nanoFramework, all these common interfaces are exposed with friendly C# APIs. Empowered with these, you can set up pins, read sensors, drive displays, and even use advanced protocols with only a few lines of code. For example, using the nanoFramework IoT device bindings, reading a BME280 temperature/pressure sensor over I²C is almost trivial—you just create an `I2cDevice`, pass it to the `Bme280` class, and call its `Read()` method. In fact, nanoFramework's APIs align closely with the .NET IoT Core libraries, so much of your code is identical between a PC or Raspberry Pi and a tiny microcontroller.

In this chapter, we'll walk through the more common interfaces and buses—GPIO, UART (Serial), SPI, I²C, ADC (analog input), PWM—and show how to use them with nanoFramework.

GPIO Pins

GPIO stands for General-Purpose Input/Output. C#-style GPIO control in nanoFramework is provided by the `System.Device.Gpio` namespace. The main class is `GpioController`, which you use to open individual pins, and you interact with each pin through a `GpioPin` object.

GPIO pins have to be in one of two possible states: High or Low. It's also common to find the equivalent names for that as True or False or even one and zero.

To use it, from your project, you have to add a reference to the `System.Device.Gpio` (nanoFramework version) NuGet package.

J. Simões, *Embedded Systems with .NET nanoFramework*, https://doi.org/10.1007/979-8-8688-2096-0_5

Let's go for the embedded version of "Hello World" and blink an LED on pin 25 (which is an arbitrary selection for demo purposes).

Figure 5-1 shows how a prototype board would look for this project.

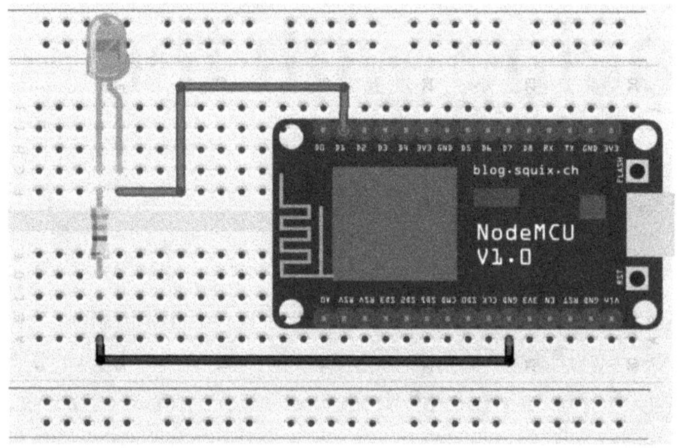

Figure 5-1. *Simple LED circuit*

The figure is simple representation of a nano device connected to an LED. Use a 100R resistor (or slightly higher). When wiring the circuit, make sure to respect the notch in the LED body so the current flows in the correct sense. Otherwise it won't LIT.

Assuming you have already a new nanoFramework application project opened and you've already added a reference to the `System.Device.Gpio` NuGet package, you'd write the following:

```
using System.Device.Gpio;

// Create a controller for the GPIO hardware
GpioController gpio = new GpioController();

// Open pin 25 as an output
GpioPin led = gpio.OpenPin(25, PinMode.Output);

while(true)
{
      // Turn LED on and off
      led.Write(PinValue.High);   // LED on (assuming active-high LED)
```

```
    Thread.Sleep(500);
    led.Write(PinValue.Low);     // LED off
    Thread.Sleep(500);
}
```

That's it—OpenPin() sets the pin mode (output in this case), and Write() sets it high or low. nanoFramework also supports pull-up and pull-down modes on input pins to avoid "floating" pins. For instance, if you have a button tied to ground, you can open the pin as an internal pull-up (so it reads high until the button is pressed):

```
GpioPin button = gpio.OpenPin(12, PinMode.InputPullUp);
PinValue state = button.Read();
```

Here pin 12 will normally read High (because of the pull-up resistor) and read Low only when the button connects it to ground.

You can also use PinMode.InputPullDown similarly (if your hardware supports it). In short, the available pin modes let you wire up almost any common digital circuit.

If you want to respond to pin changes rather than constantly polling, nanoFramework lets you register an event handler for PinValueChanged.

For example, to signal a reset event whenever the button goes from low to high, you could write the following:

```
button.ValueChanged += (sender, args) =>
{
   if( args.ChangeType == PinEventTypes.Rising)
   {
       gpioEvent.Set();
   }
};

button.DebounceTimeout = TimeSpan.FromMilliseconds(200);
```

Here we hook the ValueChanged event to the handling code, inline. We also set a debounce timeout of 200ms, which filters out any noisy glitches when the mechanical switch bounces. Debounce is a built-in feature of nanoFramework GpioPin. This is very convenient so you don't have to take care of this nuisance in your code.

Overall, using GPIO in nanoFramework is straightforward and works the same across boards—the same code can blink an LED on an ESP32, STM32, or Giant Gecko with no platform-specific tweaks (aside from pin numbers). This general GPIO API makes it trivial to turn on/off relays, read buttons, toggle sensor power pins, or do anything that requires simple digital signals.

Serial Ports

A serial port is a communication interface that sends data one bit at a time down a wire. In practice, a serial link typically uses just two data wires—one for transmitting (TX) and one for receiving (RX)—plus a common ground.

A classic RS-232 link wires the TX pin of one device to the RX pin of the other, and vice versa (with a shared ground), so each side can both send and listen at the same time. Because serial cables use fewer wires, they are simpler and cheaper to route than parallel buses. It's this simplicity and low hardware cost that means UART serial remains widely used in embedded systems and industrial devices for things like console I/O, GPS and Bluetooth modules, sensors, and instrumentation where modest data rates are sufficient. See Figure 5-2.

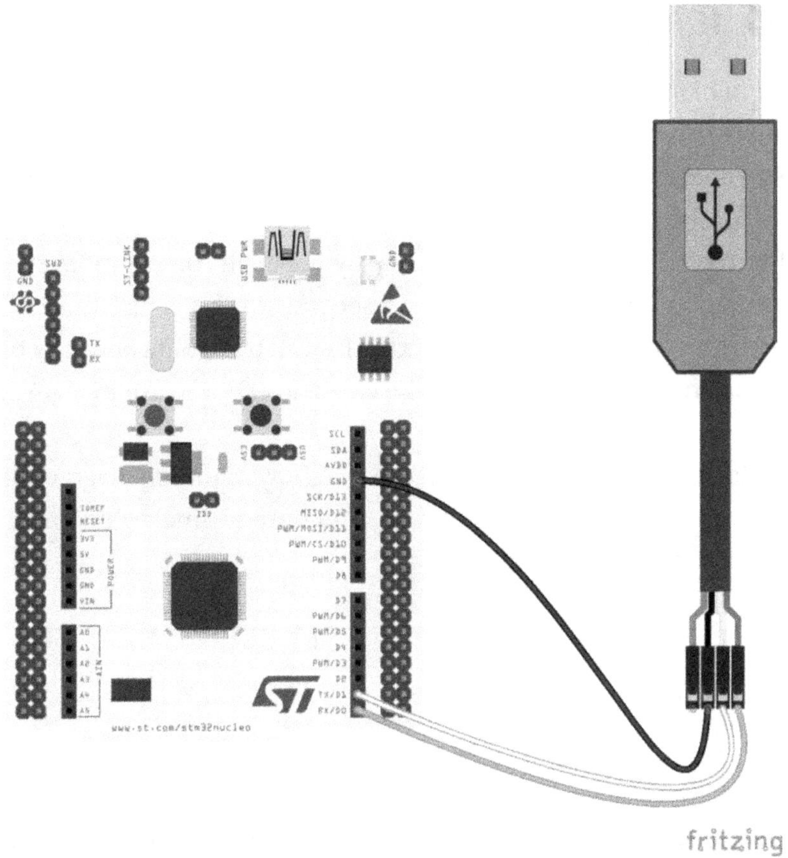

Figure 5-2. *ST Nucleo board connected to an USB serial cable*

You can see in the previous figure, the simplest possible connection from a UART in an ST Nucleo board to a USB to serial converter cable. The black wire is connected to GND, the white to TX, and the green to RX. This allows a cheap and easy connection to a PC.

The TX/RX wiring means serial links are usually full-duplex: both sides can send data simultaneously without waiting. Internally, UART hardware supports this by having separate transmit and receive buffers (shift registers) for each direction. (If only one data line were used; it would be half-duplex, but typical UARTs use two wires.) In all cases, the serial line idles at a logical “1” (mark) level, and both ends agree ahead of time on the timing (or baud rate) so bits line up.

Bits, Baud Rate, and Framing

Serial data is sent in frames (sometimes called *packets* or *characters*). Each frame carries one byte (or more) of payload along with synchronization bits. Before the actual data bits, a start bit is sent to signal "ready." Typically the line is idle-high (logic 1); then the start bit pulls it low (logic 0) for one bit-time to mark the beginning. After that come the data bits—often 8 bits (LSB first) for a standard byte. Finally, one or more stop bits (logic 1) end the frame and return the line to idle. (A second stop bit is rarely used in modern practice.) A parity bit can optionally be inserted between the data and stop bit(s) for simple error checking. Together this might be called an "8N1" format: eight data bits, No parity, 1 stop bit.

Let's take a look at a quick example. Figure 5-3 shows a timing diagram of the signal transmitting the ASCII character z (small caps) and hexadecimal value (0x7A) with a binary representation of 0-1-0-1-1-1-1-0.

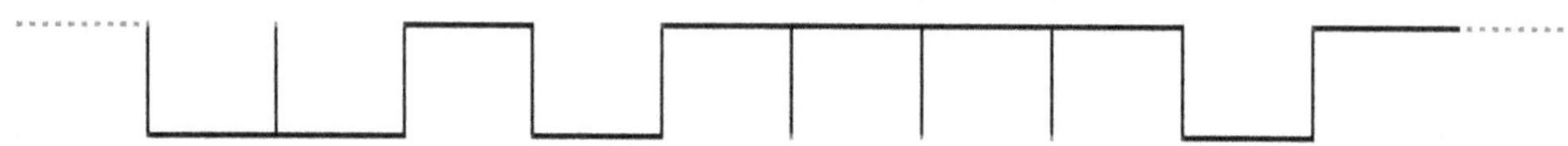

Figure 5-3. *RS-232 frame for the z charater*

Note the idle part of the signal at the start and at the end of the character. The *Start* bit (low) marks the start of the character and is used by the hardware to notice that there is start of a transmission. The individual bits follow in the respective level ending with the *Stop* bit (high). There is no parity bit in the example.

The baud rate is the number of bits per second that the serial line transmits. For example, 9600 baud means 9600 bits (pulses) per second. All UART frame parameters—baud rate, data length, parity, stop bits—must match at both ends or the data will corrupt.

The overall efficiency of an asynchronous frame like "8N1" is 80% (8 data bits out of 10 total bits per frame, counting start and stop). But this simple framing lets the receiver resynchronize on each byte without a shared clock. In fact, the receiver usually samples the incoming line at some multiple of the baud rate (for example, 16 times) and looks for the falling edge of the start bit. Once detected, it samples the data bits in the middle of each bit-time to recover the bit "level value." Because there is no separate clock line, this is called *asynchronous serial communication*.

Transmit and Receive Lines

On a hardware level, a UART or serial port chip typically provides two main data pins: TX (transmit) and RX (receive). When you wire up two devices, the TX of one goes to the RX of the other. For example, on a microcontroller board or COM port header you'll see labels like TXD and RXD (or Tx and Rx). The TX pin sends out bits in serial form, while the RX pin listens for incoming bits. Both pins use the same voltage domain (for example, TTL CMOS levels or RS-232 levels) and share a ground reference.

By having two separate lines, devices can communicate in both directions at once (full-duplex). In other words, you could be transmitting a byte while receiving another byte simultaneously. Internally, UART hardware makes this easy by using separate transmit and receive shift registers or buffers. In situations where each side transmits in turns is called *half-duplex*. Commonly serial port hardware also include hardware flow-control lines (RTS and CTS) or support for software flow control with XON/XOFF.

When using nanoFramework's `SerialPort`, you typically just specify the baud rate and framing. Under the hood, the UART peripheral drives its TX pin at that baud rate and samples the RX pin. Because the line is idle-high by convention, you will often see idle periods as continuous 1s (high) and then occasional drops to 0 for a start bit. If nothing is transmitted, the line stays in the idle (high) state indefinitely. This is illustrated in the signal representation in Figure 5-3.

The UART: How It Works

A Universal Asynchronous Receiver/Transmitter (UART) is the hardware module built into the microcontroller that handles all this timing and framing for serial communication. When you write a byte to a UART transmit register, the UART automatically prepends the start bit, shifts out the 8 data bits one at a time (least significant bit first), adds a parity bit if enabled, and then appends the stop bit(s). On the receive side, the UART watches the RX line, detects the start bit, and then samples each bit into a parallel data buffer (rebuilding your original byte).

Because of this, a UART essentially acts as a serial-to-parallel converter. It has an internal clock generator (usually 16 times or 8 times the baud rate), a shift register, and usually a FIFO buffer. This frees your CPU from having to time each bit—the UART hardware does it. If you didn't have a UART, you'd have to "bit-bang" serial output by manually toggling a pin at precise intervals, which is very CPU-intensive. In fact, very early or simple systems that lacked a UART sometimes did exactly that in software. While using an UART in nanoFramework, all the complicated configurations of the hardware peripheral and clocks are hidden from you and taken care of. You only need to worry about setting the configurations exposed in the `SerialPort` properties, and that's it. If you deploy to a different hardware, it will work the same because the HAL and the PAL (which you saw in Chapter 2) take care of setting the requested configurations for the hardware it's being deployed. This way you can "just" write and read bytes in your code.

One key aspect of all this is ensuring that both ends agree on how bits are framed. Typical serial port settings (for example, 8 data bits, no parity, 1 stop bit, known as 8N1) are just conventions that both the sending UART and receiving UART have to follow. If the sender uses 8N1 but the receiver expects 7E2 (seven bits, even parity, two stop bits), the received data will be gibberish. The UARTs don't negotiate these; you must configure them in both the sender and the receiver application to match.

Asynchronous, Full-Duplex Operation

The combination of separate TX/RX lines and framing bits means UART serial is asynchronous and full-duplex by nature. Each side uses its own clock to time bit intervals. The start bit serves as a synchronization point: when the receiver sees the line drop from idle to low, it knows a byte is coming, and it samples its own clock accordingly. This greatly simplifies wiring but does require that both sides' clocks stay reasonably close. In practice, UARTs usually allow up to about ±2-5% difference in baud rate; beyond that you can get sampling errors or framing errors.

Full-duplex means simultaneous two-way communication. Since TX and RX are independent lines, you can send data out while the other side is also sending data back. In contrast, a half-duplex system (like RS-485 in multi-drop mode) would use one wire or pair for both directions, requiring one device to wait for the other. With UART, there's no such wait—both devices can continually exchange bytes without coordination beyond matching the protocol settings.

Finally, UART serial has no clock signal embedded, so every byte is "self-contained" with its own start/stop delimiter. This makes it robust for simple point-to-point links. For example, if the line is idle for a long time, there's no problem—once data starts, the first start bit resets the timing. Because of its simplicity and low hardware cost, UART serial remains widely used in embedded systems, even though technologies like SPI or USB have taken over some tasks. It's perfect for things like console outputs, GPS modules, Bluetooth modules, and any application where modest data rates (e.g., 9600–115200 bps) are sufficient.

Serial Port in nanoFramework

Serial communication (UART/COM ports) in nanoFramework uses the `System.IO.Ports` namespace, just like on desktop .NET. The key class is `SerialPort`, which represents a serial port resource. Opening a UART is as easy as creating a `SerialPort` instance with the port name and settings.

Out of curiosity, in .NET (and Windows generally), serial ports are traditionally named COM ports (short for Communication Ports), with numbering starting from COM1, COM2, and so forth, due to historical reasons related to the original IBM PC architecture and early versions of DOS and Windows. These ports were typically mapped to standard I/O addresses and IRQ lines, often used to connect peripherals such as mice, modems, and terminals. The numbers are assigned incrementally as new serial devices (physical or virtual) are detected by the operating system. Windows inherited this naming convention.

For example, to open COM2 at 9600 baud, no parity, 8 data bits, 1 stop bit, do the following:

```
using System.IO.Ports;

// if you are on a platform that requires configuring the GPIOs function
Configuration.SetPinFunction(32, DeviceFunction.COM2_RX);
Configuration.SetPinFunction(33, DeviceFunction.COM2_TX);

// Configure serial port
SerialPort port = new SerialPort("COM2", 9600, Parity.None, 8,
StopBits.One);

// Optional: handle received data
port.DataReceived += (s, e) =>
{
    string incoming = port.ReadExisting();
    Debug.WriteLine($"Received: {incoming}");
};

// Open the port
port.Open();

// Send a line of text
port.WriteLine("Hello from nanoFramework!");
```

That's basically it—the SerialPort class has the usual methods (Read, WriteLine, ReadExisting, etc.) and events (DataReceived in this example) to handle communication. Before calling Open(), you can also set properties like Handshake, ReadTimeout, WriteTimeout. In practice, serial communication works reliably once you map your TX/RX pins correctly. For boards like ESP32 you may need to set the pin functions (e.g., with Configuration.SetPinFunction()) to match the UART you want to use, but once open the API works just like desktop .NET SerialPort.

One nice tip: if you want to treat serial communication as simple text, you can even wrap it in a StreamReader/Writer using port.BaseStream. But most often, direct WriteLine and ReadExisting are enough. In any case, the takeaway is that reading from or writing to a UART port in nanoFramework feels very familiar if you've used .NET's SerialPort, and it's just as capable. Any character-based device (GPS, Bluetooth module in text mode, PC USB-UART cable, etc.) can be controlled by this API.

A final note on the COM port availability in a nano device. The availability of COM ports depends on hardware and build-time configurations. To know which COM ports are available in a particular device, you have to either know that in advance, check the device schematic, or query this using the SerialPort.GetPortNames(), which will output a comma-separated list of the available COM ports, something like: "COM1, COM3, COM7."

Serial Peripheral Interface

The *Serial Peripheral Interface* (SPI) is a common synchronous serial bus used to connect microcontrollers to peripheral devices. It was originally developed by Motorola in the 1980s and is now a *de facto* standard in embedded systems. Because it is synchronous (uses a shared clock) and full-duplex (can send and receive at the same time), SPI can support very high data rates. You'll often see SPI used for high-speed sensors, memory chips (Flash, SRAM), ADCs/DACs, displays, and other ICs that need rapid data transfer. Unlike UART or I^2C, SPI has no defined maximum speed—many designs run SPI clocks of 10 MHz or higher, and specialized interfaces can exceed 50–100 MHz.

Four-Wire Hardware Interface

SPI uses a four-wire interface: SCLK (serial clock), MOSI (Master Out—Slave In), MISO (Master In—Slave Out), and CS (Chip Select, also called SS for Slave Select). The controller (master) generates the clock (SCLK) and drives MOSI, while each slave peripheral drives MISO back to the master. The CS line is (usually) an active-low select signal: the master pulls a slave's CS line low to enable that device and leaves it high to deselect it. When multiple slaves share an SPI bus, SCLK, MOSI, and MISO are common to all devices, but each slave gets its own CS line. Only the selected slave (CS low) is allowed to drive MISO; other slaves tri-state their MISO output. This wiring is illustrated in Figure 5-4. The master's SCLK, MOSI and MISO lines run to every peripheral, while each slave has its own CS line, originated from the master.

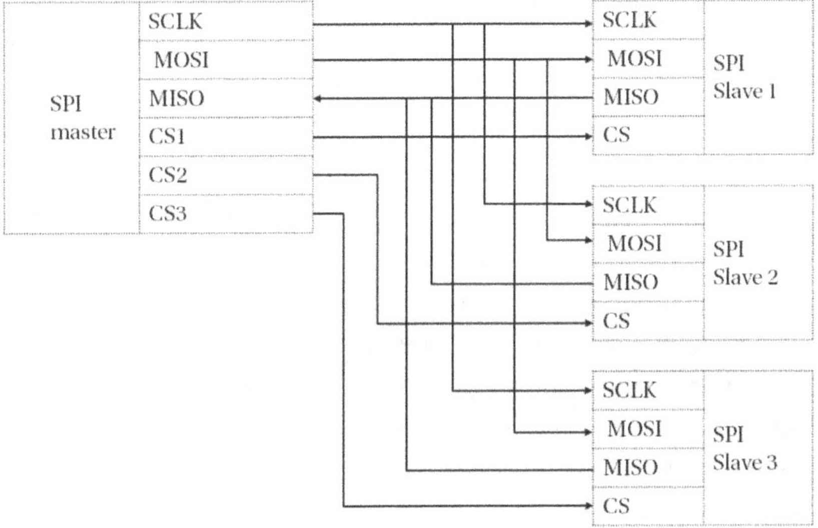

Figure 5-4. *Typical SPI wiring between one master and three slave devices*

Only the slave whose CS is pulled low will listen on MOSI and drive MISO. Therefore, one can talk to multiple devices by activating the respective CS one at a time.

Master–Slave Data Transfer

SPI transfers data in simple shift-register frames. To start a transaction, the master asserts the CS line for the target slave and begins toggling SCLK. On each clock edge, the master shifts one bit out on MOSI and simultaneously reads one bit in on MISO. Because of this, SPI is naturally full-duplex—bits flow both ways on every clock. Data is typically transferred one byte (8 bits) at a time, MSB first, but the length (in bytes) is flexible. After all bits the frame have been shifted, the master can raise CS high again to end the transaction. In practice, this means that for every bit clock, the master and slave exchange a pair of bits in sync with SCLK—one from master to slave (MOSI) and one from slave to master (MISO). To perform "read-only" operations, the master often shifts dummy data (e.g., 0xFF) on MOSI while capturing the slave's response on MISO. For "write-only" operations, the slave may ignore incoming bits. In all cases, the clock edge alignment guarantees that both sides know exactly when each bit is valid.

Clock Polarity, Phase, and Timing

SPI's clock behavior is configurable via two parameters: clock polarity (CPOL) and clock phase (CPHA). These determine exactly when bits are sampled and shifted, resulting in four SPI "modes": modes 0 to mode 3. For example, in Mode 0 (CPOL=0, CPHA=0) the clock idles low, the master drives data on MOSI at the falling edge, and both sides sample the data on the rising edge. In Mode 3 (CPOL=1, CPHA=1) the clock idles high, and sampling happens on the falling edge. The key point is that both master and slave must use the same mode so data lines are stable at the agreed sampling edge. Failing to do this will result in garbled transmission/reception.

This flexibility lets SPI adapt to peripherals' timing needs, but always remember to set the mode before communicating. Figure 5-5 shows a single-byte SPI transfer in one mode. The master pulls CS low to select the slave and then sends eight clock pulses on SCLK. On each clock, the MOSI line outputs one data bit from master to slave, while simultaneously the MISO line carries one bit from slave to master. In this example, the master's MOSI data bits are 1011...and the slave's MISO bits are 0110... (each bit is valid and sampled on the indicated clock edges). Notice the full-duplex nature: every clock edge clocks bits in both directions.

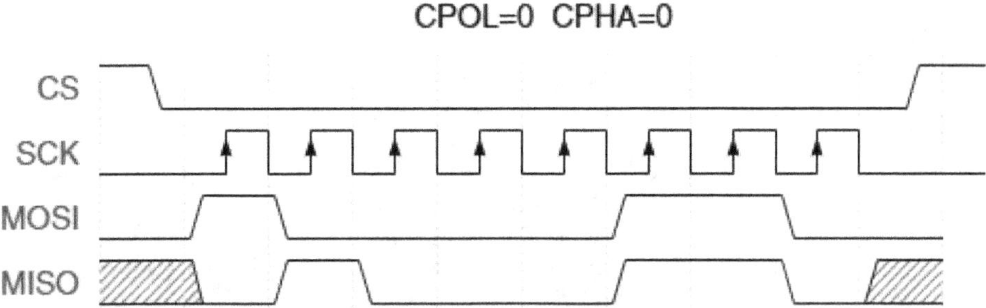

Figure 5-5. *SPI timing diagram, mode 0, 8 bit transfer*

Following the description of the I²C protocol, we'll add a brief comparison between these two protocols.

Using SPI in nanoFramework

For the rest of this section, as we walk through the SPI API, we'll write an application that controls a cascade of MAX7219 8×8 LED Matrix via SPI. The MAX7219 uses four lines for SPI: DIN (MOSI), CLK (SCLK), CS (chip select), plus VCC and GND for power.

The MAX7219 is a compact, serial-interfaced LED driver chip ideal for 8×8 (64-LED) matrices or seven-segment displays. It includes internal multiplexing and brightness control, so you need only one resistor (for current limiting, already included in the module in the schematic below) and a three-wire SPI bus (data in, clock, chip select, power) to drive all 64 LEDs. The chip supports up to a 10 MHz serial clock and can be daisy-chained (cascaded) so multiple 8×8 modules share the same SPI bus.

You'll notice that the MISO pin is "missing" in the connections. That's because this application doesn't require reading from the SPI slave device. It's only sending data with the configuration for the driver outputs. See Figure 5-6.

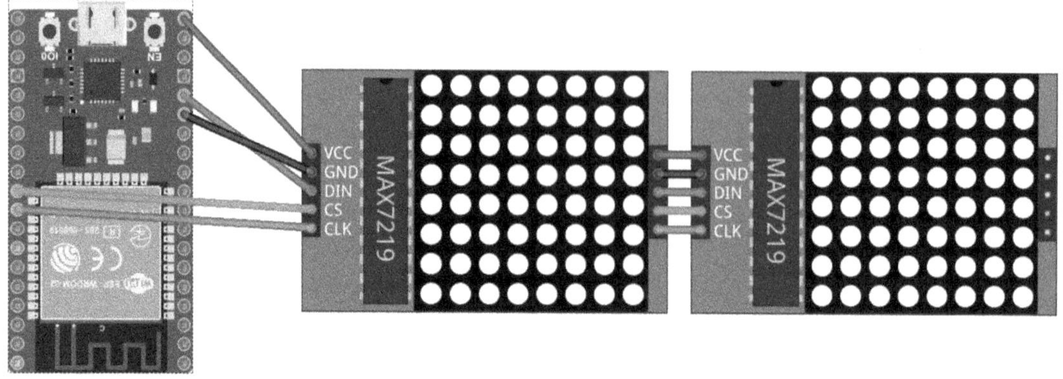

Figure 5-6. *Wiring an ESP32 module to a cascade of MAX7219*

Open a new nanoFramework application project in Visual Studio and add a reference to the MAX7219 NuGet `nanoFramework.Iot.Device.Max7219`.

Configuring SPI in .NET nanoFramework

Before talking to the MAX7219, we have to set up the SPI bus. All SPI settings are grouped in the `SpiConnectionSettings` class like this:

```
// Create SPI settings (bus 1, CS pin 42 as an example)

var settings = new SpiConnectionSettings(busId: 1, chipSelectLine: 42) {
    ClockFrequency = 10_000_000, // 10 MHz clock
    Mode = SpiMode.Mode0         // SPI Mode 0 (CPOL=0, CPHA=0)
    DataBitLength = 8,           // (default)
    DataFlow = DataFlow.MsbFirst // (default)
};

var spi = SpiDevice.Create(settings);
```

Let's take a look at the details on the code snippet.

- **BusId and ChipSelect:** The constructor takes the SPI bus ID and the pin number that will be used for CS (chip-select). If, for any reason, you prefer to drive the CS pin in your code, just pass -1 in the second parameter, and the code won't deal with the CS.

- **Clock frequency:** Set it to 10 MHz as the MAX7219 supports up to 10 MHz. So it could be lower, just there is no advantage on that.
- **Mode:** The MAX7219 expects SPI Mode0 (idle clock low, data latched on rising edge). Other modes (1–3) invert the clock phase/polarity and would corrupt the data.
- **Data bit length and flow:** The defaults of these in the `SpiConnectionSettings` class are exactly 8 bits and MSB-first; therefore, it doesn't make much difference to set these to the same values they have. Just add them for completeness.

It is worth mentioning that on platforms like the ESP32, you also need to map GPIO pins to the hardware SPI functions before creating the `SpiDevice`. Here's an example:

```
Configuration.SetPinFunction(21, DeviceFunction.SPI1_MOSI);
Configuration.SetPinFunction(22, DeviceFunction.SPI1_MISO);
Configuration.SetPinFunction(23, DeviceFunction.SPI1_CLOCK);
```

This ensures GPIO 21/22/23 acts, respectively, as MOSI/MISO/CLK for SPI1.

Now, once the pins are set, calling `SpiDevice.Create(settings)` returns a `SpiDevice` object ready to send and receive bytes.

Creating and Initializing the MAX7219 Device

With the SPI bus set up, you can instantiate the MAX7219 driver class from the `nanoFramework.IoT.Device` library. For example, to drive the two cascaded 8×8 matrices shown in Figure 5-5, use this:

```
Max7219 maxDevices = new Max7219(spi, cascadedDevices: 2);
maxDevices.Init();
```

Here `cascadedDevices` tells the driver how many 8×8 modules are chained together on the same SPI bus. If you have only one matrix, use `cascadedDevices: 1`. The `Init()` call performs the standard MAX7219 startup sequence: exits shutdown mode, turns off display-test, and sets the scan limit.

Under the hood, the library uses the SPI connection we created. Each MAX7219 chip has an 8-bit "digit" register (1–8) and an 8-bit data value. In the matrix context, each digit corresponds to one row of the 8×8 display. The driver exposes an indexer so you can write directly to a device's row. For example, to set row 0 of device 0 to a byte pattern, you would do the following:

```
maxDevices[new DeviceIdDigit(deviceId: 0, digit: 0)] = 0b10101010;
```

This does not immediately write to the hardware; it stores the value in the driver's internal buffer. The driver `CascadedDevices` property tells you how many devices are in the chain. When you have updated all th desired rows, call `maxDevices.Flush()`.

The `Flush()` method sends all buffered commands out over SPI to the MAX7219 chips. Internally, each command consists of two bytes: the first byte is the register (digit) address (1 through 8), and the second byte is the data for that row (each bit = one LED on/off). The library asserts the CS line low and clocks out 16 bits per device. For cascaded devices, the bytes for the farthest device in the chain are sent first, then the next, etc., so that all chips latch the correct row data simultaneously. In other words, one `Flush()` writes to all MAX7219 modules in sequence while CS is held active.

Example: Displaying a Static Pattern

Let's light up a simple pattern—a smiley face—on a single 8×8 matrix. First, define the 8-byte bitmap (each byte is a row, MSB = leftmost LED):

```
byte[] smiley = {
    0b00111100,
    0b01000010,
    0b10100101,
    0b10000001,
    0b10100101,
    0b10011001,
    0b01000010,
    0b00111100
};
```

Each 1 in the bit pattern corresponds to an LED turned on in that column. Now write this pattern into device 0 (the first module):

```
maxDevices.Init();

for (int row = 0; row < 8; row++)
{
    // DeviceIdDigit(deviceId: 0, digit: row) targets that row of device 0
    maxDevices[new DeviceIdDigit(0, row)] = smiley[row];
}
maxDevices.Flush();  // send the data via SPI to the MAX7219
```

This loop loads our smiley into the driver buffer, and then the call to `Flush()` pushes it to the hardware. After this code runs, the LED matrix will display the smiley face. Take a look at Figure 5-7 to see the outcome.

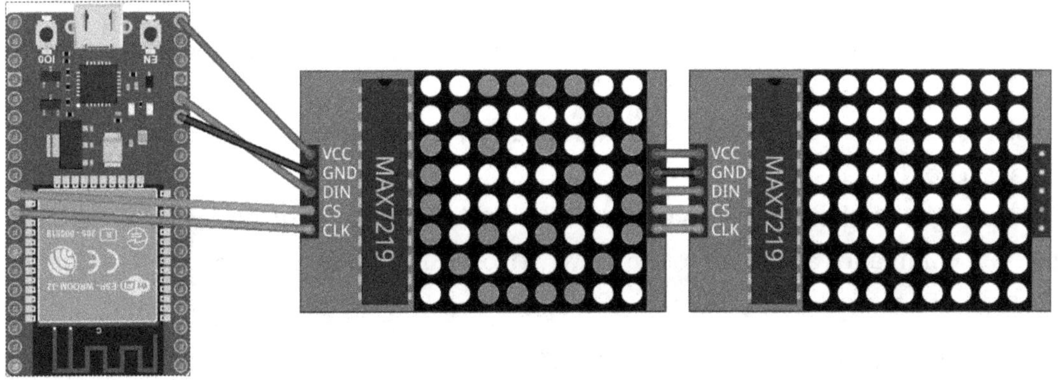

Figure 5-7. *MAX7219 module showing the smiley*

Each call to `Flush()` generates the SPI clock pulses on MOSI that shift the bytes into the MAX7219(s); when CS toggles, each chip latches the two-byte command for that row. If you had multiple cascaded matrices, you would loop over from 0 to the last device ID, filling each device's rows:

```
deviceId = 0..(devices.CascadedDevices-1)
```

The driver's `CascadedDevices` property makes it easy to adapt the same code to any number of chained displays.

Controlling Brightness and Text

By default, the MAX7219 will display at a medium brightness. This can be adjusted via code:

```
maxDevices.Brightness(7);   // set intensity
maxDevices.Flush();
```

The `Brightness(intensity)` method sets all cascaded devices to the given level (0–15).

For more creative static content, you can use the built-in `MatrixGraphics` helper to draw text or symbols with various fonts. Here's an example:

```
var writer = new MatrixGraphics(devices, Fonts.LCD);
writer.Font = Fonts.LCD;
writer.ShowMessage("HI!", alwaysScroll: false);
```

This will render "HI!" on the matrix using a small font. (If the text is wider than the display and `alwaysScroll` is false, it will show as much as fits; if true, it will automatically scroll the text across the matrix.) For static text you can choose a tiny font and set `alwaysScroll: false`.

Throughout all these examples, the SPI driver is working in the background, sending all those commands and bytes to the MAX7219 over the MOSI line. Each `Write()` or `Flush()` effectively does the following:

- Pull CS (LOAD) low on the MAX7219.
- Clocks out 16xN bits on MOSI (for N devices) at the configured `ClockFrequency`, MSB first.
- Raise CS high to latch the data in each chip.

This gives you full control of the LED matrix from C#, with familiar SPI settings. By adjusting `SpiConnectionSettings` and using the MAX7219 device API, you can draw virtually any static pattern or text on the 8×8 display in an easy and visually interesting way.

Inter-Integrated Circuit

Inter-Integrated Circuit (I^2C) is a two-wire synchronous serial bus invented by Philips in 1980. It was designed for short-distance, on-board communication between a microcontroller and peripheral chips. The beauty of I^2C derives from its simplicity: a microcontroller can control many devices (sensors, memories, DACs, etc.) with just two wires. It's widely used in embedded systems where simplicity and low cost matter more than raw speed.

You'll find I^2C in countless gadgets: for example, reading hardware monitors, temperature sensors, real-time clocks, analog-to-digital or digital-to-analog converters, LCD/OLED displays, and all sorts of chips. Because it needs only two pins (SDA for data and SCL for the clock) on your MCU, I^2C is often much easier to wire up than SPI or parallel buses.

In I^2C, all devices share the same two signal lines. Both the SDA (data) and SCL (clock) lines are open-drain (wired-AND), so they are pulled high through resistors (shown as *Rp* in the diagram). Any device can pull a line low to transmit a bit; if none is pulling it low, the pull-up resistor brings it high. Figure 5-8 shows one master (controller) and three slave (target) devices on the bus with pull-up resistors. This means multiple devices can live on the bus in parallel. However, each slave must have a unique address (or use an address-select mechanism); otherwise, they will collide on the bus.

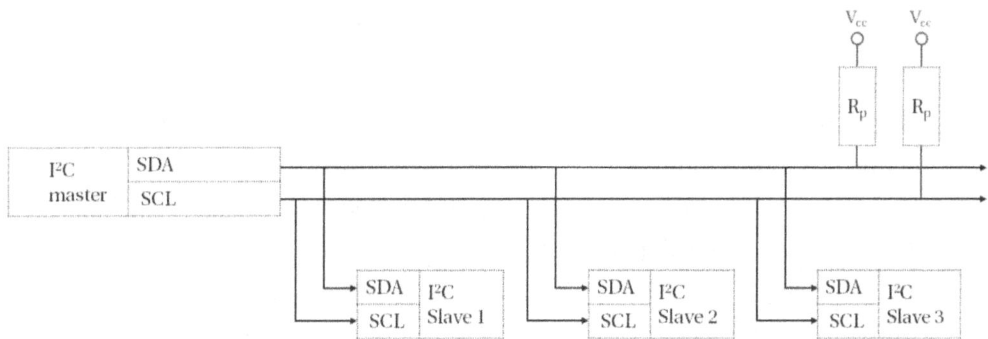

Figure 5-8. *Typical I^2C wiring between one master and three slave devices*

How I²C Data Transfer Works

Communication always happens in well-defined messages of bytes, bracketed by START and STOP conditions. Here's how a typical master-to-slave transaction goes:

1. **START condition (S):** The master begins by pulling SDA low while SCL is high. This unique transition flags all devices that a transfer is starting. (Idly, between transactions, both lines sit high.)
2. **Address + R/W bit:** Next the master sends a 7-bit address of the target it wants to talk to, plus one bit indicating a Read (1) or Write (0) operation. These 8 bits are clocked out on SDA by the master, MSB first.
3. **ACK/NACK from slave:** The addressed slave (if present) then pulls SDA low during the next clock pulse to ACK (acknowledge) the address. If SDA stays high (NACK), it means no slave recognized that address.
4. **Data bytes:** If ACK, the master and slave proceed to exchange data one byte (8 bits) at a time. After each data byte, the receiver (whether master or slave) sends a 1-bit ACK in the same way (low = OK). The data bits must be stable on SDA while SCL is high and can only change when SCL is low.
5. **STOP condition (P):** When done, the master releases SDA high while SCL is high This stop transition signals the end of the transfer and frees the bus for others. Alternatively, the master can issue a repeated START (pull SDA low again while SCL is high) to keep control of the bus for a new transfer without a STOP. This situation is often used for combined read/write transactions.

Figure 5-9 illustrates this flow.

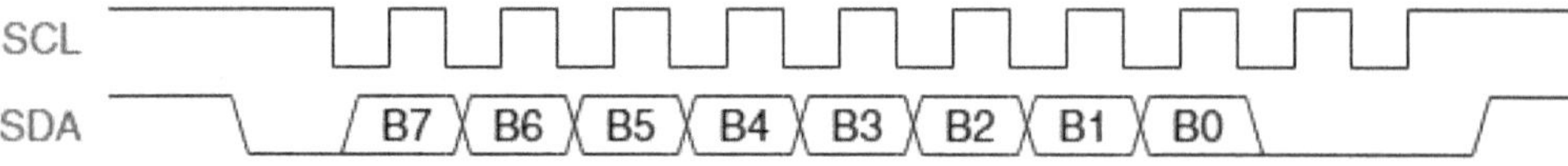

***Figure 5-9.** I²C frame*

I²C data timing diagram: the master issues a START (S) and then clocks out bits B1, B2, ..., while SDA is stable when SCL is high and finishes with a STOP (P). After each 8-bit frame, the receiver drives SDA low on the nineth clock as an ACK. (If SDA is high instead, that's a NACK meaning "no more data" or "not present." In write operations the master drives data and the slave acks; in read operations the slave drives data and the master acks. Both address and data are sent MSB-first.)

Advanced I²C Features

Here are the features:

- **Multimaster arbitration:** I²C allows multiple masters on the same bus. If two controllers start transmitting at the same time, arbitration resolves who wins. Each transmitter monitors SDA while it drives it. If a master writes a 1 (releases SDA) but sees the line low (because another master is holding it low), it loses arbitration and stops. The winner proceeds without data corruption. Arbitration is automatic and deterministic—you don't need extra hardware for it.
- **Clock stretching:** Normally the master drives SCL, but a slow slave can hold SCL low after a byte to pause the clock (and let the slave catch up). The master must then wait until SCL actually goes high before continuing. This "clock stretching" is built into I²C as a flow-control mechanism. Not all devices "stretch," so if you have timing issues, make sure your masters and slaves agree on this behavior.
- **Repeated START:** A master can issue another START condition without a STOP in between (called a *repeated start*). This is used, for example, when a master wants to switch from writing to a slave to reading from it without giving up the bus. The slave knows to treat the next START as part of the same overall transaction, since no STOP was seen.

Common Pitfalls and Troubleshooting

Here are some common mistakes when dealing with I^2C:

- **Missing/weak pull-ups**: Since I^2C lines are open-drain, you must have pull-up resistors on SDA and SCL. If you omit them (or choose very large values), the lines never reliably go high. In fact, without proper pull-ups there will be no communication—the MCU can't generate a valid START or address on the bus. A good rule of thumb is pull-ups in the 1 to 10k range, adjusted for your bus capacitance and speed. Most of the platforms supported by nanoFramework have GPIOs with configurable pull-ups, meaning you may want to rely on them and save the external components.
- **Address conflicts**: Two devices with the same I^2C address will "fight" on the bus. If you see garbled data or neither device working, check that every slave has a unique address. Some chips let you change their address via pins or registers; otherwise, you may need an I^2C multiplexer/switch.
- **Long wires or noise:** I^2C was intended for board-level short links. The total bus capacitance should stay under ~400 pF, which limits practical length to a few meters (and that is already stretching it). Long cables or a noisy environment will slow signal edges and can cause data errors. If you need longer runs, keep speeds low and consider shielding or twisted pair. Also ensure all devices share a common ground; mismatched grounds can corrupt I^2C signals.
- **Too-fast clock/timing mismatches:** Make sure the I^2C clock speed and modes match your devices. Typical standard mode is 100 kHz and fast mode is 400 kHz. If you try to run faster than a slave or the bus can support, errors will ensue. For example, if pull-ups are too large, rise times become slow, and at high speed SDA may not reach valid levels in time. If a slave is slow, it should stretch the clock, but not all masters support indefinite stretching. If you see missing ACKs or corrupted data, try a lower clock rate and verify pull-up sizing.

I²C in nanoFramework

To showcase the I²C nanoFramework API, we'll use the Bosch BMP280 over I²C. We'll go through the process of configuring the I²C bus, create an `I2cConnectionSettings` with the bus ID, and communicate with the sensor.

In Visual Studio, open a new project from an application project template, and add a reference to `nanoFramework.System.Device.I2C`. We'll start by configuring the I²C like this:

```
int busId = 1;
var i2cSettings = new I2cConnectionSettings(busId, Bmp280.
DefaultI2cAddress);
I2cDevice i2cDevice = I2cDevice.Create(i2cSettings);
```

In some platforms, like ESP32, you must also map the correct pins to I²C functionality before creating the device. For ESP32, if you were to use bus one, you would call the following:

```
Configuration.SetPinFunction(21, DeviceFunction.I2C1_DATA);
Configuration.SetPinFunction(22, DeviceFunction.I2C1_CLOCK);
```

Figure 5-10 illustrates a typical wiring: VIN to 3.3V, GND to ground, SDI/SDA to I²C data, and SCK/SCL to I²C clock (matching the "General" and "I²C" mappings).

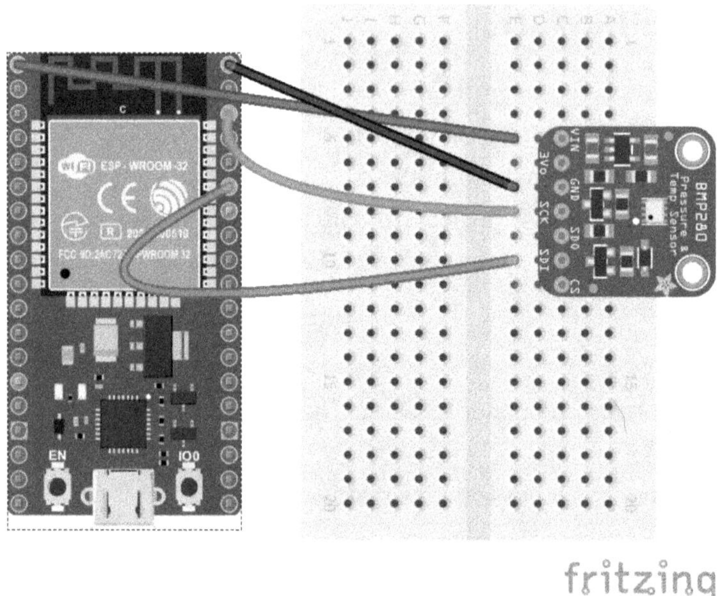

Figure 5-10. *I^2C schematic for BMP280*

In this setup, VIN powers the sensor, GND is common ground, and the SDI/SDA and SCK/SCL pins carry the I^2C data and clock. On the microcontroller side, make sure the pins are configured for I^2C (e.g., using `Configuration.SetPinFunction()` on ESP32 before you create the `I2cDevice`.

Once the I^2C device is ready, instantiate the BMP280 binding over that bus. The `Bmp280` class has a constructor taking the `I2cDevice`:

```
using var bmp = new Bmp280(i2cDevice);
```

You can then configure oversampling and other settings via properties on the `Bmp280` object. For example, setting higher resolution:

```
bmp.TemperatureSampling = Sampling.LowPower;
bmp.PressureSampling    = Sampling.UltraHighResolution;
```

Here, `Sampling.UltraHighResolution` means 16x oversampling (highest precision) for pressure, and `Sampling.LowPower` means minimal oversampling for temperature. As default the sensor powers up in sleep mode; you can set the power mode using `bmp.SetPowerMode(Bmx280PowerMode.Forced)` for single-shot reads or bmp.SetPowerMode(Bmx280PowerMode.Normal) for continuous measurements. To read data, call the Read() method, which returns a Bmp280ReadResult object containing both temperature and pressure. Like this:

```
Bmp280ReadResult result = bmp.Read();
Temperature temp    = result.Temperature;
Pressure    pres    = result.Pressure;
```

The Bmp280ReadResult object has Temperature and Pressure properties (of types Temperature and Pressure) that hold the measured values. You can then use the extensions DegreesCelsius or Hectopascals on these to get human-readable numbers:

```
Debug.WriteLine($"Temperature: {temp?.DegreesCelsius:0.0} °C");
Debug.WriteLine($"Pressure:    {pres?.Hectopascals:0.00} hPa");
```

You may also use the lower-level methods bmp.TryReadTemperature(out Temperature) and bmp.TryReadPressure(out Pressure) if you need to check validity or read only one value.

Calculating Altitude

The BMP280 binding includes a convenient altitude calculation. Once you have a pressure (and optional temperature), you can compute altitude above sea level. The TryReadAltitude() method uses an assumed sea-level pressure to do this. Like this:

```
if (bmp.TryReadAltitude(out Length altitude))
{
    Debug.WriteLine($"Altitude: {altitude.Meters:0.##} m");
}
```

By default, TryReadAltitude(out Length) uses the standard sea-level pressure (≈1013.25 hPa) to compute meters above sea level. If you want to use a specific local sea-level pressure, use the overload:

```
Pressure localSeaLevel = Pressure.FromHectopascals(1015.0);
bmp.TryReadAltitude(localSeaLevel, out Length altitude);
```

This returns a Length (distance) in meters. Internally the binding uses the standard barometric formula (taking temperature into account) to get altitude.

Calibration Registers

Under the hood, the BMP280 has factory calibration registers that store compensation coefficients. These are 8-bit register pairs at addresses 0x88–0xA1 (named calib00...calib25 in the datasheet), which correspond to compensation words dig_T1...dig_T3 and dig_P1...dig_P9. These raw calibration values are unique to each sensor and are used to correct the raw readings. The nanoFramework BMP280 binding automatically reads these calibration registers during initialization (in its default configuration routine) and applies them in its calculations. In other words, when you call `Read()` or `TryReadTemperature/Pressure()`, the returned values are already compensated by those factory coefficients. You generally do not need to manage the calibration registers yourself; the API handles this internally.

Practical Configuration Tips

Here are some tips:

- **I²C Address:** The BMP280 supports two I²C addresses. The default is 0x76 if the address (SDO pin) is left low. If SDO is pulled high, it will use the secondary address 0x77 by creating your settings with `Bmp280.SecondaryI2cAddress`.
- **Sampling and Filtering:** Use `TemperatureSampling` and `PressureSampling` to balance accuracy versus speed. Higher oversampling (e.g., `UltraHighResolution`) gives more accurate pressure readings at the cost of longer measurement time. You can check how long a measurement takes with `bmp.GetMeasurementDuration()` if you need to wait in software. You can also set `bmp.FilterMode(IIR filter)` and `bmp.StandbyTime` for normal mode to reduce noise.
- **Power Mode:** In *Forced* mode, the sensor wakes up, takes one reading, and then goes back to sleep—ideal for low-power applications. In *Normal* mode, it continuously takes measurements with pauses defined by the standby time. When the object is instantiated in the constructor, the sensor starts in sleep mode by default. For example, to do a single-shot measurement, you could follow this:

```
bmp.SetPowerMode(Bmx280PowerMode.Forced);
var data = bmp.Read();
bmp.SetPowerMode(Bmx280PowerMode.Sleep);
```

Or you can simply call `Read()` when in forced mode (the binding may internally handle one-shot automatically). In Normal mode `bmp.SetPowerMode(Bmx280PowerMode.Normal)`, the sensor will keep cycling continuously (and you can read the latest values anytime). Choose the mode that better fits the power/latency requirements of the application you are coding.

- **Board Pins:** Always ensure your board's I²C pins are correctly assigned. Many nanoFramework platforms come with default I²C pins, but boards like the ESP32 require `Configuration.SetPinFunction(...)` calls as shown earlier. On boards with multiple I²C buses, match the `busId` in your settings to the one you have configured.

SPI vs I²C

SPI and I²C are both popular master–slave serial buses, but they have different trade-offs.

- ***Wiring***: I²C uses only two bidirectional lines (SDA and SCL) and relies on 7-bit addresses to identify devices. SPI uses four wires (SCLK, MOSI, MISO, plus one CS per device). That means SPI requires an extra GPIO for each slave's CS, whereas I²C can "clip on" many devices to the same two-wire bus using addresses.
- ***Speed***: Because SPI uses push-pull drivers and no addressing overhead, it can run much faster than I²C. Typical I²C speeds are 100–400 kHz (up to a few MHz in fast modes), while SPI often runs in the 10–50 MHz range or higher. In practice you'll find SPI on high-bandwidth peripherals like memory cards, displays or fast sensors, whereas I²C is common for simpler, slower devices (clocks, temp sensors, etc.).

- ***Communication***: SPI's separate MOSI/MISO lines mean true full-duplex transfers (master can send and receive simultaneously). By contrast, I^2C is half-duplex (the same SDA line is shared for sending and receiving) and includes protocol overhead (start/stop conditions and ACK bits). However, I^2C supports multimaster on the same bus and has built-in acknowledgments, while SPI has a simpler protocol with no handshaking (the master just clocks bits and expects the right responses).

In summary, SPI is a simple and speedy point-to-point bus—no addressing, just one select line per device—whereas I^2C is a two-wire, addressable multidrop bus with slower speeds. Depending on the requirements (wire count versus speed versus simplicity versus hardware availability), you'll choose the one that is a better fit for the task at hand.

ADCs

Microcontrollers are digital by nature: they process information in the form of binary ones and zeros. However, the real world is analog—think of temperature sensors, light intensity, battery voltage, or audio signals, all of which vary continuously. To bridge this gap, analog-to-digital converters (ADCs) are used. An ADC takes an analog voltage and converts it into a digital number that software can process.

How an ADC Works: Bits, Resolution, and Sampling

At the core, an ADC measures the voltage at its input and translates this into a digital value with a certain *resolution*, expressed in *bits*. For example, a 12-bit ADC can represent an input in $2^{12} = 4096$ discrete steps. If the reference voltage is 3.3 V, each "step" (also called a Least Significant Bit, LSB) is as follows:

$$\text{LSB size} = V_{ref} / (2^{\wedge n - 1})$$

So with 3.3 V and a 12-bit ADC:

$$\text{LSB} = 3.3\text{ V} / 4095 \approx 0.0008\text{ V} \approx 0.8\text{ mV}$$

The higher the resolution (the more bits), the smaller each step, and the more precisely the ADC can distinguish between input voltages.

Sampling rate is another critical parameter: it's the number of times per second the ADC takes a measurement. For slowly changing signals (like the temperature in a room), a low sample rate is fine; for faster signals (like audio), a higher rate is essential. Otherwise, information will be lost.

ADC Architectures in Microcontrollers

Most MCUs use either a *Successive Approximation Register (SAR)* ADC or, less commonly, a *Sigma-Delta (ΣΔ)* ADC:

- **SAR ADC:** This is the most common type in general-purpose MCUs (STM32, ESP32, etc.). SAR ADCs are fast, reasonably accurate, and provide n-bit parallel output by performing a binary search of the input voltage. Conversion is typically in the microsecond range—great for many sensor inputs.
- **Sigma-Delta ADC:** Used for higher precision and lower speed (often in audio applications). Sigma-Delta ADCs oversample the input and use digital filtering to achieve very high resolution, but at the cost of speed.

MCUs typically map each ADC "channel" to a specific pin, meaning you can read several analog inputs—sometimes one at a time (multiplexed), sometimes in parallel depending on the hardware.

Reference Voltage and Input Range

The *reference voltage* (V_{ref}) is critical. It's the highest voltage the ADC can accurately measure; anything above this will just "saturate" the reading at the max value. Some MCUs use the main supply (e.g., 3.3 V), while others provide a dedicated, thus more stable V_{ref} pin. For accurate readings, especially in noisy environments, using a clean, low-noise reference is important. Using appropriate filtering techniques make a huge difference on providing a clean stable reference, which is paramount for accurate sampling.

The input range of the ADC is usually 0 V to V_{ref}, but not always! Some MCUs allow for differential inputs (measuring the difference between two pins) or bipolar ranges ($\pm V_{ref}/2$).

Practical Considerations: Noise, Impedance, and Averaging

Here are some practical considerations:

- **Noise:** Analog inputs are sensitive to electrical noise. Long wires, high-impedance sources, or fast-switching digital circuits nearby can all cause readings to "jump" unexpectedly. To fight this, it's common to average multiple readings in software or use analog filtering (a simple RC filter) at the hardware level.
- **Input impedance:** ADCs work best when driven by a low-impedance source (like an op-amp or buffer). Directly connecting a high-impedance sensor can result in slow or inaccurate conversions because the ADC's internal sample-and-hold capacitor may not charge/discharge properly.
- **Averaging and calibration:** Many sensors and applications benefit from taking multiple samples and averaging to reduce noise and improve repeatability. For precision, sometimes calibration is needed (measuring known voltages and correcting the result in software).

Typical Usage in .NET nanoFramework

As usual, we'll start with a fresh project created from the application template. Add a reference to the NuGet package `nanoFramework.System.Device.Adc`.

In .NET nanoFramework, ADCs are accessed through the `System.Device.Adc` namespace. This namespace offers an API, with classes like `AdcController` and `AdcChannel`.

An `AdcController` represents the ADC hardware block, and you "open" channels (usually numbered) on it. Please note that an MCU can have one or more ADC blocks. Or it can have the channels grouped for some technical reason. So, be sure to check the schematic of the module you're using or the MCU datasheet to be fully aware how this is organized.

Take the following code snippet:

```
using System.Device.Adc;

// Create the controller (there's normally only one per MCU)
AdcController adc = new AdcController();

// Optional: check range
int min = adc.MinValue;    // e.g. 0
int max = adc.MaxValue;    // e.g. 4095 for 12-bit ADC
Console.WriteLine($"ADC range: {min} to {max}");

// Open analog channel 0 (mapped to a specific pin per board)
AdcChannel channel0 = adc.OpenChannel(0);

// Read raw value (integer between min and max)
int rawValue = channel0.ReadValue();

// Or read a ratio (0.0 to 1.0)
double ratio = channel0.ReadRatio();

Console.WriteLine($"Raw: {rawValue}  Ratio: {ratio:P1}");
```

Typically, each channel corresponds to a fixed analog-capable pin on the MCU (for example, "channel 0" might be pin PB2 or whatever). The `MinValue` and `MaxValue` let you know the resolution—e.g., a 12-bit ADC usually has max 4095. As we've seen, the bits of resolution determine how many discrete steps your voltage is split into. If you need to convert that raw number into a voltage or scaled value, you can use the known reference voltage (often 3.3V or 5V) and simple math. For quick-and-dirty percentage, `ReadRatio()` is handy. For example, if you have a potentiometer between 0V and V_{ref}, the ratio will go from 0.0 (0V) to 1.0 (V_{ref}) as you turn the knob. One more pro tip: ADC readings can be a bit noisy. nanoFramework `AdcChannel` includes a `ReadValueAveraged(int sampleCount)` method to help with that. As with any ADC, good practices recommend that multiple samples should be taken then and averaged in order to get a stable reading. So you could do this to take 10 quick samples and average them:

```
int smoothValue = channel0.ReadValueAveraged(10);
```

This improves accuracy when the sensor or ADC is noisy. Under the hood, you don't need to do any special setup besides `OpenChannel()`. On some boards, you might need to configure the pin function (similar to PWM or I^2C), but often the nanoFramework image already has ADC pins enabled. Just remember which channel number matches each pin (check the board's schematic or the build configuration). Otherwise, reading an analog voltage is just as easy as digital I/O: open a channel and call `ReadValue()`.

DACs

Just as ADCs allow microcontrollers to "see" the analog world, *digital-to-analog converters* (DACs) let them "speak" to it. While MCUs work natively in digital values—zeros and ones—sometimes we need to generate true analog voltages: outputting a waveform to a speaker, generating control voltages for analog circuits, or simulating sensor outputs for testing. This is where DACs come in.

How a DAC Works: Resolution, Steps, and Voltage Range

A DAC converts a digital value (a number, say 0 to 4095 for 12 bits) into a corresponding analog voltage. The output voltage is proportional to the digital input and the configured reference voltage:

$$V_{out} = (\text{DigitalValue} / (2^n - 1)) \times V_{ref}$$

For example, with a 12-bit DAC and a 3.3 V reference:

- Writing a digital value of 0 outputs 0 V.
- Writing the maximum value (4095) outputs close to 3.3 V.
- Each increment increases the voltage by about 0.8 mV (as in the ADC example).

Resolution (in bits) determines how finely you can control the output voltage. More bits mean smoother and more precise analog output.

DAC Architectures in Microcontrollers

Common DAC implementations in MCUs include:

- **Resistor String DACs**: Use a string of resistors and switches to select voltages—simple and robust, often found in lower-end MCUs.
- **R-2R Ladder DACs**: Use a clever resistor network for compact, efficient conversion—popular in many MCUs.
- **Sigma-Delta DACs**: Less common but can achieve high resolution by oversampling and filtering, sometimes used for audio output.

Most MCUs provide one or more DAC "channels," each connected to a dedicated analog output pin. Some support buffered output, so you can connect loads directly; others recommend an external buffer for best performance.

Reference Voltage and Output Range

The DAC reference voltage (V_{ref}) sets the highest output voltage it can generate. Often, this is tied to the microcontroller's supply voltage (e.g., 3.3 V), but some MCUs allow a separate, more accurate V_{ref} for improved stability.

The output range is typically from 0 V up to (but not exceeding) $V_{ref.}$ It's important to remember that the DAC output is only as good as its reference—if V_{ref} is noisy or drifts, so will your analog output!

Practical Considerations: Output Impedance, Settling, and Filtering

Here are practical considerations:

- **Output Impedance**: Many MCU DACs have moderate output impedance. For best accuracy and response, connect a buffer amplifier if driving heavy loads or low-impedance circuits.
- **Settling Time**: It takes a short time for the output to stabilize after a new value is set. This is called the settling time and limits how fast you can update the DAC reliably.

- **Filtering**: To create smooth analog waveforms (especially audio), a simple RC low-pass filter can remove the steps from the output. This is crucial if you use the DAC for sound, voltage control, or precise analog signals.
- **Noise:** Keep traces short, use proper analog layout. Good decoupling of V_{ref} is a must.

Typical Usage in .NET nanoFramework

Start with a fresh nanoFramework application project and add the `nanoFramework.System.Device.Dac` NuGet package. The main API classes are `DacController` (which manages the DAC hardware) and `DacChannel` (which represents an individual output channel).

```
using System.Device.Dac;

// Create the DAC controller
DacController dac = new DacController();

int max = (int)Math.Pow(2.0, dac.ResolutionInBits);
// e.g. 4095 for 12-bit DAC
Console.WriteLine($"DAC range: 0 to {max}");

// Open output channel 0 (maps to a specific analog pin)
DacChannel channel0 = dac.OpenChannel(0);

// Set output to half scale (midpoint voltage)
int halfScale = (max + 1) / 2;
channel0.WriteValue(halfScale);
```

Each DAC channel maps to a fixed output pin on your MCU (check your board's schematic for the exact pin assignments). You can write any value from `MinValue` to `MaxValue`. To produce a specific voltage, calculate the corresponding digital value as shown earlier.

PWM

Pulse Width Modulation (PWM) is a powerful yet simple technique used by microcontrollers to simulate analog outputs using digital signals. Since microcontrollers inherently operate digitally—meaning their output pins are either "ON" (logic HIGH) or "OFF" (logic LOW)—they can't directly produce continuous analog voltages. Instead, they use PWM to approximate analog behavior, such as controlling brightness in LEDs, adjusting motor speeds, generating audio signals, or creating servo control pulses.

How PWM Works

PWM generates an analog-like signal by rapidly switching a digital pin on and off. This produces a waveform consisting of pulses, each pulse having two key properties:

- **Period (T)**: The total duration of one complete on-and-off cycle
- **Duty Cycle (D)**: The proportion of the period where the signal is ON (active high), typically expressed as a percentage

For example, a PWM signal with a 50% duty cycle is ON exactly half the time and OFF half the time, producing an average voltage exactly half of the full logic HIGH voltage.

If the duty cycle increases to 75%, the pin stays HIGH three-quarters of the cycle, delivering a higher average voltage.

The "analog" effect arises because loads (like LEDs, motors, or speakers) average out the pulses due to their inertia or built-in low-pass filtering characteristics.

Duty Cycle and Average Voltage

The average voltage output by a PWM signal depends directly on the duty cycle:

$$V_{average}=V_{max} \times \text{DutyCycle}$$

If your microcontroller pin outputs 3.3 V at logic HIGH, then:

- 25% duty cycle results in an average of 0.825 V (25% × 3.3 V).
- 50% duty cycle results in an average of 1.65 V.
- 75% duty cycle results in an average of 2.475 V.

By continuously adjusting this duty cycle, you can produce a smoothly varying output, closely approximating an analog voltage or controlling device power.

PWM Frequency: Selecting the Right Speed

The frequency at which PWM pulses repeat is crucial. For simple LED brightness control, any frequency above around 100 Hz is typically acceptable because human eyes cannot perceive flicker at that rate or higher. For motor control, frequencies from a few kHz to tens of kHz are common, as higher frequencies reduce audible noise from motor coils.

However, too high a frequency can lead to unnecessary switching losses and inefficiencies in transistor circuits. Finding the "sweet spot" involves balancing frequency (to minimize flicker or noise) and efficiency (to reduce power consumption and heat).

PWM in Microcontrollers

PWM is typically implemented in microcontrollers using dedicated hardware timers:

The timer counts up (or down) at a defined clock speed.

The microcontroller compares the timer's current value with a set duty cycle threshold.

When the timer is below this threshold, the output pin is held HIGH; when the timer exceeds it, the pin switches LOW.

This repeats continuously, generating a stable PWM waveform.

Most microcontrollers (ESP32, STM32, AVR, etc.) have hardware timer peripherals explicitly designed for PWM generation. This hardware assistance offloads the PWM generation from the CPU, ensuring accurate timing, low CPU overhead, and stable signals.

PWM and Analog Devices: Real-world Applications

These are real-world applications:

- **LED Brightness Control**: PWM is widely used for dimming LEDs smoothly without using linear regulators (saving energy and reducing heat).

- **Motor Speed Control**: By controlling the average power delivered to motors, PWM precisely adjusts their speed or torque.
- **Servo Control**: PWM signals define the angle position of servo motors, with standard pulse widths representing specific angles.
- **Audio Generation**: PWM signals combined with low-pass filters can produce audio signals, creating simple sound effects or tones.

PWM in nanoFramework

In nanoFramework, PWM is supported via the `System.Device.Pwm` namespace, centered around the `PwmChannel` class.

As usual, start with a clean project created from an application template. Add a reference to the NuGet `nanoFramework.System.Device.Pwm`.

It's okay to use the same hardware setup as in the GPIO section, so we'll assume an LED connected at pin. Figure 5-11 shows the hardware setup, for convenience.

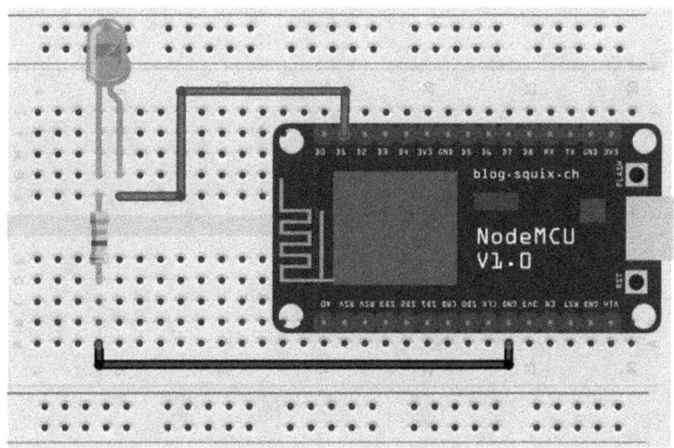

Figure 5-11. *Simple LED circuit (to feed from PWM output)*

Here's a simple example of this. To drive an LED on pin 18 with a 4kHz PWM at 0% duty (off), do the following:

```
using System.Device.Pwm;
```

```
// this will run on ESP32: first configure the pin for PWM function
Configuration.SetPinFunction(18, DeviceFunction.PWM1);

// Create a PWM channel on pin 18, 4kHz frequency, 0% duty
PwmChannel pwm = PwmChannel.CreateFromPin(
    18,
    frequency: 4_000,
    dutyCycle: 0);

// Start the PWM
pwm.Start();
```

The LED will be off because duty cycle was 0. Now let's adjust the duty cycle to 50% so we can see the LED lit at "half" brightness with `pwm.DutyCycle = 0.5;`.

Let's have more fun and automate the fade up and down using a loop. Check the following code snippet assuming that we'll be using the same pwm object created earlier:

```
double dutyCycle = 0.0;
bool fadingUp = true;

while (true)
{
    pwm.DutyCycle = dutyCycle;

    // Adjust duty cycle
    if (fadingUp)
    {
        dutyCycle += 0.01;
        if (dutyCycle >= 1.0)
        {
            dutyCycle = 1.0;
            fadingUp = false;
        }
    }
    else
    {
        dutyCycle -= 0.01;
        if (dutyCycle <= 0.0)
```

```
            {
                dutyCycle = 0.0;
                fadingUp = true;
            }
        }

        Thread.Sleep(200);
    }
```

This loop gradually increases and decreases the PWM duty cycle between 0.0 and 1.0 to create a smooth fading effect on the LED. The `fadingUp` flag determines whether the brightness is currently increasing or decreasing, and `Thread.Sleep(200)` controls the speed of the fade.

It's never too much to remind that in some MCUs (like ESP32), you must configure the pin's alternate function first so that the hardware knows it's a PWM output (in this example). That's the purpose of the code `Configuration.SetPinFunction(...)`.

On other chips (like many STM32 boards), PWM-capable pins are marked as timers in the datasheet, and often you can create the channel directly without special configuration. Once `CreateFromPin` returns a `PwmChannel` object, you control it with simple methods like `Start()`, `Stop()`, and the `DutyCycle` (0.0 to 1.0). You can even change `Frequency` at runtime on some hardware. Keep in mind that the duty cycle is the fraction of time the signal is high—e.g., 0.75 means it's high 75% of each period.

Driving a servo motor, for instance, might involve setting a 50 Hz PWM and changing duty between 5% and 10%. Or fading an LED is just a matter of smoothly adjusting `DutyCycle` over time (e.g., in a loop). The nice part is that once set up, the PWM runs in hardware without CPU overhead—you just tweak the numbers in code.

Practical Considerations and Best Practices

The following are best practices:

- **Noise and Filtering:** For sensitive analog applications (like audio), always consider filtering the PWM output with a simple RC low-pass filter to create a smoother DC voltage or audio waveform.

- **Frequency:**
    - **LEDs**: Use 100 Hz to 1 kHz to eliminate visible flicker.
    - **Motors**: 5–20 kHz to avoid audible noise.
    - **Servos**: Typically 50 Hz (20 ms period) with 1–2 ms pulse widths.
- **Efficiency and Heat:** PWM helps improve efficiency (over linear control methods) by reducing heat dissipation. However, transistor switches in PWM circuits must be chosen carefully—fast-switching MOSFETs or transistors are best, minimizing switching losses and heat buildup.

Other Interfaces

Beyond the interfaces and protocols, which are considered the most commonly used ones in the embedded system world, .NET nanoFramework supports many more ways to connect with the outside world. Let's review briefly some of them:

I^{2}S Audio: The `System.Device.I2s` namespace lets you send audio data to an I^{2}S DAC or amplifier. This works in the same style as an ADC: you simply open the channel and write samples to the I2S bus to produce sounds. This opens up possibilities like sound playback or VoIP on devices that have I^{2}S-capable hardware.

Modbus: If you need industrial communication, there's a Modbus library over serial port. There available several APIs under `ModbusClient` and `ModbusServer` classes. For instance, `new ModbusClient("COM3")` lets you read/write coils and registers on Modbus-RTU devices. There's even built-in support for using RS-485 transceivers (MAX485 chips) if you wire up the RTS pin for direction control. In short, you can talk to PLCs or other Modbus gear right from your nanoFramework application.

MQTT: Message Queuing Telemetry Transport is a lightweight messaging protocol designed for constrained devices and low-bandwidth networks, making it ideal for IoT applications.

The .NET nanoFramework simplifies MQTT implementation with libraries that allow developers to establish connections to MQTT brokers and exchange messages effortlessly. This protocol is highly efficient for real-time updates and is widely adopted in scenarios like home automation, industrial monitoring, and remote control systems.

1-Wire: The popular 1-Wire bus (for DS18B20 temperature sensors and such) is supported via `nanoFramework.Device.OneWire` library. It uses a combination of UART pin to generate the precise timing. Once initialized, you can use the APIs available that implement the 1-Wire commands like `Reset()`, `WriteByte()`, `ReadByte()` on the `OneWireHost` class to poll 1-Wire devices.

Networking (Ethernet & Wi-Fi): Several .NETnanoFramework boards have Wi-Fi (especially ESP32) or Ethernet (some STM32 dev boards). The `System.Device.Wifi` API lets you scan for networks and connect to a Wi-Fi access points. For example, `WifiNetworkHelper.ConnectDhcp(ssid, password)` can bring up Wi-Fi and obtain an IP via DHCP. Once connected, you can use `System.Net.Sockets, HttpClient`, `MQTT`, AMQPLite and others, almost exactly as in desktop .NET. In fact, much of the Internet stack API is the same—you can open a `Socket`, send HTTP requests, etc. The main difference is that you are on a tiny MCU, so make sure you keep the code light. Networking and connection to the cloud is covered with more detail on another chapter.

LoRa/LoRaWAN: Provide robust wireless communication solutions for IoT applications that demand low power and long-distance connectivity. LoRa operates using radio frequencies and is ideal for transmitting small packets of data over several kilometres. LoRaWAN, a network protocol built on top of LoRa, offers additional features such as secure communication, scalable network architecture, and device management. In the context of .NET nanoFramework, LoRa and LoRaWAN integration allow developers to leverage these technologies for IoT projects.

By utilising libraries specifically designed for LoRa communication, developers can build applications that manage device registration, transmit sensor data, and monitor network status, all on a microcontroller platform.

Displays/UI: Graphical displays (OLEDs, TFTs, e-ink, etc.) are also supported in the IoT device library. For instance, SSD1306 and SH1106 OLED displays have a managed driver in the nanoFramework.Iot.Device.Ssd13xx library. Using it is quite simple and looks like this:

```
I2cDevice i2c = I2cDevice.Create(new I2cConnectionSettings(1,
Ssd1306.DefaultI2cAddress));

using (Ssd1306 display = new Ssd1306(i2c, Ssd13xx.
DisplayResolution.OLED128x64))
{
    display.ClearScreen();
    display.DrawString(0, 0, "Hello from nano!", 0xFF, true);
    display.Display();
}
```

This code fills the OLED with text. Many drawing primitives (`DrawPixel`, `DrawLine`, `DrawBitmap`, etc.) are available, so you can create nice UIs. The beauty is that these libraries are part of the same IoT device repo, so again it feels just like using .NET IoT Core on a Raspberry Pi—but it's running on a micro controller.

What ties all these together is the `nanoFramework.IoT.Device` repo and the .NET IoT Core alignment. This repo contains dozens of sensor, display, and communication drivers (temperature sensors, gas sensors, IMUs, small screens, e-paper displays, etc.). It's designed so that if you know the .NET IoT driver on desktop, you can use the nanoFramework equivalent with minimal changes. In practice, many examples are identical. And in that repo you'll find sample code for all those. In short, any interface or sensor you might want or need to use is likely already covered by a nanoFramework library or sample.

Summary

As you can see, .NET nanoFramework makes hardware I/O a breeze. You open pins, start serial ports, configure SPI/I^2C buses, and call methods—all in familiar C#—without wrestling with register maps or having to know the fine details of each hardware platform or vendor. The framework's cross-platform nature means your code will run on different microcontrollers with virtually no changes. In this chapter, we covered the core interfaces—GPIO, UART, SPI, I^2C, ADC, and PWM—with examples. We also mentioned other options (I^2S, Modbus, 1-Wire, networking, graphical displays, etc.) and the rich IoT device binding library that offers more than 100 bindings for dozens of devices. In every case, the code is concise and high-level. Microcontrollers aren't supposed to be scary low-level beasts anymore—with .NET nanoFramework they're just tiny friendly computers you program in C#. So go ahead, wire up that sensor or LED, add a reference to the required NuGet packages, write a few lines of C#, and let nanoFramework handle the nasty bits. It really is that easy!

Additional Resources

Learn more about the topics in this chapter at the following locations:

nanoFramework Docs: `https://docs.nanoframework.net`

IoT bindings repo: `https://github.com/nanoframework/nanoFramework.IoT.Device`

CHAPTER 6

An IoT Embedded Device

The Internet of Things (IoT) is transforming industries by connecting physical devices—ranging from simple sensors to complex automation controllers—to digital networks. IoT devices enable real-time monitoring, control, and data-driven decision-making in fields as diverse as manufacturing, utilities, transportation, and smart infrastructure.

At its core, an IoT device consists of a microcontroller-based system capable of interfacing with sensors and actuators, processing data locally, and communicating with other systems or the cloud. These capabilities allow for remote monitoring, automated control, predictive maintenance, and seamless integration with cloud services or artificial intelligence.

This chapter marks a pivotal step in this book. Moving beyond individual interfaces and protocols, you will design and build a fully integrated IoT solution that addresses real-world industrial and commercial challenges.

To ground these concepts, we will build a fully automated pool controller using the industrial-grade Orgpal's PALTHREE board and .NET nanoFramework. This project goes beyond hobby-level experimentation, introducing you to a practical IoT scenario that integrates advanced sensing, automation, and cloud connectivity.

You'll learn how to interface the PALTHREE with industry-standard 4–20 mA sensors for monitoring critical water parameters such as pH, chlorine, turbidity, or temperature. The chapter covers the entire process—from reliable sensor acquisition and robust dosing logic for chemical pumps to reporting status and alerts to the cloud. All control and monitoring will be performed on a platform engineered for demanding, always-on environments, ensuring the skills you develop are directly transferable to industrial and commercial applications.

By the end of this chapter, you will have a solid grasp of both hardware and software integration for industrial IoT and a complete, working example that can serve as a foundation for more complex systems in the future.

J. Simões, *Embedded Systems with .NET nanoFramework*, https://doi.org/10.1007/979-8-8688-2096-0_6

Note To keep this chapter a reasonable size, you'll find short code snippets to illustrate the explanation. The complete solution with all the code is available at github.com.

Overview of Typical Supported Boards

When building IoT devices with .NET nanoFramework, a variety of hardware platforms are available—each with distinct advantages for different use cases and environments.

- **ESP32 (Espressif):** No longer just for hobbyists, recent ESP32 models feature high-performance dual-core and single-core MCUs, with ample RAM and flash. These chips are packed with features: multiple ADCs, DACs, touch inputs, PWM, cryptography accelerators, and various connectivity options. With their robust peripherals and improved reliability, modern ESP32 boards are now strong candidates for both prototyping and commercial/industrial deployments, especially where wireless or cost-effective solutions are needed.
- **STM32 Series (STMicroelectronics):** A mainstay of industrial and professional projects, STM32 MCUs are known for their robust industrial-grade performance, longevity, and extensive suite of peripherals (advanced ADCs, timers, serial ports, hardware security, etc.). Many STM32-based boards—such as the PALTHREE—offer a solid platform for critical or long-lived deployments where reliability and expandability are essential.
- **Others (NXP, TI, Silicon Labs):** .NET nanoFramework also supports MCUs from NXP (LPC series), Texas Instruments, and Silicon Labs, broadening hardware options for specialized or high-security environments. Silicon Labs, in particular, offers MCUs designed for ultra-low power, wireless mesh networking, and applications with stringent certification needs.

Selecting the right board is crucial, as it determines available peripherals, networking capabilities, expansion options, and long-term support.

Criteria for Selecting Hardware for IoT Projects

Selecting the ideal hardware platform or microcontroller (MCU) for an IoT project is rarely a simple checklist exercise. Each application has its own constraints and priorities, so this section is presented as a series of guiding questions. There are no universally right or wrong answers—the purpose is to provoke thoughtful consideration of your project's true needs, helping you avoid costly surprises down the road.

As you read, watch for real-world pitfalls and cautionary notes based on common mistakes seen in both prototyping and commercial deployments.

Analog Inputs and Measurement Accuracy

Here are the questions:

- Do you require one or more analog channels for sensors (such as temperature, pressure, or 4–20 mA transducers)?
- Should you use external signal conditioning chips or circuits to improve measurement quality, range, or robustness?
- Is galvanic isolation required to protect your MCU and system from ground loops, electrical surges, or interference?
- What is the required resolution and sample rate for accurate measurements in your application?

Pitfall: Many platforms offer ADCs, but some may not have enough effective resolution, high noise, or shared pins that limit simultaneous use.

Example: A temperature control system deployed with a low-grade ADC led to unstable readings and costly field service visits.

Digital I/O Capabilities

Here are the questions:

- How many digital inputs and outputs are necessary?
- Should you select a larger MCU with more GPIOs or use an external GPIO expander (such as I^2C or SPI-based chips) to increase I/O count?
- Do you need features such as hardware interrupts, open-drain outputs, or input filtering (for counting pulses or reading contact closures)?

Pitfall: Overlooking the need for input isolation or debounce circuits can cause erratic readings from mechanical switches or noisy environments. Relying on CPU-intensive processing for debouncing or high-frequency GPIO handling can also consume excessive processor cycles and impact overall system performance. In complex or time-sensitive applications, consider using a more powerful MCU, hardware-accelerated peripherals, or distributing the workload with dedicated coprocessors or microcontrollers to ensure smooth and reliable operation.

PWM, Timers, and Output Control

Here are the questions:

- Is hardware PWM needed for dimming, speed control, or signal generation?
- Are advanced timers required for precise event timing or waveform capture?

Pitfall: Some MCUs multiplex PWM/timer functions with other peripherals; confirm you can use the needed features simultaneously. Direct Memory Access (DMA) channels are also frequently shared with timers, ADCs, or other peripherals, which may lead to resource conflicts or unexpected limitations. Carefully review the MCU's datasheet and reference manual to understand any DMA channel sharing, especially for applications with multiple simultaneous high-speed peripherals.

Communication Interfaces

Here are the questions:

- Which protocols must be supported?
- Is UART/RS-232/RS-485 for industrial communication required?
- Is there a need to interface with I^2C or SPI sensors or peripherals?
- CAN or LIN for automotive or industrial bus integration?

Pitfall: The number of serial ports on a board is often limited, and software-based solutions are less reliable.

Example: A gateway device designed with only one UART had to be redesigned when a second serial device needed to be added late in development.

Networking Requirements

Follow the common options:

- What network interface is best suited?
- Ethernet for high reliability and bandwidth
- Wi-Fi or Bluetooth for wireless operation (note: evaluate coverage, security and certification requirements)
- Cellular or LoRa for remote and wide-area deployments

Pitfall: Wireless is convenient, but industrial settings with metal enclosures or interference can make Wi-Fi/Bluetooth unreliable.

Example: A building automation system installed in a basement regularly lost connectivity due to Wi-Fi signal loss.

Processing Power and Memory

- Does your application involve complex local processing, buffering, or edge analytics?
- Does the MCU offer enough RAM and Flash to handle all tasks, firmware, and libraries?

- Should you invest in the next model up in the MCU series for more internal memory?
- Is it more appropriate to use an external Flash or RAM chip? External memory can provide greater capacity but often at the cost of additional GPIO usage, board complexity, and timing penalties.
- Is the performance impact of slower external access is acceptable for your application, and are the added cost and hardware complexity justified compared to a higher-specification MCU?

Pitfall: Underestimating memory needs can block future feature upgrades or even basic stability if unexpected tasks are required post-deployment. Memory is relatively inexpensive compared to the costs of redesigns or missed features, so consider your choice carefully. When in doubt, opt for external memory—this allows you to design your PCB to support extra RAM or Flash chips, which you can choose not to populate in lower-cost versions or offer as a premium SKU for more demanding applications.

Expandability and Modular Design

Here's the question:

- Does the board really need to support expansion, or is it better to keep the design as simple as possible? Don't add expansion capability "just in case"—if your use case doesn't clearly require it, extra headers and PCB space only increase costs and complexity. You're often better off releasing a new version of your hardware when future expansion needs are identified, rather than carrying the burden of unneeded expandability in every unit.

Pitfall: While it is important not to overdesign with unnecessary expansion, a lack of realistic planning for future needs can leave you with no upgrade path. If expansion is not required for your immediate application, avoid adding cost and complexity—but do consider how you might respond if future requirements arise, such as by planning a revision or designing modular options for future product lines.

Power Supply and Electrical Protection

Here are the questions:

- Is the hardware compatible with the site's voltage (e.g., 12–24 V DC common in industry)?
- Are onboard protections in place (fusing, surge protection, reverse polarity)?
- Does your system require redundant power supplies or backup options for safety-critical or high-availability applications?
- Are there industry, medical, or safety regulations (e.g., IEC, UL, ISO, IECEx, ATEX) that specify power supply design, redundancy, or fail-safe operation?
- Is the power system sufficient to support all connected loads, including expansion boards and actuators, under all operating scenarios?
- Are connectors and terminals sturdy enough for repeated maintenance, harsh environments, and secure wiring?
- Does the design facilitate maintenance and upgrades, such as easily accessible fuses, modular power blocks, or labeled connectors?

Pitfall: Insufficient power budget, poor signal quality, or slow transient response are common causes of device failure in industrial IoT.

Example: A telemetry device deployed in the field randomly failed in extreme temperatures because the power supply couldn't maintain voltage required by LTE modem during transmission due to current peaks.

Mechanical, Thermal, and Environmental Suitability

Here are the questions:

- Can the board operate reliably in your deployment environment?
- What is the service temperature and humidity range?

- Is the product subject to vibration and mechanical shock?
- Does the environment calls for ingress protection (dust, water)?
- Is the device designed with ease of maintenance in mind, with proper access for the technicians who will service it?

Pitfall: Indoor-rated PCBs or connectors quickly fail outdoors or in pump rooms exposed to condensation, insects, or cleaning chemicals. Poor access to connectors and parts that require regular service can lead to costly or impractical maintenance operations, sometimes preventing repairs altogether and significantly increasing operational costs.

Certification and Compliance

Here is the question:

- Are there regulatory or safety certifications required for your target market (CE, UL, FCC, industry-specific standards)?

Pitfall: Skipping certification planning can block market entry or lead to expensive, late-stage redesigns.

Longevity and Supply Chain

Here are the questions:

- Is the board (and MCU) likely to be available and supported for the expected lifetime of your project, especially for production deployments?
- Does the vendor provide a clear roadmap and active support channels?

Pitfall: Relying on short-lived hobby boards or MCUs discontinued with little notice has led many companies to costly redesigns or lost business.

Considering the previous general criteria—as well as others that may be specific to your project—you can now narrow your search to an MCU platform or series that is the best fit for your application.

At this point, you should also carefully weigh whether it makes sense to use a ready-to-use OEM module or take on the challenge of designing and producing a custom board. Even if you have strong in-house PCB design capabilities, never underestimate the complexity and potential pitfalls that come with a fully custom hardware approach. Evaluate the total cost, including unit price at your expected production volume, the engineering time investment, and the risk of delays. Factor in parts procurement (availability of MCUs, passive and active components), maintainability (ease of repair and servicing in the field), stocking (minimum order quantities, inventory management), and product longevity (expected lifecycle and vendor commitment). Assess the level of long-term support and documentation available from the OEM vendor, as this will often make a significant difference in your ability to keep your devices running reliably over years of operation.

Ask yourself: how does the chosen board integrate into the overall product architecture? Does it offer the right mechanical and electrical fit? Will it allow you to meet product certification and support requirements down the line? Assess the level of support and documentation available from the OEM vendor, as this will often make a significant difference in your time-to-market and ability to troubleshoot issues during development or mass production.

No matter how thorough your analysis is, always prototype before committing to a final platform. When in doubt, seek advice from hardware vendors or engineering firms with real-world experience in nanoFramework-based systems. Early and well-informed decisions pay off by streamlining your project and helping avoid costly surprises or budget overruns later.

.NET nanoFramework empowers you with tremendous flexibility from the very beginning. You can quickly and easily come up with a proof of concept (even using a different platform or hardware more suitable for prototyping) to perform the required validations before committing to the hardware that will make it to the final version.

Hardware Overview

Having considered all of this, for this chapter's capstone project we will use the PALTHREE board as our hardware platform. PALTHREE stands out due to its robust industrial-grade design, feature set, and proven compatibility with .NET nanoFramework. This makes it an ideal choice for demonstrating a real-world, professional IoT automation system that can serve as both a development platform and a production-ready solution.

The PALTHREE Board: A Robust Industrial Controller

With the hardware selection rationale established, let's take a closer look at the PALTHREE board that will serve as the platform for our capstone project. Figure 6-1 shows this board.

Figure 6-1. *PALTHREE board with LCD fitted*

The following are the technical highlights of this board:

- **Microcontroller:** STM32F769NI (ARM Cortex-M7, 216 MHz).
- **Memory:** 2 MB Flash, 512 kB SRAM, Dual 8 MB external SDRAM.
- **External Storage:** 16 MB SQSPI NOR Flash; SD card slot and USB host (for data logging or backup, board-dependent).
- **Power Input:** 12–24 V DC, with over-voltage and reverse polarity protection.
- **Auxiliary Connectors:** USB A x 2, micro USB for Visual Studio debug, JTAG.

- **Analog Inputs:** The PALTHREE leverages the microcontroller's on-chip ADCs to provide high-resolution analog input capabilities. By default, the board includes a dedicated circuit for a single 4–20 mA current loop input—allowing direct connection to one industrial process sensor (such as pH, chlorine, or turbidity). This current loop interface provides electrical noise immunity and is a *de facto* standard in process automation.
- **Expandable Analog Acquisition:** While the on-board hardware supports only one native 4–20 mA channel, the board's expansion headers allow for the integration of external analog front-end modules or multichannel 4–20 mA receiver boards. This enables the system to scale up to support multiple simultaneous analog process sensors, which are vital for applications requiring comprehensive monitoring (such as full water quality analysis in a pool controller). All the channels support active and passive 4-20mA (loop-powered and nonloop-powered wiring).
- **Versatile Digital I/O:** The board features an array of GPIOs, configurable as inputs or outputs for digital interfacing. Outputs are intended for controlling external relay modules, solid-state relays, or direct-drive opto-isolators. Inputs can be used for safety interlocks, pump status monitoring, level switches, or other automation signals.
- **Industrial-Grade Power Input and Protection:** PALTHREE supports a wide DC voltage input, with onboard protections against over-voltage and reverse polarity. This ensures stable, uninterrupted operation even in challenging electrical environments.
- **Ethernet Connectivity:** The inclusion of a 10/100 Mbps Ethernet port provides robust, deterministic network communication—critical for automation systems requiring secure and reliable data transfer.
- **Expansion Capability:** The board's expansion connectors are designed for compatibility with a range of off-the-shelf industrial I/O modules and communication transceivers (e.g., RS-485, 4-20mA Input and Output, LoRa, Wi-Fi, and others). This flexibility allows users to adapt the platform to complex control and monitoring requirements.

- **Mechanical and Environmental Durability:** All connectors and PCB construction are rated for industrial temperature ranges and mechanical stress, ensuring long-term reliability in field installations.
- **Mechanical:** 162x123x26 (WxLxH) without LCD mounted.
- **.NET nanoFramework Support:** The PALTHREE is natively supported by .NET nanoFramework, with dedicated firmware images continuously maintained and delivered through the nanoFramework cloud build pipelines. This ensures that developers can always flash the latest version—incorporating new features, fixes, and improvements—directly onto the board. The firmware is ready to use out of the box.

Reading Analog 4–20mA Sensors

Let's look at a real-world example.

Quick Primer

The 4-20mA current loop is a standard way to connect industrial sensors to controllers in environments where reliability is critical. Instead of sending a voltage (which can drop or pick up noise over long cables), the sensor transmits a small current proportional to the measured value: 4mA represents the minimum (zero), and 20mA represents the maximum value of the sensor's range.

Why use current instead of voltage? Current remains constant over long wires, so you get accurate readings even with cables running tens of meters through electrically noisy environments. Also, using a "live zero" (4mA instead of 0mA for minimum value) means wiring faults—like a broken cable or unplugged sensor—can be detected immediately, since they would register as 0mA.

So, how does the microcontroller read the current? The controller doesn't measure current directly. Instead, it places a precision resistor (called a *shunt*) between the current loop and ground. The sensor current flows through this resistor, creating a voltage that can be read by the controller's analog-to-digital converter (ADC).

You can see in Figure 6-2 the solution available in the PALTHREE board. There is a dedicated amplifier (INA196A with gain = 20) and a 4.99Ω shunt resistor. When the sensor sends 4mA, the voltage across the resistor (after amplification) is about 0.4V; at 20mA, it's about 2V.

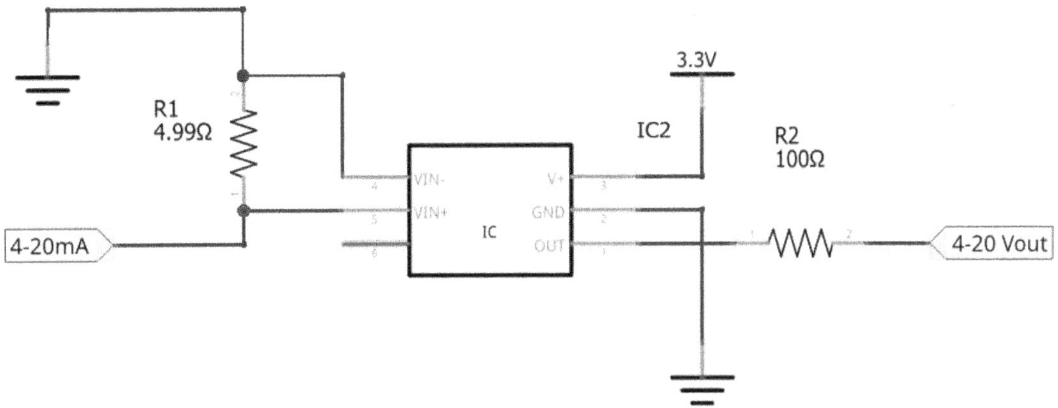

***Figure 6-2.** Schematic of a 4-20mA receiver*

Check the math here, using the equation $V_{out} = I_{sensor} \times R_{shunt} \times Gain$.

$$\text{At 4 mA: } V_{out}(4\,\text{mA}) = 0.004 \times 4.99 \times 20 = 0.399\text{V}$$

$$\text{At 20 mA: } V_{out}(20\,\text{mA}) = 0.020 \times 4.99 \times 20 = 1.996\text{V}$$

So, the amplified voltage presented to the ADC will range from approximately 0.4V (minimum) to 2.0V (maximum) for 4-20mA sensor currents. This stays within the safe range for the STM32F769 ADC.

Bottom line: 4-20mA sensors let you reliably measure real-world values over long distances, and the proper signal conditioning makes connecting them to a microcontroller pretty straightforward, even if you're more comfortable with software than hardware.

Code

With the hardware theory and signal conditioning established, let's see how to acquire a real pH sensor reading in code. If you're new to analog-to-digital conversion, review Chapter 4 for an in-depth look at the nanoFramework ADC API and its usage patterns.

The following is an example class for robust pH sensor readings. This class handles both sampling/averaging and conversion from voltage to physical pH units.

```
public class PhSensor
{
    private const float _phMin = 0; // pH at 4mA
    private const float _phMax = 14; // pH at 20mA
```

```
    private readonly AdcChannel _adc;
    private readonly float _shuntResistor;
    private readonly float _gain; // INA196A gain

    public PhSensor(
        AdcController adcController,
        int adcChannel,
        float shuntResistor = 4.99f,
        float gain = 20f)
    {
        _adc = adcController.OpenChannel(adcChannel);
        _shuntResistor = shuntResistor;
        _gain = gain;
    }

    public float ReadPh(int samples = 10)
    {
        float total = 0f;

        for (int i = 0; i < samples; i++)
        {
            total += _adc.ReadValue();
        }

        float averageRaw = total / samples;

        // Convert ADC reading to voltage (assume 12-bit ADC, 3.3V ref)
        float voltage = (averageRaw / 4095f) * 3.3f;

        // Calculate current in mA: I = Vout / (R_shunt * Gain)
        float current_mA = voltage / (_shuntResistor * _gain) * 1000f;

        // Map 4-20mA to pH range
        float phValue = _phMin + ((current_mA-4f) / 16f) * (_phMax-_phMin);
        phValue = Math.Max(_phMin, Math.Min(_phMax, phValue));

        // Return pH
        return phValue;
    }
}
```

Instantiating a PhSensor should be straightforward:

```
AdcController controller = new AdcController();
PhSensor phSensor = new PhSensor(controller, 0);
```

And to take a pH reading:

```
float phValue = phSensor.ReadPh();
```

For further details on configuring ADCs and handling other channels, you may want to take a look at Chapter 4.

Recall that 0 mA in a 4–20 mA sensor system typically means the sensor is disconnected or faulty. This will correspond to the ADC reading roughly 0V.

Challenge: Try improving the PhSensor class to reliably detect and signal this condition. This will let your software alert the operator or trigger a safe fallback state when a sensor is unplugged or malfunctions for any reason.

For the sake of brevity, we'll skip implementing the classes to represent the chlorin, turbidity, and temperature sensors. The underlying concepts are the same as with the PhSensor class, and therefore it shouldn't present any major challenges.

Worth noting: The PALTHREE board is equipped with only a single native 4–20 mA input. To connect the remaining sensors required for our pool monitoring device, we need to add an expansion board that provides additional 4–20 mA input channels. In our project, this expansion board will be connected to the first expansion connector on the PALTHREE. This is a common pattern in industrial systems, where modular expansion allows you to scale up the sensor count as needed without redesigning the main controller. See Figure 6-3.

Figure 6-3. *Expansion board for 4–20mA inputs*

Monitoring Water Quality

Once the sensors are integrated and the analog readings are reliable, the next step is to implement a periodic monitoring loop. This routine is at the heart of automated water quality management.

Choose an appropriate sampling frequency. For pool applications, reading each sensor every few minutes (e.g., every 5 minutes) balances timely intervention with resource efficiency. It would be wise to make this sample rate value part of a general configuration class so it could be changed programmatically by the pool owner using the UI interface or remotely from the cloud connection.

Despite being connected to the cloud, the system should be self-sufficient and not rely on a continuous cloud connection for critical decisions or real-time actions. Local processing—commonly referred to as *edge computing*—offers several key advantages. First, it ensures the system can continue operating, making decisions and keeping the water safe and balanced even if connectivity is lost. Second, processing data locally reduces communication costs, as it eliminates the need to constantly send raw data to the cloud and wait for instructions. This saves bandwidth and reduces latency, enabling immediate reactions to changing water conditions.

In our working example, the local decision logic is simple and efficient, and pushing this responsibility to the cloud would add unnecessary complexity. However, in more advanced scenarios—such as systems that require image processing, pattern recognition, or predictive analytics—edge computing can be even more valuable. Modern microcontrollers, including those supported by .NET nanoFramework, are increasingly capable of running lightweight AI frameworks, which allow for sophisticated, real-time analysis on resource-constrained devices. This makes it possible to perform advanced tasks (optimizing chemical dosing based on historical trends) directly at the edge, with all the advantages of speed, resilience, and reduced communication cost.

Getting back to the implementation of the required processing, the controller should immediately compare each new sensor reading against safe operating thresholds:

- If the **pH** is out of range, trigger the dosing pump to adjust pH.
- If **chlorine** is low, activate the chlorine dosing system.
- If **turbidity** is high (cloudy water), log an alert or, if desired, trigger filtration/notification.

The same recommendation made for the sample rate applies to the thresholds. These should be part of a general configuration class to make it easy to store/adjust from the UI and cloud backend.

Developing more in the edge computing front, in addition to monitoring thresholds, the system should incorporate dynamic adjustment capabilities. For instance, instead of relying solely on fixed limits, the software could adapt based on external conditions such as seasonal changes, usage patterns, or historical data. This approach would make the system more proactive, allowing it to anticipate trends and optimize water quality management before issues arise rather than reacting to them.

Furthermore, robust error-handling mechanisms are essential to ensure the reliability of such automated systems. These mechanisms should detect and manage sensor malfunctions, communication delays, or unexpected deviations in readings. For example, if a sensor consistently reports values outside expected parameters despite regular calibration, the controller could flag the issue and switch to backup thresholds or a predefined safe operation mode until the sensor is repaired or replaced.

The integration of fail-safe protocols guarantees that even in the event of partial system failure, the pool remains safe. Such protocols might include default chemical dosing routines or manual override options for pool owners, ensuring uninterrupted operation regardless of technical issues.

Here is an example of a simplistic loop to sample sensors and implement a minimalist control logic:

```
while (true)
{
    // Take sensor readings
    float ph = phSensor.ReadPh();
    float chlorine = chSensor.ReadChlorineLevel();
    float turbidity = turbiditySensor.ReadTurbidity();

    // Simple local decision logic
    if (ph < GeneralConfiguration.PhLowThreshold
        || ph > GeneralConfiguration.PhHighThreshold)
    {
        Log("pH out of range: " + ph);

        TriggerPhDosingPump();
    }

    if (chlorine < GeneralConfiguration.ChLowThreshold)
    {
        Log("Chlorine low: " + chlorine);

        TriggerChlorinePump();
    }

    if (turbidity > GeneralConfiguration.TurbidityThreshold)
    {
        Log("Turbidity high: " + turbidity);

        TriggerTurbidityAlert();
    }

    // Log readings for traceability
    Log($"ph={ph}, chlorine={chlorine}, turbidity={turbidity}");

    Thread.Sleep(GeneralConfiguration.SampleRate);
}
```

Here's a practical exercise for you: try refining your monitoring loop to detect errors (like disconnected sensors or out-of-range values), missed pump activations, or excessive pump running time. You might also implement time-based averaging or min/max recording to make your solution even more robust.

Logging and Traceability

Implementing a robust logging module is essential for traceability and diagnostics—critical for debugging, compliance, and trend analysis. In this project, let's assume logging can be enabled or disabled through a property in the general configuration class, making it easy to adapt to different deployment or debug needs.

A simple approach is to log to a file on the SD card using the nanoFramework `Logging` library. This approach ensures that pump activations, system boots, threshold crossings, and significant events are all stored for later review, even if the device is temporarily offline. The logging class writes to a stream (a file on the SD card), supporting efficient and flexible logging that scales well with real-world usage.

Here's an example implementation:

```
public class LoggerModule
{
    private StreamWriter _logStream;
    private readonly bool _enabled;

    public LoggerModule(string logFilePath, bool enabled)
    {
        _enabled = enabled;

        if (_enabled)
        {
            var fileStream = new FileStream(
                logFilePath,
                FileMode.Append,
                FileAccess.Write);

            _logStream = new StreamWriter(fileStream);
        }
    }
```

```
    public void Log(string message)
    {
        if (!_enabled)
        {
            return;
        }

        string logLine = $"{DateTime.UtcNow:yyyy-MM-dd HH:mm:ss}
        {message}";

        _logStream.WriteLine(logLine);
        _logStream.Flush();
    }

    public void LogBoot() => Log("System boot");
    public void LogPumpOn(string pump) => Log($"{pump} pump ON");
    public void LogPumpOff(string pump) => Log($"{pump} pump OFF");
    public void LogThresholdCrossed(string sensor, float value) =>
    Log($"{sensor} threshold crossed: {value}");
    public void LogSystemEvent(string message) => Log($"{message}");

    public void Close()
    {
        if (_logStream != null)
        {
            _logStream.Flush();
            _logStream.Dispose();
        }
    }
}
```

Logging is enabled or disabled through a setting in the configuration class, allowing you to easily adapt the system for development, troubleshooting, or production. Once enabled, you use the `LoggerModule` to log all relevant events like system boot, pump activations, threshold crossings, and general events.

For practical deployments, all logs are written to the SD card. The recommended approach is to store one plain-text file per day (named with the date, such as *2024-07-02.txt*), creating a new file either on each boot or at midnight. This makes it straightforward to trace problems, review system behavior, or perform compliance checks. SD cards are especially practical for field devices. When needed, the card can be removed and the log files downloaded to any PC, ensuring that complete operational history is accessible even if the device is offline for extended periods.

Actuating Pumps for Chemical Dosing

Chemical dosing pumps play a crucial role in automated water quality management, providing the precise addition of treatment chemicals in response to real-time measurements and operating conditions. In professional pool management and industrial water treatment, effective dosing is not simply about running a pump—it demands robust feedback control, flow-proportional adjustment, rigorous safety, and careful calibration.

Quick Primer on 4–20mA pump control

Dosage pumps used for pool and industrial water treatment are often controlled by a 4-20 mA current loop input, which allows for precise and proportional adjustment of chemical injection rates. In practice, the current value sent to the pump determines the instantaneous dosing rate—the higher the current within the 4-20 mA range, the faster the pump delivers chemicals. This control signal is typically maintained for as long as dosing is required, with the rate continuously adjustable by software according to real-time sensor readings. In most systems, the software periodically re-evaluates water quality data and updates the current output as needed, ensuring the chemical dosing is both accurate and responsive to changing pool conditions. Some pumps may also support time-based dosing or combined control strategies, and some use flowrate of liquid, but for this project, the 4-20 mA signal directly sets the delivery rate in real time, allowing for simple yet highly effective feedback control based on the latest measurements.

In our project, we'll use the second expansion connector on the PALTHREE to connect an analog output expansion board. This board provides the required 4-20 mA outputs for direct connection to dosing pumps, as well as 0-10 V outputs for compatibility with other actuator types. See Figure 6-4.

***Figure 6-4.** Expansion board for 4-20mA and 0-10V output*

The expansion board generates the output current via a digital-to-analog converter (DAC), which feeds an operational amplifier and a MOSFET network that acts as a current sink. This design allows the board to produce a stable, programmable output current that matches the setpoint determined by your software. The pump's control circuit is then connected in series with this output, enabling closed-loop control of chemical dosing from your application code.

Considering that the circuitry of this board includes advanced electronics concepts beyond the scope of the current work, we'll skip the schematic entirely and also any explanation about it. Readers interested in the underlying analog output design are encouraged to consult the manufacturer documentation for the expansion board.

The expansion board's DAC output governs the current sink to achieve the 4–20 mA current range. Specifically, the board converts a voltage from 0 to 2V into a corresponding current value, calculated by dividing the voltage by 100.

Let's compute this for the limit values:

- Setting the DAC to output to 0.4 V results in a current output of:

  0.4 V / 100 = 4 mA.

- Setting it to output 2 V generates a current of:

  2.0 V / 100 = 20 mA.

This approach is both clever and straightforward, making it an excellent choice for precise chemical dosing control.

The DAC fitted in the expansion board is a Texas Instruments DAC63004. This is a 12-bit smart DAC with several connection options. In the expansion board its wired to use a I²C connection. We'll skip the detailed explanation about Digital Analog Converters which was covered in Chapter 4. Still, we need to know a couple of details about the part and the setup in order to get those output values correct.

The DAC will be using its internal voltage reference of 1.21 V. As explained, the maximum voltage we need is 2.0 V, so to maximize the resolution, we should use the V_{out} gain set to 2.0, which gives us a top output voltage of $1.21 \times 2.0 = 2.42$ V.

Quick Primer on pH Compensation

The goal is to bring the pool water's pH into the desired range (typically 7.2–7.6 for pools). The controller software, often employing a Proportional-Integral-Derivative (PID) controller, compares the measured pH to the setpoint to calculate the precise amount of acid to be dosed. The PID controller helps enhance precision by dynamically adjusting the acid addition rate based on real-time feedback, minimizing overshoot and ensuring the process remains stable. As a curiosity, know that most pool systems only need acid dosing, as pH tends to drift upward due to aeration and chlorine use.

Example computation:

- Suppose you have a 50 m^3 (50,000 L) pool.
- The measured pH is 8.0, but the target pH is 7.4.
- The chemical manufacturer specifies:

  "To decrease pH by 0.2 units in 10 m^3 of water, add 200 mL of acid."

So, to decrease the pH by 0.6 units in 50 m^3:

1. Calculate how much pH you need to adjust:

$$\Delta pH = 8.0—7.4 = 0.6$$

2. Determine the required acid dose:

   Each 0.2 units in 10 m^3 needs 200 mL.

   For 50 m^3:

   5 × (200 mL per 0.2 pH) = 1,000 mL per 0.2 pH

   For 0.6 pH:

   1,000 mL × (0.6 / 0.2) = 3,000 mL

So, 3 liters of acid are needed to bring the pool from pH 8.0 to 7.4. Knowing this, it has to be translated into a pump command. The PID controller plays a critical role here by regulating the pump command through a 4–20 mA signal, ensuring the acid injection is optimized based on the pump's calibration (e.g., the pump delivers 1 L/hour at 12 mA). The software often runs the pump gradually, with repeated cycles and periodic measurement, allowing the PID controller to refine the dosing process and reduce the risk of overshooting.

Quick Primer on Chlorine Compensation

Chlorine compensation involves maintaining the necessary chlorine levels in the pool to ensure effective disinfection. The process starts with measuring the current free chlorine levels and comparing them against the target value, often influenced by pool usage and environmental factors like sunlight and debris.

Calculate the adjustment needed:

- ΔChlorine = Target—Current (e.g., 3 ppm—1.5 ppm = 1.5 ppm)

Determine the required chlorine dose:

- For a 50 m^3 pool, each ppm increase requires approximately 50 g of chlorine.

  1.5 ppm × 50 g/ppm = 75 g of chlorine needed.

The dosing system uses a calibrated pump, controlled by the same PID mechanism as with pH adjustment. The pump command is regulated through a 4–20 mA signal, with the chlorine injected gradually in cycles to avoid overshooting. The PID controller refines the process through periodic water testing, ensuring precise and efficient dosing.

Chlorine levels are also impacted by pH, as higher pH can reduce chlorine efficacy. Therefore, pH adjustments and chlorine dosing often work in tandem to maintain optimal water quality. Advanced systems may include sensors to measure both free chlorine and combined chlorine, providing a more comprehensive view of pool conditions.

Quick Primer on Turbidity Compensation

Turbidity compensation in a pool is about maintaining clear water by measuring how "cloudy" it is and then taking corrective actions if the turbidity gets too high.

How does it work in practice? In a pool system, the turbidity compensation process is essential for maintaining water clarity. It begins with a turbidity sensor, typically optical, which measures the concentration of suspended particles in the pool water. The sensor provides an output in units like NTU, usually is 0 to 100, indicating the water's cloudiness level. When the turbidity measurement exceeds a predefined threshold, such as 1.0 or 2.0 NTU, the system identifies the need for corrective action. Instead of adding chemicals like in pH adjustment, this system prolongs the operation of the pool's filtration and circulation system. In more advanced setups, it may also apply clarifying agents, known as *flocculants*, which promote the settling of particles or enhance their capture by the filtration system.

The smooth operational integration of these mechanisms ensures that the water remains clear and free from excessive cloudiness. Combined with advanced monitoring systems for chlorine levels and pH balance, this approach provides a holistic framework for managing pool conditions effectively, guaranteeing both chemical precision and visual purity.

Coding It

Now that we know everything about chemicals dosage pumps, how to compensate those parameters, and the hardware we have to connect to, let's tackle the code for our pool controller!

Because the code for the pool controller will grow very quickly and will necessarily get into a certain complexity level, we won't be listing all of it here for the obvious reasons. Instead, we'll focus and dissect the relevant snippets. The full code base is made available in a GitHub repository companion to this book.

Let's start with a component that will be reused multiple times: the dosage pump controller.

As we're fortunate and we're developing with .NET nanoFramework, we can *just* grab building blocks that will make our life easier. There is a binding for the DAC63004 that we can reference from our C# project.

Let's create a `DosagePumpController` class that takes the I²C bus ID as the constructor parameter, instantiates a `Dac63004` object, and creates and initializes four `DosagePump` classes, which, in turn, implements the required API to allow controlling the pump.

Because it's using hardware resources, the `DosagePumpController` class has to implement the `IDisposable` pattern so it can dispose of those resources gracefully.

The constructor will look like this:

```
public DosagePumpController(int i2cBusId)
{
    I2cConnectionSettings settings = new(
        i2cBusId,
        Dac63004.DefaultI2cAddress);

    _i2CDevice = I2cDevice.Create(settings);

    _dac = new(_i2CDevice);

    ConfigureDac();

    Pumps = new DosagePump[4];
    Pumps[0] = new DosagePump(_dac, Channel.Channel0);
    Pumps[1] = new DosagePump(_dac, Channel.Channel1);
    Pumps[2] = new DosagePump(_dac, Channel.Channel2);
    Pumps[3] = new DosagePump(_dac, Channel.Channel3);
}
```

In `ConfigureDac()` method the configuration of the DAC63004 is taken care of, which consists of configuring the channels to voltage output mode, setting the V_{out} gain and enabling the internal reference.

```
private void ConfigureDac()
{
    // all channels are set to voltage output mode
    _dac.ConfigureChannelMode(Channel.Channel0, Mode.VoltageOutput);
    _dac.ConfigureChannelMode(Channel.Channel1, Mode.VoltageOutput);
    _dac.ConfigureChannelMode(Channel.Channel2, Mode.VoltageOutput);
    _dac.ConfigureChannelMode(Channel.Channel3, Mode.VoltageOutput);

    // gain for all channels is set to 2
    _dac.ConfigureChannelVoutGain(Channel.Channel0, VoutGain.Internal2x);
    _dac.ConfigureChannelVoutGain(Channel.Channel1, VoutGain.Internal2x);
    _dac.ConfigureChannelVoutGain(Channel.Channel2, VoutGain.Internal2x);
    _dac.ConfigureChannelVoutGain(Channel.Channel3, VoutGain.Internal2x);

    // Enable internal reference voltage
    _dac.InternalRefEnabled = true;
}
```

Looking at the DosagePump class, the constructor is quite simple:

```
internal DosagePump(Dac63004 dac, Channel channel)
{
    _dac = dac ?? throw new ArgumentNullException();
    _channel = channel;
}
```

You'll notice that it has a validation for the dac parameter and stores the channels it was assigned to. The constructor visibility is set to internal because we don't want to expose it beyond the DosagePumpController.

The only aspect left to address is how the API should allow control over the pump's output current. In .NET, this can be implemented as either a method (such as SetCurrent()) or a property (such as Current). Both approaches are valid and align with .NET guidelines and good practices.

For this class, I prefer using a property named Current. This style is often cleaner, allows the current value to be easily read back by the caller, and aligns well with .NET's idiomatic use of properties for directly-settable values.

Exposing it as a property and including a backing field to store the value looks like this:

```
private ElectricCurrent _current;

public ElectricCurrent Current
{
    get => _current;
    set => SetCurrent(value);
}
```

You might be wondering if this is misleading, since the underlying hardware—specifically the DAC—actually outputs a voltage, not a current. Here's where the *abstraction principle* comes in: the role of a class is to abstract away implementation details and expose a clear, meaningful interface to the caller. From the perspective of the application, the "current" to set the pump is what matters; how it's physically generated is an internal *detail*. By exposing a `Current` property, the class makes it obvious what the developer can control, while hiding the complexity of voltage conversion, amplification, and current loop circuitry.

Now that this is clarified, let's look at the implementation:

```
private void SetCurrent(ElectricCurrent current)
{
    // validate range: 4-20 mA
    if (current.Milliamperes < 4.0
        || current.Milliamperes > 20.0)
    {
        throw new ArgumentOutOfRangeException();
    }

    _current = current;

    // convert to voltage absolute value (0-2.0 V)
    // 4mA = 0.4 V, 20mA = 2.0 V
    double voltageValue = _current.Amperes * 100.0;
```

```
    // Convert to 12-bit value (0-4095)
    // max voltage is Vref x gain = 1.21 × 2.0 = 2.42 V
    int dacValue = (int)(( voltageValue / 2.42) * 4095);

    _dac.SetChannelDataValue(_channel, dacValue);
}
```

The parameter value is verified to ensure it falls within the expected range; otherwise, an `ArgumentOutOfRangeException` will be thrown. An alternative approach involves clamping the parameter value to the appropriate range. However, this would obscure from the caller that the current value was incorrect, potentially leading to erroneous assumptions and subsequent errors.

Follows the conversion of the parameter to the value that will be sent to the DAC channel. You'll notice that it's following the algorithm we've discussed in the primer on the expansion output board.

Here's a step-by-step computation for a 12 mA setpoint:

1. Take the current value (12mA) in A and multiply by 100:

   `voltageValue` is $0.012 \times 100 = 1.2$

2. Convert this to the DAC value, considering the full scale value of 2.42 V and that a 12-bit DAC has 4,096 steps:

   `dacValue` is $(1.2 / 2.42) \times 4095 \simeq 2030$

The last line in the method set the value of the DAC channel corresponding to this pump to the computed value. The call to `SetChannelDataValue()` goes through the paces of communicating with the DAC chip through the I^2C and setting the appropriate registers to make that happen.

Please note the usage of `ElectricCurrent` object in the previous code. This is a handy class available from the *UnitsNet* collection that allows you to represent electrical current values together with their units (such as milliamperes, amperes, or microamperes). It provides type safety, readable code, and easy conversions between units, reducing errors and making your calculations both more expressive and less error-prone.

As a final note, *UnitsNet* offers a wide range of other NuGet packages for working with commonly used units—covering everything from temperature and length to pressure and speed—which can help you write safer, more readable code throughout your .NET nanoFramework projects.

Now that we have a working DosagePumpController class, we can move to implement the PhController.

For that class, we need the configurations for the controller, the dosage pump that is assigned to it, the pH sensor, an API to start and stop it and last, and not the least, a control loop that reads the sensor and computes the control to the pump.

As there are common configurations among the various controllers, let's create a base class for this.

```
public class ControllerConfigBase
{
    public float Kd { get; set; } = 0.05f;
    public float Ki { get; set; } = 0.1f;
    public float Kp { get; set; } = 2.0f;
}
```

The first three properties are the parameters for a PID controller, whose default values are reasonable parameters for a controller with this usage.

The PhControllerConfig class will derive from this one, like this:

```
public class PhControllerConfig : ControllerConfigBase
{
    // default value is 7.2 pH
    public float TargetPh { get; set; } = 7.2f;
    public float ChemicalStrength { get; set; } = 1.0f; // mg/L per mL
}
```

Here's the constructor of PhController:

```
public PhController(
    PhSensor sensor,
    DosagePump pump,
    float poolVolume,
    PhControllerConfig config)
{
    _sensor = sensor;
    _pump = pump;
    _poolVolume = poolVolume;
    Config = config;
}
```

Two properties have to exist and be accessible externally to allow changes from the caller:

```
public PhControllerConfig Config { get; set; }
public float PhValue { get; set; }
```

There are also a couple of fields that are required because of the PID implementation (`_integral` and `_lastPhDelta`), and `_running` serves as flag for the thread running the control loop to allow stopping and (re)starting it.

```
private bool _running;
private float _integral;
private float _lastPhDelta;
```

The control loop will look like this:

```
private void ControlLoop()
{
    while (_running)
    {
        // read the pH value from the sensor
        PhValue = _sensor.ReadPh();

        // compute the difference from target pH
        float phDelta = Config.TargetPh-PhValue;

        // Simple PID control
        _integral += phDelta;
        float derivative = phDelta-_lastPhDelta;
        float output = Config.Kp * phDelta + Config.Ki * _integral +
        Config.Kd * derivative;

        // Calculate required chemical dose (in mL or mg, depending on
        ChemicalStrength units)
        float requiredDose = output * _poolVolume / Config.
        ChemicalStrength;
```

```
            // Map requiredDose to pump current (mA) as needed for your system
            double pumpCurrent = _pump.PumpMinCurrent.Milliamperes
                        + (requiredDose * (_pump.PumpMaxCurrent.Milliamperes-_
                        pump.PumpMinCurrent.Milliamperes));

           // Clamp to valid range (from the pump's configuration)
           pumpCurrent = Math.Clamp(pumpCurrent, _pump.PumpMinCurrent.
           Milliamperes, _pump.PumpMaxCurrent.Milliamperes);
            _pump.Current = ElectricCurrent.FromMilliamperes(pumpCurrent);

            // store the last delta for derivative calculation
            _lastPhDelta = phDelta;

            // sleep untill the next cycle
            Thread.Sleep(TimeSpan.FromMinutes(1));
        }
}
```

The comments in the code should make it self-explanatory, but still let's highlight some aspects. There's a loop controlled by `_running` that starts reading the pH sensor and computes the delta from the reading to the set point value.

A simple implementation of a PID controller computes the required chemical dose to start injecting in the pool, considering the PID parameters, the chemical strength of the compensating acid, and the pool volume.

Then it proceeds to calculate the current required for the dosage pump taking into account the configuration parameters. Note the clamping operation there to ensure that the computed value does not exceed the admissible values for the pump. With this value it updates the current for the pump, stores the delta value, and goes to sleep until the next iteration.

The `ChlorineController` controller will have a similar implementation, so we'll skip it.

For `TurbidityController` controller there is a slightly different implementation, considering that turbidity isn't corrected with injection of a chemical, rather making the filter system work more time and/or with more power.

The constructor is as simple as this:

```
public TurbidityController(
    TurbiditySensor sensor,
    TurbidityControllerConfig config)
{
    _sensor = sensor;
    _config = config;
}
```

And the control loop something like this:

```
private void ControlLoop()
{
    while (_running)
    {
        TurbidityValue = _sensor.ReadTurbidity();

        if (TurbidityValue > _config.Threshold)
        {
            // Run filter with extra power
            _config.FilterGpioPin.Write(PinValue.High);
        }
        else
        {
            // disable extra power from filter
            _config.FilterGpioPin.Write(PinValue.Low);
        }

        Thread.Sleep(TimeSpan.FromMinutes(1));
    }
}
```

This operates by sending a signal that controls the additional power of the filter run.

Connecting to the Cloud

Now that we have developed a reasonably functional pool controller, we can incorporate Internet connectivity to complete the IoT concept. Cloud connectivity is an essential component of most modern controllers. There are various methods to achieve this, ranging from large providers that offer multiple building blocks for solution composition to in-house solutions that are effective for a certain number of devices deployed within a specific geography. Each method has its own advantages and disadvantages. There is generally no universal solution or consensus on a standard architecture or approach.

Having said all that, for out pool controller project, and for the sake of the example we'll leverage the *nanoFramework.Azure.Devices* library to connect securely to Azure IoT Hub, enabling both robust telemetry reporting and dynamic remote configuration.

The Azure Devices SDK for nanoFramework handles device authentication, secure MQTT communication, and cloud message formatting. Initial configuration (such as device connection string or X.509 certificate) is stored in the device's configuration class.

This section will examine the specifics of various interactions with the cloud. Detailed instructions for setting up and configuring the client, along with other relevant information, are provided in Chapter 7.

Presuming we have a requirement to send the daily telemetry, we can create a `DailySummary` class that will become the payload.

```
public class DailySummary
{
    public DateTime Timestamp { get; set; }
    public float PhMin { get; set; }
    public float PhMax { get; set; }
    public float ChlorineMin { get; set; }
    public float ChlorineMax { get; set; }
    public float TurbidityMin { get; set; }
    public float TurbidityMax { get; set; }}
```

To send a message to the IoT Hub, it's a matter of serializing it in a JSON payload and sending it, like this:

```
AzureClient.SendMessage(JsonConvert.SerializeObject(summary));
```

We'll leverage on the concept of digital twin and will update properties of the device in the cloud according to what is sent to the pump controller.

To adhere to the Don't Repeat Yourself (DRY) principle, it is recommended to incorporate a call to the new method ReportToCloud() within the SetCurrent() method in the DosagePump class. This approach ensures streamlined and efficient code management.

```
private void ReportToCloud()
{
    if (_propertyName is not null)
    {
        TwinCollection propertyToUpdate = new()
        {
            { _propertyName, _current }
        };

        AzureClient.UpdateReportedProperties(propertyToUpdate);
    }
}
```

The previous code depends on a global variable AzureClient and a new property in the DosagePump that holds the name of the property to use for reporting.

As an example of an alert situation and how that can be handled, let's imagine that we want to push an alert if the pH raises above 9.0. To accomplish this, let's add a new method CheckSafetyValue() to the PhController class, which is called right after the sensor reading is taken in ControlLoop().

```
private bool CheckSafetyValue()
{
    if(PhValue > SafetyPhMax)
    {
        // force the pump to stop
        _pump.Current = ElectricCurrent.FromMilliamperes(_pump.
        PumpMinCurrent.Milliamperes);

        // send error message to Azure
        Program.AzureClient.SendMessage($"{{\"safety_alert\":\"pH out of
        range {PhValue}\"}}");
```

```
        // flag abnormal condition
        return false;
    }

    return true;
}
```

With this new method, let's update the `ControlLoop()` in our `PhController`.

```
private void ControlLoop()
{
    while (_running)
    {
        // read the pH value from the sensor
        PhValue = _sensor.ReadPh();

        if(!CheckSafetyValue())
        {
           // safe pH value

           (...)
        }

        // store the last delta for derivative calculation
        _lastPhDelta = phDelta;

        // sleep untill the next cycle
        Thread.Sleep(TimeSpan.FromMinutes(1));
    }
}
```

We'll execute the usual adjustment of the pump value only if the pH is within a safe value; otherwise, the `CheckSafetyValue()` method will take care of sending an alert and stop the pump.

To literally close the loop and illustrate the cloud to device (C2D) communication, let's consider that our pool controller, among other convenient features, has the possibility to be configured remotely. nanoFramework Azure SDK has support for an IoT Hub feature that is perfect for this purpose: direct method invocation. These are added to the Azure client as method callbacks, and we can add as many as we need. Here's how that is set up:

```
AzureClient.AddMethodCallback(UpdateConfiguration);
```

And here's the implementation of the callback handler.

```
private static string UpdateConfiguration(int rid, string payload)
{
    try
    {
        BaseConfiguration newConfig = (BaseConfiguration)JsonConvert.
        DeserializeObject(payload, typeof(BaseConfiguration));

        if (newConfig == null)
        {
            return $"{{\"result\": \"Failed to parse new
            configuration\"}}";
        }
        else
        {
            GeneralConfiguration.Update(newConfig);
        }

        return "{{\"result\": \"OK\"}}";
    }
    catch (Exception ex)
    {
        Log("Error parsing a configuration update: " + ex.Message);

        return $"{{\"result\": \"{ex.Message}\"}}";
    }
}
```

This section illustrated how to bring cloud connectivity into the pool controller demo project, not to exhaustively describe all the possibilities. There are other features in Azure IoT Hub that can be leveraged to add value to a product. We'll cover all those more in depth in Chapter 7. If and when you choose to add these features to a project you're working on, be careful to choose the ones that bring added value, truly enhancing the product features and making it a better solution. Stay away from bringing cloud connectivity if that's not necessary, and don't do it just because it's fancy.

Local storage and Persistence

In embedded systems, the ability to store and retrieve data locally is fundamental—sometimes even mission-critical. Whether saving configuration settings, holding temporary sensor readings, logging intermediate computations, or persisting larger datasets that don't fit in system RAM, reliable local storage allows devices to operate autonomously and recover gracefully from power failures or system resets.

Real-world embedded applications make heavy use of local storage:

- In industrial automation, programmable logic controllers (PLCs) routinely save their configuration, last process state, and error logs in nonvolatile memory, so machinery can resume normal operation after an outage with minimal intervention.
- Medical devices, such as infusion pumps or diagnostic equipment, store calibration data and critical patient logs locally, ensuring they can continue to function safely even when connectivity is unavailable.
- Consumer products, like smart thermostats, use persistent storage to remember user preferences and scheduling, providing a seamless experience even after a firmware update or unexpected restart.
- Data loggers—found everywhere from weather stations to fleet management systems—buffer large volumes of sensor data in flash memory, uploading batches when network connectivity is restored.

The needs for storage can be broadly classified:

- Short-lived storage: Temporary computation buffers, rolling logs, or state snapshots—valuable for brief periods or until data is transmitted.
- Long-term storage: Calibration parameters, cryptographic keys, device identity, or usage statistics, often written rarely but read frequently.
- Recovery data: System status or task queues saved at intervals, enabling the system to pick up where it left off after a crash or reset.

Choosing the right storage medium is critical in embedded design.

- *EEPROM* is popular for small amounts of configuration data due to its simplicity, but its endurance (limited number of writes) and speed may be a constraint for high-frequency updates.
- *SPI Flash* is ubiquitous in applications needing megabytes of storage, like firmware images, event logs, or over-the-air updates, but it comes with considerations around block erases and wear leveling.
- *FRAM* is gaining traction in mission-critical applications (e.g., automotive black boxes, energy meters) thanks to its high endurance and fast access—ideal for logging events or system status without the write fatigue of flash or EEPROM.
- *SD Cards and eMMC* are available as removable (SD, microSD) or soldered (eMMC) NAND flash modules. They have high capacity (up to gigabytes), have low cost per bit, and use industry-standard interfaces. They usually have a large physical footprint, require a file system and power-loss data integrity must be handled;.

Other factors—power consumption, write speeds, cost, and the complexity of managing data integrity—also influence the storage strategy.

Table 6-1 sumarizes all this.

Table 6-1. *Comparison of Local Storage Technologies*

Memory Type	Endurance	Speed	Use Cases
EEPROM	100K cycles	Slow	Config, logs, IDs
(Q)SPI Flash	10K-100K	Fast/very fast	Large logs, random files, OTA/IFU
FRAM	10^12+	SRAM-like	Critical logs, frequent save
MRAM	Unlimited	SRAM-like	Process state, configs
SRAM (battery-backed)	Unlimited	Very fast	Fast process state
SD/eMMC	Varies	Fast	Big data, files
NOR Flash	100K	Moderate	Firmware XIP, boot
NVRAM	Varies	Fast	Network, PLCs

Working with Local Storage in nanoFramework

PALTHREE is well-equipped when it comes to local storage. In addition to a pair of high-capacity SPI flash chips that easily cover the needs of most embedded applications, the board also boasts an SD card slot for removable storage and a USB-A port for plugging in USB thumb drives. This versatility means you can tailor your storage strategy to your application's requirements—whether you need high-speed access, removable media, or robust long-term persistence.

As with most things in .NET nanoFramework, you benefit from a robust abstraction layer that makes local storage straightforward and consistent to use, regardless of the underlying hardware.

Under the hood, .NET nanoFramework uses the reliable *littlefs* filesystem for serial flash devices, while *FatFS* powers access to SD cards and USB mass storage devices. This means you don't have to worry about the quirks of each storage medium; nanoFramework takes care of those details, presenting you with a unified and familiar API.

As a developer, this translates into simplicity and flexibility: you interact with all storage types using the standard `System.IO.FileSystem` API, just as you would on a desktop .NET application. Need to save a configuration file to flash or write a data log to an SD card? The process is the same—just specify the correct drive letter for your target medium, and you're good to go.

All you need to know is which drive corresponds to each storage medium in your system. From there, file and directory operations work exactly as expected, freeing you to focus on your application logic.

Back to our pool controller, let's take advantage of all this to further improve it.

Something convenient would be to have the general configuration and the various controllers' parameters stored so they can be loaded at boot time and configure the system accordingly. A `StorageManager` class is in order for this. Each configuration class has implemented a method to read the serialized content from a file and deserializes it into the respective config class. There is a symmetric method that serializes the configuration and stores it. For performance we'll be using the nanoFramework `Runtime.BinaryFormatter` class, which uses a very compact binary format. We could have used a Json serializer instead. That could be preferable if, for example, the settings should be editable by a human.

Here's the method that saves the GeneralConfiguration:

```
public static void SaveGeneralConfiguration(BaseConfiguration config)
{
    byte[] encodedConfig = BinaryFormatter.Serialize(config);
    File.WriteAllBytes(GeneralConfigFile, encodedConfig);
}
```

The following is the symmetric one that loads it. Note the Try prefix to give the hit that it may not be successful.

```
public static BaseConfiguration TryLoadGeneralConfiguration()
{
    if (!File.Exists(GeneralConfigFile))
    {
        return null;
    }

    byte[] encodedConfig = File.ReadAllBytes(GeneralConfigFile);

    return BinaryFormatter.Deserialize(encodedConfig) as BaseConfiguration;
}
```

At boot time we call LoadConfigurations().

```
private static void LoadConfigurations()
{

    BaseConfiguration baseConfiguration = StorageManager.
    TryLoadGeneralConfiguration();

    if (baseConfiguration == null)
    {
        Log("No general configuration found, using defaults.");

        // If no configuration exists, create a new one with default values
        baseConfiguration = new BaseConfiguration();

        // Update the general configuration with default values
        GeneralConfiguration.Update(baseConfiguration);
```

```
        // Save the default configuration to storage
        StorageManager.SaveGeneralConfiguration(GeneralConfiguration.
        ToBaseConfiguration());
    }
    else
    {
        Log("General configuration loaded.");
        GeneralConfiguration.Update(baseConfiguration);
    }

    // Load pH controller configuration
    PhControllerConfig phControllerConfig = StorageManager.
    TryLoadPhControllerConfig();
    if (phControllerConfig == null)
    {
        Log("No pH controller configuration found, using defaults.");
        phControllerConfig = new PhControllerConfig();
    }
    else
    {
        Log("pH controller configuration loaded.");
    }

    // remaining code removed for conviniece
}
```

Whenever there is an update in the parameters pushed from the cloud or locally, we just update the stored copy of the configuration. Like this:

```
StorageManager.SaveTurbidityControllerConfig(turbidityControllerConfig);
```

To follow up on the logging topic discussed earlier in this chapter, local storage—such as an SD card—has been used to store event logs. This section describes expanding storage options to other available media, which may be more suitable for certain tasks. Although configurations could also be saved to an SD card, this approach is less robust due to the possibility of the card being removed or file system issues requiring reformatting. By utilizing a storage medium that is permanently integrated into the device, such as a serial flash chip soldered to the PCB, there is a higher level of reliability for storing configurations and ensuring they are accessible during system startup.

User Interface

The user interface (UI) is one of the most critical aspects of any embedded system. Even the most technically advanced product, packed with innovative features and clever solutions, can fail if users find it difficult or confusing to operate. No matter how impressive the underlying technology or how many problems the product solves, if the UI is lacking, users simply won't be able to take full advantage of what's on offer—or might not use the product at all. Think of the UI as the gateway between your technology and its intended audience: if this gateway is blocked or unclear, users will quickly become frustrated and may abandon the product altogether.

Ease of Use Is Not Optional

Ease of use is not a luxury—it's a necessity. Imagine a digital thermostat in a hotel room that guests struggle to set, or a piece of industrial equipment with menus so complex that operators resort to trial and error. In both cases, the technology's potential is wasted. A good UI should allow users to achieve their goals quickly and confidently, often without needing a manual.

For example, consider our pool controller project with a simple LCD and four buttons. If you need a lengthy combination of button presses just to start or stop the pump, usability suffers. But if there are clear labels and direct actions—one button to start, one to stop, and two for navigation—most users will be able to operate it without help.

Know Your Users

Understanding your users is the foundation of great UI design. Who are they? Are they experienced technicians, casual users, or perhaps older adults who less familiar with technology? The interface should be tailored to their expectations and capabilities.

Example:

A home energy monitor for families should present data in simple terms—like "today's cost in euros" and "usage compared to yesterday." By contrast, an installer interface might need to expose advanced configuration menus, but those can be tucked away behind a password or a special key combination to avoid overwhelming the average user.

Context Matters

Where and how your device will be used directly impacts UI choices. Will it be outside, possibly exposed to rain and sunlight? Is the operator likely to be wearing gloves or working in low light?

Examples:

> **Outdoor Equipment:** Use large, mechanical buttons with tactile feedback rather than a small touch screen, which becomes difficult to use with gloves or when wet.
>
> **Industrial Display:** Place a backlight on the screen and opt for high-contrast, large-font displays for visibility in both bright and dim environments.
>
> **Medical Devices:** Design the interface for quick operation—consider color-blind accessibility, and avoid relying solely on color to communicate status.

Don't overlook small details. If your device uses a touch screen, make sure the buttons are big enough for gloved hands and are spaced to prevent accidental presses.

Usability and Testing

No matter how carefully you plan, assumptions can be wrong. That's why usability testing is essential. Bring in real users—ideally those who match your target audience—and observe how they interact with the prototype. You'll quickly spot patterns: confusion over a button's purpose, difficulty navigating menus, or trouble reading the screen.

For example, during testing of an agricultural sensor, you might find that farmers can't read the display in direct sunlight or struggle to press small buttons while wearing work gloves. These insights allow you to make practical adjustments before the product launches.

If your budget allows, bring in a UI/UX expert—their experience can streamline the design process and help you avoid common pitfalls. Even if resources are tight, push for expert involvement whenever possible, as their insight can be invaluable.

Universal Design: Aim for the Least Common Denominator

By focusing on accessibility and simplicity, you widen your potential user base. A well-designed UI for the "least common denominator" doesn't mean dumbing down the product—it means removing unnecessary complexity and ensuring everyone can succeed, regardless of their background or abilities.

For example, an emergency stop button should always be large, red, and clearly labeled so that anyone, regardless of training, can find and activate it in a crisis. Expert users will appreciate an efficient workflow, but the clear layout ensures even a first-time operator won't be lost.

Back to Code

Back to our pool controller project and the platform we're using on the PALTHREE board; you'll notice that the model we're using includes a text LCD. It has a modest size with 2 lines, 16 characters, single color. It has backlight and provides high contrast. Considering that the controller doesn't require that much user interaction and feedback, the default 2x16 LCD should suffice to cover the product needs.

In addition to the LCD, the board offers plenty of GPIOs, giving us flexibility in user input design and on-board relay (optically isolated) to be used for turning on relays for alarms, local strobe light, or other needs. For this project, we'll stick with a time-tested approach for embedded systems: a keypad with four keys—Up, Down, Select/Enter, and Back, but a full 4x4 matrix keypad is supported also. This minimal set covers typical menu navigation and user actions, ensuring the interface remains straightforward and accessible, even for less experienced users. This hardware configuration strikes a balance between usability, robustness, and simplicity, perfectly matching the needs of our application.

Next, let's see how to bring this interface to life in code, handling display output and keypad input for an effective and user-friendly experience.

To be accessible throughout the application namespace, let's create a static class LcdManager.

```
public static void Init()
{
    if (_lcd != null)
    {
        // LCD already initialized
        return;
    }

    var i2cSettings = new I2cConnectionSettings(1, 0x27);
    var i2cDevice = I2cDevice.Create(i2cSettings);
    _lcd = new Lcd1602(i2cDevice);

    _lcd.Clear();
    ShowBootMessage();

    _running = true;
    _updateThread = new Thread(IdleUpdateLcd);
    _updateThread.Start();
}
```

This method initializes the LCD display, calls a method to show a boot message, and starts a background thread to update the LCD when idle. Please note that we're using another .NET nanoFramework IoT binding library for the character LCD.

Let's take a look at the IdleUpdateLcd method that runs on its own thread:

```
private static void IdleUpdateLcd()
{
    while (_running)
    {
        if (!_paused)
        {
            _lcd.Clear();

            _lcd.SetCursorPosition(0, 0);
            _lcd.Write($"pH:{Program.PhController0.PhValue:F1} Cl:{Program.
            ChlorineController0.ChlorineValue:F1}");
```

```
            _lcd.SetCursorPosition(0, 1);
            _lcd.Write($"Turb:{Program.TurbidityController0.
            TurbidityValue:F1}");
        }

        Thread.Sleep(1_000);
    }
}
```

This code segment is rather obvious; it updates the LCD display with the latest reading from pH, chlorine, and turbidity values. It clears the LCD, sets cursor positions, writes the formatted sensor readings into the two available lines, and then pauses for one second before repeating.

Now let's create a `KeypadController`, whose `Init()` method looks like this:

```
public static void Init(GpioController gpioController)
{
    _gpio = gpioController;

    _back = _gpio.OpenPin(BackPin, PinMode.InputPullUp);
    _up = _gpio.OpenPin(UpPin, PinMode.InputPullUp);
    _down = _gpio.OpenPin(DownPin, PinMode.InputPullUp);
    _select = _gpio.OpenPin(SelectPin, PinMode.InputPullUp);

    _back.DebounceTimeout = DebounceTime;
    _up.DebounceTimeout = DebounceTime;
    _down.DebounceTimeout = DebounceTime;
    _select.DebounceTimeout = DebounceTime;

    _back.ValueChanged += BackHandler;
    _up.ValueChanged += UpHandler;
    _down.ValueChanged += DownHandler;
    _select.ValueChanged += SelectHandler;
}
```

Each of those handlers contains a quick update of the respective properties:

```
private static void UpHandler(object sender, PinValueChangedEventArgs e)
{
    _upPressed = e.ChangeType == PinEventTypes.Falling;
    UpChanged.Set();
}
```

The state of each key is exposed through a *Name*`Pressed` property, and to allow other code to subscribe to async changes in the key state, it exposes also a `ManualResetEvent`.

The remaining classes are those necessary for managing menu display and related functionalities, such as presenting menu items, responding to key presses, and handling value editing. Because of the complexity and length of this code, its detailed implementation falls outside the scope of this chapter. The solution available in the repository demonstrates one possible approach to addressing these requirements. As with many programming challenges, there is no single universal method, so this example should be regarded as a reference.

Final Considerations

As we're reaching the end of this chapter and having went through the project of our pool controller, it's worth pausing to reflect on some essential software engineering practices that can make or break the success of any embedded IoT device—especially when using a robust and modern framework like .NET nanoFramework. Embedded development is not just about getting the device to work; it's about ensuring that it will continue to work reliably, safely, and maintainable over the years and across many units in the field.

Embrace Separation of Concerns and Threading

One of the first habits to adopt is to split system logic into clearly defined, well-separated tasks—ideally with each class or module having a single responsibility. In C#, this means leveraging object-oriented principles to create small, focused classes, and using threads to keep critical tasks (like sensor sampling, cloud communication, or UI updates) running independently. This approach avoids tightly coupled code, makes maintenance easier, and reduces the risk that a fault in one part of the system will cascade into others. Proper use of threading and synchronization primitives (such as `Monitor` or `ManualResetEvent`) is essential to maintain system responsiveness and to avoid deadlocks or race conditions—particularly in resource-constrained devices where blocking the main execution loop is a common pitfall.

Design for Robustness from the Ground Up

Unlike desktop or cloud software, embedded systems operate in unpredictable environments and are often left unattended for long periods. Coding for robustness means building in hardware watchdogs and periodic self-checks to ensure that the device can recover automatically from faults. Always ensure fail-safe default states: if a sensor fails or a communication link drops, the system should fall back to a safe condition, log the incident, and, where appropriate, attempt recovery or notify a human operator. Defensive programming—anticipating what can go wrong and explicitly handling those cases—can be the difference between a product that quietly keeps working and one that causes headaches (or worse, safety incidents) in the field.

Unit Tests from the Start

Write unit tests as you add new features, not as an afterthought. With nanoFramework support for unit testing, there is no excuse not to validate key modules early and often. Testing helps catch regressions and edge cases before they become hard-to-diagnose bugs in production. We'll be covering the test framework in Chapter 8. Consider also developing integration tests that run on real hardware, simulating typical user scenarios and interactions between subsystems.

Make Safety Non-negotiable

Electrical safety must be a primary consideration from the very first design stage. This applies not only to hardware layout (clearances, fusing, isolation) but also to software: never assume that external wiring is correct or that actuators and sensors will always behave as expected. Build in checks for fault conditions, and ensure that your software cannot cause dangerous situations (such as over-dosing chemicals, or failing to shut down relays when required). Consider adding explicit "safe mode" or "lockout" logic, particularly when interfacing with high voltages, motors, hazardous chemicals, and such.

Plan for Maintenance and Calibration

Every real-world device will eventually need periodic maintenance, recalibration, or replacement of parts. This is true for both sensors (which drift over time) and actuators (which wear out). Code with this in mind: provide routines for calibration, allow easy triggering of maintenance cycles (manually or remotely), and keep logs of usage hours, calibration events, and service interventions. Well-maintained devices are safer, last longer, and deliver better data.

Leverage Telemetry and Historical Data

Go beyond basic logging: design your system to gather operational telemetry, record historic data, and analyze usage patterns. This data can be invaluable for preventative maintenance, troubleshooting, or improving future versions of the product. In cloud-connected scenarios, retrieving all this data is a no-brainer. Use telemetry to drive product enhancements and support teams with real-world feedback.

Document Everything

Start thinking about documentation right from the very first design stage—not as an afterthought but as a core, strategic part of the project. Allocate time and budget specifically to ensure documentation is complete, accurate, and up-to-date. This is one of the smartest investments you can make in any embedded system project, but it is all too often underrated or neglected. Where possible, explicitly assign a dedicated team member or even a small group to own the documentation process. Make sure documentation evolves alongside the product and does not get left behind as schedules slip or priorities change.

Documentation should cover not just the main application code but also configuration files, calibration procedures, hardware revisions, maintenance logs, firmware releases, and field interventions. Good diagrams, bills of materials, and field notes are as valuable as code examples. Having all of this well recorded is essential for future maintenance, onboarding new developers, supporting end users, and even for certification or audits.

Never underestimate the cost of poor documentation: it can be the reason a team wastes weeks trying to understand old decisions, or why a customer loses confidence in a product. By contrast, clear, living documentation speeds up troubleshooting, simplifies updates and adaptations, and increases the long-term value of your product.

Prioritize Simplicity and Readability

In embedded systems, clarity beats cleverness. Resist the urge to over-optimize or implement needlessly complex abstractions, especially in resource-limited environments. Code that is simple to understand is easier to debug, maintain, and audit for safety or compliance. Choose clear naming, consistent formatting, and leave comments where context or intent may not be obvious.

Build for Updates and Long-Term Support

Design the system to support firmware updates in the field, whether via SD card, USB, or secure in-field-updates (IFU) methods. Plan for how you will issue updates, recover from failed upgrades, and manage device versions. In the fast-evolving world of IoT, the ability to update deployed devices is critical for security, compliance, and product evolution.

Respect Power and Environmental Constraints

Always keep in mind the power budget, thermal profile, and environmental requirements of your hardware. Use low-power sleep modes where possible, manage peripherals to avoid unnecessary energy drain, and monitor for environmental extremes (such as overheating or moisture ingress) that could affect device longevity. Where relevant, add software monitoring and self-protection logic.

Practice Secure-by-Design Principles

IoT devices are often exposed to networks and potentially hostile environments. Make security a foundational part of the architecture: store secrets securely, authenticate all communications, validate incoming data, and regularly audit the codebase for vulnerabilities. Leverage .NET nanoFramework available cryptographic libraries and secure communication APIs.

Good embedded systems are not accidental—they are engineered deliberately with a focus on reliability, safety, and maintainability. By making these practices part of your everyday workflow, you will not only avoid the most common pitfalls but also create devices that you and your users can truly rely on.

Summary

This chapter brought together essential concepts and practical steps for developing reliable IoT devices, using an automated pool controller as a real-world case study. The chapter begins with hardware selection, showing how to choose industrial-grade components like the PALTHREE while considering durability, expandability, and safety requirements.

It then explains how to interface with 4–20 mA industrial sensors at both the hardware and software levels, enabling accurate measurement of water quality parameters such as pH, chlorine, turbidity, and temperature. Special emphasis was given to robust local processing, which allows the system to operate safely and make autonomous decisions even when disconnected from the cloud.

The logic and best practices for actuating chemical dosing pumps were also covered, including flow-proportional dosing calculations, configuration management, calibration routines, and traceability. The chapter highlighted the importance of alarms, fault tolerance, and regulatory compliance throughout the design.

Clear code examples and configuration strategies demonstrate how .NET nanoFramework can be used to build, deploy, and manage industrial IoT devices.

With these foundations, you should be now better equipped to design safe, scalable, and maintainable systems ready for real-world use.

Additional Resources

You can learn more at the following locations:

nanoFramework System.IO.FileSystem: `https://github.com/nanoframework/System.IO.FileSystem`

nanoFramework Logging Library: `https://github.com/nanoframework/nanoFramework.Logging`

nanoFramework DAC63004 Binding: `https://github.com/nanoframework/nanoFramework.Device.Dac63004`

UnitsNet library: `https://github.com/angularsen/UnitsNet`

PALTHREE product page: `https://www.orgpal.com/palthree-iot-azure`

IoT bindings repo: `https://github.com/nanoframework/nanoFramework.IoT.Device`

Washington State University Chemigation Worksheet (FS227E): `http://irrigation.wsu.edu/Content/Fact-Sheets/FS227E.pdf`

CHAPTER 7

Nano Devices, Big-Time Connectivity

In today's world, connectivity is at the heart of nearly every embedded system. Whether it's a sensor reporting temperature data from a remote field, a smart home device turning on the lights before you arrive, or an industrial controller optimizing production lines in real time, the ability to connect and communicate over networks—or directly with the cloud—unlocks a universe of new capabilities.

Modern embedded systems are no longer isolated black boxes. Instead, they're becoming active participants in larger ecosystems, sharing data, responding to remote commands, and integrating seamlessly with other devices and services. This shift is driven by the exponential growth of the Internet of Things (IoT) but also by evolving user expectations: people now want devices that are not only smart but also connected, adaptive, and secure.

From IoT sensors scattered across a smart city to factory-floor controllers in Industry 4.0 to connected appliances at home and wearables on your wrist—networked embedded devices are everywhere. Achieving reliable, efficient, and secure connectivity is no longer a bonus feature; it's a fundamental requirement.

In this chapter, we'll explore how .NET nanoFramework brings rich networking capabilities to tiny devices, demystifying technologies and showing how you can quickly move from "hello world" to robust, networked solutions—whether that means connecting to the cloud, linking devices through LoRa or TI EasyLink, communicating over BLE, or using cellular standards like LTE and NB-IoT.

J. Simões, *Embedded Systems with .NET nanoFramework*, https://doi.org/10.1007/979-8-8688-2096-0_7

Network Connectivity Basics

Before diving into protocols and coding, it's crucial to understand the foundational elements of connecting embedded devices to networks. Getting the basics right lays the groundwork for reliable and scalable solutions.

IP Networking: IPv4 and IPv6

The backbone of most modern digital communication is the good old Internet Protocol (IP). IPv4 uses 32-bit addresses (e.g., 192.168.1.10) and remains the most widely used, especially in local networks. However, with billions of devices coming online, IPv6 (128-bit addresses) is increasingly important for its vast address space and built-in security features.

IPv4 is simple and familiar, but limited to ~4.3 billion unique addresses. IPv6 solves this with an astronomical number of possible addresses, as well as enhancements such as simplified packet headers, better multicast support, and automatic address configuration (SLAAC).

nanoFramework supports both IPv4 and IPv6 versions, where platform hardware and the network stack allow. Currently, IPv6 is supported only on ESP32-based devices, including the ESP32, ESP32-S2, ESP32-C3, and ESP32-S3 series. This enables seamless device integration with existing networks and future-proofs solutions.

Connectivity Protocols

It supports these protocols:

- **Ethernet:** The most robust and deterministic wired connection. This is preferred for stationary and industrial environments due to low latency, high reliability, and electrical noise immunity.
- **Wi-Fi:** This brings wireless freedom to embedded devices. nanoFramework provides APIs to scan, connect, and even set up devices as access points. Common in consumer and office settings, Wi-Fi offers decent bandwidth but can be power-hungry and is prone to interference.

- **Bluetooth Low Energy (BLE):** Designed for ultra-low power and short-range connectivity, BLE is great for wearables, medical devices, and proximity-based applications. BLE uses the Generic Attribute Profile (GATT) for structured data exchange.
- **LoRa:** Meaning Long Range, this low-power, wide-area wireless technology is ideal for remote sensors and devices that need to communicate over long distances—sometimes several kilometers. LoRa itself defines only the physical and data link layers, allowing for proprietary or point-to-point networking. It's typically used for simple, infrequent, or event-based messaging due to its limited bandwidth and duty cycle restrictions.
- **LoRaWAN:** LoRa Wide Area Network (LoRaWAN) builds on LoRa by adding an open networking protocol and architecture for secure, large-scale, multidevice networks. LoRaWAN introduces gateways that relay messages between end devices and a central network server, enabling star-topology networks and Internet/cloud integration. It handles device authentication, message encryption, adaptive data rates, and seamless device roaming. While both use LoRa radios, LoRaWAN enables managed, scalable deployments, whereas "plain" LoRa is for simpler or custom topologies.
- **EasyLink (TI):** Texas Instruments proprietary sub-GHz wireless protocol, designed for simple, low-power, point-to-point or star networks. This is useful in environments where standards like LoRa or Zigbee aren't feasible and where TI hardware is available.
- **OpenThread:** This is an open-source implementation of the Thread mesh networking protocol, built on IEEE 802.15.4. Thread provides secure, scalable, self-healing mesh networks for IoT applications. It is based in IPv6, allowing devices to directly participate in the broader Internet and supporting robust device-to-device and device-to-cloud connectivity.

Key Design Considerations

These are key design considerations:

- **Bandwidth:** Some applications—such as high-frequency data acquisition or machine vision—require high bandwidth, but most embedded and IoT scenarios (telemetry, sensor data) are low bandwidth. Choosing the right protocol (for example, Wi-Fi for high-speed data such as remote machine diagnostics or process monitoring, LoRa for energy-efficient long-range sensor telemetry in distributed industrial installations) is vital.
- **Latency:** Time-critical applications (e.g., motor control, real-time alerts) need low-latency connections. Wired Ethernet and Thread typically offer lower latency than long-range wireless protocols.
- **Power Consumption:** Battery-powered devices must minimize communication overhead. BLE and LoRa are optimized for ultra-low power use, while Wi-Fi and Ethernet can drain batteries quickly.
- **Range:** Consider the maximum distance between nodes or to the access point. LoRa excels at long range, BLE is strictly short-range, and Wi-Fi and Ethernet vary based on the environment and infrastructure.
- **Security:** All networked devices are exposed to threats. Always consider encrypted channels (TLS for IP traffic), device authentication, and periodic security updates. Some protocols (Thread, BLE) have built-in security mechanisms, but application-layer security is often needed.

By understanding these basics, developers can make informed choices and architect robust, efficient, and future-ready networked embedded systems.

Network Sockets in .NET nanoFramework

Lets delve into network sockets and learn how to use them in nanoFramework projects. If you're already familiar with the network API of .NET you'll recognize most, if not all of this.

A Brief on Sockets and TCP/UDP

At the heart of most network communications are sockets—a low-level abstraction allowing your device to send and receive data over the network. Sockets provide a programming interface for two main protocols:

- **TCP (Transmission Control Protocol):** Reliable, connection-oriented, and stream-based. Ideal for scenarios where data integrity and order matter (e.g., device telemetry, configuration, remote commands).
- **UDP (User Datagram Protocol):** Unreliable, connectionless, and message based, no acknowledge, no resend without user code. Great for low-latency applications, sensor bursts, or streaming where occasional data loss is acceptable (e.g., real-time sensor readings, device discovery).

.NET nanoFramework uses the same .NET APIs for working with both TCP and UDP sockets, making it straightforward to port or reuse code from desktop or other .NET platforms.

Creating and Using Sockets

The `System.Net.Sockets` namespace provides TCP and UDP support via the `TcpClient` and `UdpClient` classes, plus direct `Socket` APIs if you need to go deep in the network layers for some advanced usage.

This is the simplest possible TCP client example:

```
using System.Net.Sockets;
using System.Text;

using var client = new TcpClient();
client.Connect("192.168.1.20", 12345);

var stream = client.GetStream();
byte[] data = Encoding.UTF8.GetBytes("Hello, world!");
stream.Write(data, 0, data.Length);
```

```
// Receive response
var buffer = new byte[128];
int received = stream.Read(buffer, 0, buffer.Length);
string response = new string(Encoding.UTF8.GetChars(buffer, 0, received));

stream.Close();
```

Here is a snippet of a simple UDP send/receive example:

```
using System.Net;
using System.Net.Sockets;

using var udp = new UdpClient();
var serverEndpoint = new IPEndPoint(IPAddress.
Parse("192.168.1.100"), 8888);
byte[] message = Encoding.UTF8.GetBytes("Sensor data");
udp.Send(message, message.Length, serverEndpoint);

// To receive
var localEndpoint = new IPEndPoint(IPAddress.Any, 8888);
byte[] received = udp.Receive(ref localEndpoint);
```

The server is sitting on a device with the IP 192.168.1.100, which is accepting connections from clients connecting from *any* address.

Handling Errors and Reconnections

Network code in embedded environments must be resilient. Common issues include dropped Wi-Fi connections, cable disconnects, IP address changes, or server timeouts. Make sure to always do the following:

- Check return values and catch exceptions (e.g., `SocketException`, `TimeoutException`).
- Implement reconnection logic with exponential backoff where appropriate.
- Monitor the network interface status and gracefully close and reopen sockets as needed.

Connecting Devices with NetworkHelper

The `nanoFramework.Networking.NetworkHelper` class (part of the `System.Net` library) makes connecting your device to Ethernet or Wi-Fi networks much easier. The latter uses the Wi-Fi-specific APIs available in the `Wi-FiNetworkHelper` class (part of the `System.Device.Wi-Fi` library). These abstracts away low-level network stack details and manages interface configuration, such as DHCP, static IP, and Wi-Fi credentials.

You can code a connection to Wi-Fi as follows:

```
using nanoFramework.Networking;

var success = NetworkHelper.ConnectWi-Fi("MySSID", "password",
requiresDateTime: true);

if (!success)
{
    Debug.WriteLine($"Error: {NetworkHelper.Status}");
    // Optionally, inspect NetworkHelper.HelperException for more detail
}
```

The `requiresDateTime` parameter is part of the helper library. It tells the helper that the application requires a valid date and time to function, typically because of certificate validation. Requesting this causes the helper to wait for a SNTP to receive updated date and time information from the Internet, signaling that the system has network connection *and* a valid date and time.

There are several ways to configure Wi-Fi credentials when connecting your device to a network. You can provide them directly in code, like in the previous snippet.

Another option is to program them securely using `nanoff` CLI. This is particularly useful in production environments, for example when programming an application to perform a QA self-test during manufacturing. With `nanoff`, you can provision Wi-Fi credentials in the device's storage using the following CLI options:

```
nanoff --config --Wi-Fi-ssid "MySSID" --Wi-Fi-password "MyPassword"
--target <DEVICE-TYPE> --port <COM-PORT>
```

This approach keeps credentials out of your application code and enables batch programming or test automation workflows. The Wi-Fi profile is securely stored internally on the device, is not retrievable by nanoFramework APIs, is added to the device's credentials collection, and remains stored until explicitly deleted.

The last alternative is to set them through the Visual Studio Device Explorer using the Network Configuration editor. You can see how it looks in Figure 7-1 and Figure 7-2.

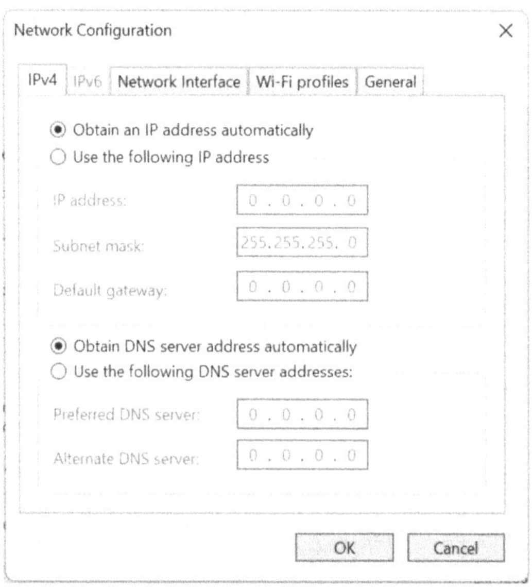

***Figure 7-1.** IP configuration in Network Configuration dialog*

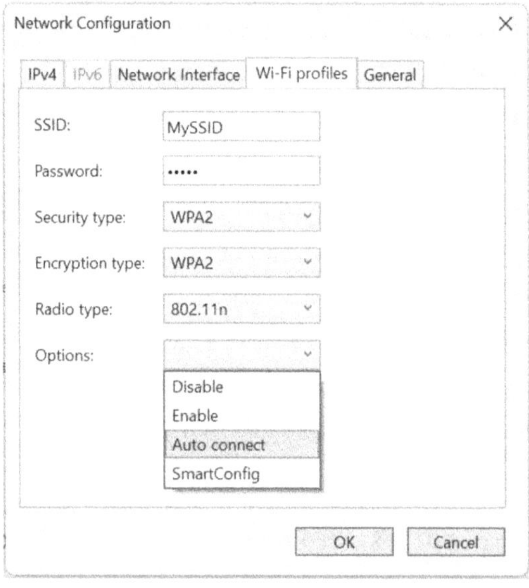

***Figure 7-2.** Wi-Fi configuration in Network Configuration dialog*

Please note in the options for the Wi-Fi profile being edited. If *Auto connect* is selected, this profile will be active at all times, and the nano device will connect to this network whenever it's in reach. As you've probably figured out by now, using *Disable* and *Enable*—which can be accessed programmatically—allows you to manage which networks the device is allowed to connect.

If you've previously stored Wi-Fi credentials on your device (using *nanoff* or the Visual Studio Device Explorer as we've just seen), you can reconnect to the network without hardcoding SSID or password in your application. `NetworkHelper` will use the saved Wi-Fi profile without the need to provide them in your code. This is especially useful in deployed or production scenarios where credentials management is separated from application code.

```
using nanoFramework.Networking;

var success = NetworkHelper.ConnectWi-Fi(requiresDateTime: true);
if (!success)
{
    Debug.WriteLine($"Reconnect error: {NetworkHelper.Status}");
}
```

This approach lets you keep your application generic and reusable.

The helper works for both Wi-Fi and Ethernet connections, handling network time setup, DHCP or static IPs, and interface initialization.

For Ethernet this works exactly the same way: you make use of `NetworkHelper`. Here's how to connect using DHCP and automatically handle interface restarts:

```
using nanoFramework.Networking;

var success = NetworkHelper.ConnectEthernet(
    requiresDateTime: true,
    onConnected: () => Debug.WriteLine("Ethernet connected!"),
    onDisconnected: () => Debug.WriteLine("Ethernet disconnected,
    attempting reconnect..."));

if (!success)
{
    Debug.WriteLine($"Ethernet error: {NetworkHelper.Status}");
}
```

To use a static IP address instead of DHCP, simply pass a `NetworkInterfaceSettings` object:

```
using nanoFramework.Networking;
using System.Net;

var netSettings = new NetworkInterfaceSettings
{
    Address = IPAddress.Parse("192.168.1.99"),
    SubnetMask = IPAddress.Parse("255.255.255.0"),
    GatewayAddress = IPAddress.Parse("192.168.1.1"),
    DnsAddresses = new IPAddress[] { IPAddress.Parse("8.8.8.8") }
};

var success = NetworkHelper.ConnectEthernet(netSettings: netSettings,
requiresDateTime: false);

if (!success)
{
    Debug.WriteLine($"Ethernet (static) error: {NetworkHelper.Status}");
}
```

These helpers wrap the tedious workflow required to connect, reconnect, and configure network interfaces, ensuring robust connectivity for both dynamic (DHCP) and fixed (static IP) configurations in the most common application scenarios.

HTTP Client and Web Requests

Reliable HTTP communication is fundamental for connected devices—whether you're sending telemetry, pulling configuration, or integrating with cloud platforms. In .NET nanoFramework, `HttpClient` is the recommended class for these tasks, replacing the obsolete `WebRequest`. The design closely mirrors the modern .NET ecosystem while being resource-conscious for embedded devices.

HTTP is pervasive across IoT and industrial automation:

- Pushing telemetry data to a cloud API using HTTP POST
- Pulling live configuration or schedules from a management server with HTTP GET

- Periodic status checks and diagnostics with REST endpoints
- Secure device registration, firmware activation, or remote actuation

Patterns and Practical Samples

The `System.Net.Http` API offers synchronous and event-driven patterns. While calls are blocking by default, the lightweight event mechanism can be used to monitor progress or handle long operations without blocking main device logic.

Here's how one would send a POST request with a JSON payload:

```
using System.Net.Http;
using System.Text;

var httpClient = new HttpClient();

string jsonPayload = "{\"temperature\":24.5,\"machineId\":101}";

var content = new StringContent(jsonPayload, Encoding.UTF8,
"application/json");

HttpResponseMessage response = httpClient.Post("http://factory-cloud.com/
api/telemetry", content);

if(response.IsSuccessStatusCode)
{
    Debug.WriteLine("Data sent successfully.");
}
else
{
    Debug.WriteLine($"Error: {response.StatusCode}");
}

// Only dispose httpClient at the very end of its usage
response.Dispose();
```

Here is an HTTP GET and JSON parsing:

```
using System.Net.Http;
using nanoFramework.Json;

var httpClient = new HttpClient();

HttpResponseMessage response = httpClient.Get("http://factory-cloud.com/
api/config?device=101");

if(response.IsSuccessStatusCode)
{
    string payload = response.Content.ReadAsString();
    Debug.WriteLine($"Received: {payload}");
    DeviceConfig config = (DeviceConfig)JsonConvert.
    DeserializeObject(payload, typeof(DeviceConfig));
}

// Only dispose httpClient at the very end of its usage
response.Dispose();
```

Tip `HttpClient` is designed to be reused throughout your application's lifecycle. There is no need to create a new instance for each request (you really should not do this)—simply instantiate it once and use it for all subsequent HTTP calls. This approach is more efficient and helps avoid resource exhaustion on memory-constrained devices. Always dispose of your `HttpResponseMessage` instances after use to free resources. Otherwise, you may be start see exceptions about sockets becoming unavailable.

Working with Headers and Authentication

Custom headers are easy to set, allowing authentication (API keys, tokens, etc):

```
httpClient.DefaultRequestHeaders.Add("Authorization", "Bearer {token}");
```

You may add content-type such as `httpClient.DefaultRequestHeaders.Add("Content-Type", "application/json")` or custom tracking headers as required by your industrial backend, like `httpClient.DefaultRequestHeaders.Add("X-Device-Id", deviceId)`.

By default, `HttpClient` uses a 100-second timeout for requests. You can change this default by setting the `Timeout` property, like this:

```
httpClient.Timeout = TimeSpan.FromSeconds(10);
```

Implementing retries is recommended for transient errors, such as temporary network drops or overloaded servers.

.NET nanoFramework takes security very seriously; therefore, every network-capable platform includes support for SSL/TLS out of the box. Adjusting the previous sample code, it would look like this:

```
// Load a root CA cert in PEM or DER format (here baked into code as PEM)
string rootPem = @"
-----BEGIN CERTIFICATE-----
MIIDrzCCApegAwIBAgIQCDvgVpBCRrGhdWrJWZHHSjANBgkqhkiG...
-----END CERTIFICATE-----";
httpClient.HttpsAuthentCert = new X509Certificate(rootPem);

// Optionally, set TLS version if needed (defaults to Tls12)
httpClient.SslProtocols = System.Net.Security.SslProtocols.Tls13;
```

The nanoFramework implementation of `HttpClient` was coded as efficiently as possible. Still, constrained targets have tight RAM limits. When processing responses, avoid keeping large JSON or text documents in memory—prefer streaming or parsing partial responses whenever possible. Always close sockets when they are no longer needed, and dispose of responses as soon as you are done processing them.

Real-Time Communication with WebSockets and SignalR

Traditional HTTP-based communication is inherently request-response and often too slow or inefficient for scenarios where data must be delivered instantly as it changes. Mostly, this is because every time an HTTP request is made, it involves a fair amount of ceremony: resolving the server address, opening a TCP socket, possibly negotiating TLS security, and performing the initial HTTP negotiation—all before any useful data is actually transmitted. This introduces significant latency and overhead for each individual message, making HTTP less suited for scenarios where updates must flow continuously or interactively.

In industrial IoT and interactive applications, there's a strong need for real-time communication—a mechanism for the server to push updates to connected devices as soon as events occur and for devices to immediately send data or commands back. Real-time protocols are crucial in scenarios like live dashboards, remote control of equipment, safety monitoring, alarms, collaborative robotics, and user-facing interfaces.

WebSockets

WebSockets provide a low-latency, bidirectional, persistent connection between client and server over a single TCP port (usually 80 or 443). Based on the HTTP protocol and running over TCP, WebSockets maintain an open socket for the duration of the connection, which consumes resources on embedded systems. Keeping a socket open and maintaining the connection "alive" prevents the device from entering deep sleep or low-power modes that require all network connections to be closed. This setup enables both sides to send and receive messages at any time without the overhead of repeatedly opening HTTP requests. For embedded systems, WebSockets are often used for remote control, telemetry streaming, device-to-cloud messaging, or receiving configuration updates, but developers should consider the trade-offs between real-time communication needs and device power management. Even for "always on" devices, you should use persistent connections like WebSockets only if it makes sense for the application requirements.

A WebSocket connection begins as a standard HTTP request. During the initial handshake, the client sends a special Upgrade header in the HTTP request, asking the server to switch protocols from HTTP to WebSocket. If the server supports WebSockets, it responds with an agreement to upgrade, switching the communication channel from HTTP to the full-duplex WebSocket protocol. At this point, the HTTP connection is "upgraded" and transformed into a persistent, bidirectional socket. Both the client and server can then send and receive data frames asynchronously at any time, without waiting for a request or response cycle. The framing and message boundaries are handled at the protocol level, supporting both text and binary payloads efficiently. This enables applications to push updates, notifications, telemetry, and control messages in real time, while also reducing the latency and overhead associated with creating new HTTP connections for each interaction.

The following is a minimal example of a WebSocket client:

```
using System;
using System.Net.WebSockets;
using System.Net.WebSockets.WebSocketFrame;
using System.Text;

var ws = new ClientWebSocket(new ClientWebSocketOptions
{
    KeepAliveInterval = TimeSpan.FromSeconds(30)
});

ws.MessageReceived += (sender, e) =>
{
    var frame = e.Frame;
    if (frame.MessageType == WebSocketMessageType.Text)
    {
        var msg = Encoding.UTF8.GetString(frame.Buffer, 0, frame.
        MessageLength);
        Debug.WriteLine("Received: " + msg);
    }
};

// Optional: send custom headers on handshake
var headers = new ClientWebSocketHeaders();
headers["userId"] = "nano";
ws.Connect(new Uri("wss://example.com/realtime"), headers);

// Send a text message
ws.SendString("Hello from nanoFramework!");

// WebSocket runs  -  you can handle incoming messages via the
event handler

// When done:
ws.Close(WebSocketCloseStatus.NormalClosure, "Done");
```

The code snippet should be pretty self- explanatory. For completeness, let's go over the key differences from the full .NET API:

- Uses a synchronous `Connect()` method, not async/await
- Supports `KeepAliveInterval`, custom headers via `ClientWebSocketHeaders`, and message framing
- Events (`MessageReceived`) handle incoming frames, so there is no polling required
- Methods like `SendString()` and `SendBytes()` replace generic `Send<T>()`

SignalR

SignalR is a Microsoft real-time library that builds on top of WebSockets (with fallback to other techniques when unavailable) and provides an abstraction for broadcasting messages, group communication, and client-to-server RPC calls. In .NET nanoFramework, SignalR is supported with a simplified client API for embedded devices—ideal for real-time data visualization (e.g., live dashboards), remote monitoring, and remote actuation/control.

SignalR Client

The `nanoFramework.SignalR.Client` library enables embedded devices to connect to SignalR hubs (usually hosted in ASP.NET Core at the server end). Compared to desktop .NET, the nanoFramework client has a subset of the full API. The following are the major differences:

- Only client-to-hub and server-to-client messaging is supported (streaming and advanced negotiation are not).
- No built-in reconnection, authentication, or automatic fallback to long polling.
- The API is synchronous.

Here's an example of connecting to a SignalR hub and sending data:

```
using nanoFramework.SignalR.Client;
using System.Threading;

var hub = new HubConnection("wss://my.signalr-hub.com/hub");

hub.On("ReceiveMessage", (args) =>
{
    var msg = args[0].ToString();
    Debug.WriteLine("Message from server: " + msg);
});

// Start the connection
hub.Start();

// Send a message to the hub
hub.Invoke("SendMessage", "Hello from nano device!");

Thread.Sleep(10000); // Keep running for 10 seconds for demonstration

hub.Stop();
```

Typical use cases for this technology are as follows:

- **Real-time dashboards:** Devices push sensor readings or status updates to a server, which then broadcasts to live dashboards.
- **Remote control:** Operators send commands to devices via SignalR, instantly updating actuators or settings.
- **Collaborative robotics or distributed systems:** Devices keep each other in sync using the SignalR hub as a message broker.

Leveraging on .NET nanoFramework SignalR and WebSocket libraries even the smallest devices can participate in modern, low-latency, interactive systems.

MQTT and AMQP Messaging Protocols

Messaging-oriented protocols are designed to enable efficient, scalable, and reliable communication between distributed systems—especially important in IoT and embedded scenarios where devices often need to exchange small, frequent messages, sometimes with many clients and servers interacting simultaneously. Unlike HTTP, which is request-response, messaging protocols are typically asynchronous and decoupled, supporting patterns like publish/subscribe (pub/sub) and message queuing.

Differences from WebSockets and Choosing the Right Protocol

While MQTT and AMQP are both messaging protocols, they are fundamentally different from WebSockets in their design and intended use. WebSockets provide a persistent, bidirectional communication channel that is ideal for low-latency, real-time updates between a client and server, often with custom message handling on each side. However, WebSockets are typically point-to-point and require careful management of socket connections, which can be resource intensive for large fleets of devices or on constrained embedded systems.

In contrast, MQTT and AMQP implement a broker-based architecture that decouples message senders (publishers) from receivers (subscribers) using topics or queues. This approach enables scalable, asynchronous messaging patterns where devices do not need to maintain continuous direct connections with every endpoint. MQTT is especially optimized for lightweight telemetry, device-to-cloud communication, and scenarios where low bandwidth and reliability are key. AMQP is better suited for enterprise environments, supporting advanced features like message routing, transactions, and robust security.

Here are some aspects to consider to help you decide which one is best suited for the task you have at hand:

- Use WebSockets when you need direct, low-latency, bidirectional communication—such as remote user interfaces, interactive controls, or real-time streaming data where every millisecond counts.
- Choose MQTT when your application requires lightweight, scalable, publish/subscribe messaging, particularly in IoT and sensor networks where bandwidth and device resources are constrained.
- Select AMQP when your scenario demands enterprise features such as transactional messaging, guaranteed delivery, complex routing, or integration with business systems and cloud services.

MQTT

Message Queuing Telemetry Transport (MQTT) is a lightweight, publish/subscribe messaging protocol designed for resource-constrained devices and low-bandwidth, high-latency, or unreliable networks. The architecture consists of clients and a central broker. Clients publish messages to topics or subscribe to topics to receive messages. The broker serves as the central element responsible for receiving all messages, filtering them by topic, and distributing them to subscribed clients. The publish/subscribe model allows devices (clients) to publish messages to named topics and subscribe to topics of interest, effectively decoupling senders from receivers and enabling flexible data flow. MQTT defines three quality of service (QoS) levels: 0, which ensures delivery at most once (fire and forget); 1, which guarantees delivery at least once but may produce duplicates; and 2, which guarantees exactly once delivery without duplicates, though it involves higher overhead. The delivery here is relative to the broker, as QoS is negotiated per hop.

Here is an MQTT client implementation using the `m2mqtt` library:

```
using nanoFramework.M2Mqtt;
using nanoFramework.M2Mqtt.Messages;

var client = new MqttClient("myfactory.westeurope.ts.eventgrid.azure.net");

// register handler for received messages
client.MqttMsgPublishReceived += client_MqttMsgPublishReceived;

string clientId = Guid.NewGuid().ToString();
var ret = client.Connect(clientId);
if (ret != MqttReasonCode.Success)
{
    Debug.WriteLine($"ERROR connecting: {ret}");
    client.Disconnect();
    return;
}
```

Assuming the MQTT client has successfully connected, it can subscribe to the topic `home/temperature` with QoS 2, like this:

```
client.Subscribe(new string[] { "home/temperature" }, new MqttQoSLevel[] {
MqttMsgBase.ExactlyOnce });
```

Similarly, a connected MQTT client can publish to the `home/temperature` topic with QoS 2, like this:

```
client.Publish("home/temperature", Encoding.UTF8.GetBytes(strValue), false,
MqttQoSLevel.ExactlyOnce, false);
```

The boolean parameters in the middle are adjusting the duplicate and retain flags.

With a simple API for connecting, subscribing, and publishing, MQTT clients can quickly integrate into complex systems in scenarios where bandwidth and power usage are critical. Therefore, it is perfect for IoT use cases.

AMQP

Advanced Message Queuing Protocol (AMQP) is a robust, standardized protocol for business messaging, cloud systems, and IoT, most commonly found in enterprise and cloud IoT backends like Azure IoT Hub or RabbitMQ. At its core, AMQP defines a flexible messaging architecture centered around brokers (such as RabbitMQ or Azure Service Bus) that manage message routing through constructs like queues, topics, and exchanges. This allows AMQP to support a variety of communication patterns, including both point-to-point (direct queue delivery) and publish/subscribe (topics and exchanges for broadcasting to multiple subscribers). Devices connect as clients to these brokers, sending and receiving messages with support for rich metadata, transactional operations (ensuring exactly-once delivery and rollback on failure), explicit acknowledgments, message persistence, flexible routing, and advanced security controls. As a result, AMQP is heavier than MQTT but offers powerful features suited for complex, high-reliability, and scalable messaging scenarios.

The following code snippet is a practical usage example of AMQPnetlite connecting to Azure IoT Hub:

```
using Amqp;
using Amqp.Framing;

string senderAddress = "devices/" + _deviceId + "/messages/events";
string receiverAddress = "devices/" + _deviceId + "/messages/deviceBound";
string hostName = _hubName + ".azure-devices.net";
string userName = _deviceId + "@sas." + _hubName;
```

```
// Connect to AMQP broker
var connection = new Connection(new Address(hostName, 5671, userName,
_sasToken));
Session session = new Session(connection);

SenderLink sender = new SenderLink(session, "sender-link", senderAddress);

ReceiverLink receiver = new ReceiverLink(session, "receiver-link",
receiverAddress);
receiver.Start(100, OnMessage);
```

This is how you send a message with a temperature reading:

```
Message message = new Message();
message.ApplicationProperties = new Amqp.Framing.ApplicationProperties();
message.ApplicationProperties["temperature"] = temperature;

// send message with temperature
sender.Send(message, null, null);
```

Considering that we've set a handler in the receiver to process received messages, here's an example on how that works:

```
private static void OnMessage(IReceiverLink receiver, Message message)
{
    // command received
    int setTemperature = (int)message.ApplicationProperties["settemp"];
    Debug.WriteLine($"received new temperature setpoint:
    {setTemperature}");
}
```

To wrap up this section, let's summarize the comparison of MQTT versus AMQP:

Feature	MQTT	AMQP
Footprint	Very lightweight	Heavier (full-featured)
Pattern	Pub/Sub only	Pub/Sub, queues, transactions
QoS Levels	0, 1, 2	Granular, transaction support

(continued)

Feature	MQTT	AMQP
Best For	Device telemetry, IoT, sensors	Enterprise, cloud, hybrid IoT
Broker Options	Mosquitto, HiveMQ, Azure IoT Hub	RabbitMQ, Azure, cloud backends
Security	TLS/SSL, simple auth	TLS/SSL, SASL, advanced

Efficient Data Exchange with MessagePack

MessagePack is a binary serialization format developed as an attempt to have an efficient alternative to JSON, with a strong focus on compactness and speed. Its cross-language design and open specification have made it a popular choice across a wide range of platforms. For embedded systems, where bandwidth and memory are limited, MessagePack is exceptionally well-suited. Unlike JSON or XML, which are text-based and require significant parsing overhead, MessagePack efficiently encodes data in a compact binary form, reducing both transmission time and device resource usage. MessagePack produces much smaller payloads compared to JSON and especially XML. Its serialization and deserialization routines are optimized for low-latency, making it ideal for devices that need to quickly exchange structured data, telemetry, or settings with the cloud or other devices. This efficiency is particularly valuable in scenarios such as sensor networks, remote monitoring, and real-time control where every byte and CPU cycle counts.

The following is a practical serialization/deserialization example using the .NET nanoFramework API:

```
using nanoFramework.MessagePack;

[MessagePackObject]
public class SensorReading
{
    public int Id { get; set; }
    public float Value { get; set; }
    public long Timestamp { get; set; }
}
```

```
var reading = new SensorReading { Id = 1, Value = 25.6f, Timestamp =
DateTime.UtcNow.Ticks };

// Serialize
byte[] dataBuffer = MessagePackSerializer.Serialize(reading);

// transmit data somewhere...

byte[] receiveBuffer = new byte[300];
// receive data from somewhere...

// Deserialize
var newSetpoint = MessagePackSerializer.Deserialize(typeof(ValveSetPoint),
receiveBuffer) as ValveSetPoint;
```

You'll find a similar usage pattern as with the already mentioned `JsonConverter`. In the previous example, following the serialization, the `dataBuffer` array would be, most likely, the payload that sends that sensor reading over a network connection. Inversely, following the reception of a binary payload containing a serialized object, the call to `MessagePackSerializer.Deserialize()` would convert that into a `ValveSetPoint` object that the application would use appropriately.

MessagePack encoding typically produces payloads that are two to four times smaller than JSON. Binary formats also serialize and deserialize significantly faster, resulting in lower CPU and energy usage. Running on a nano device, MessagePack typically serializes a class in about half the time the JSON converter does and slightly faster when deserializing. In practical terms, this means more responsive devices, lower data costs, and better battery life for wireless IoT endpoints.

Integrating with Cloud Platforms

Cloud platforms such as Microsoft Azure and Amazon AWS offer a comprehensive set of services that go far beyond simple device connectivity. These platforms provide scalable infrastructure, secure device provisioning, message brokering, data storage, analytics, and integration with broader services like AI, alerting, dashboards, and automated workflows. By leveraging a commercial solution, you benefit from robust security models, compliance features, global reliability, and out-of-the-box integration with enterprise systems. However, this often comes at the cost of service fees, vendor lock-in, and less flexibility for custom or niche use cases. Rolling your own in-house solution provides ultimate control and customization but requires significant effort to achieve a comparable level of security, scalability, and reliability. Therefore, give it a good thought before you decide to roll your own.

Azure IoT

In Microsoft own words, Azure IoT Hub is a managed service that acts as a central message hub in a cloud-based IoT solution. It enables reliable and secure communication at scale between an IoT application and its attached devices. Almost any device can be connected to an IoT hub. Several messaging patterns are supported, including device-to-cloud messages, uploading files from devices, and request-reply methods to control your devices from the cloud. IoT Hub also supports monitoring to help you track device creation, device connections, and device failures. IoT Hub scales to millions of simultaneously connected devices and millions of events per second to support your IoT workloads. You can integrate IoT Hub with other Azure services to build complete, end-to-end solutions. Examples include Azure Event Grid, Azure Logic Apps, Azure Machine Learning or Azure Stream Analytics, and the Azure Data Explorer time-series database.

The following are some features and highlights that are fully supported by nanoFramework APIs:

- Device identity with certificates
- Device provisioning service (DPS) for secure onboarding.
- Scalable messaging infrastructure with support for AMQP, MQTT, and HTTP protocols
- Twin services for device state management, updates and reported property sync
- Telemetry and event publishing
- Cloud-to-device (C2D) command reception
- Direct methods and command handling
- Secure MQTT and AMQP over TLS

Practical Examples

The following are some examples on several usage topics and typical scenarios.

Connecting a Device

Assuming the device is already registered in the IoT Hub, this can be done with a couple of lines, like this:

```
using nanoFramework.Azure.Devices.Client;
using nanoFramework.Azure.Devices.Client.Transport;

var deviceClient = new DeviceClient(
       Secrets.IotHub,
       Secrets.DeviceName,
       Secrets.SasKey,
       azureCert: new X509Certificate(
                   Resource.GetBytes(Resource.BinaryResources.AzureRoot)),
       modelId: "dtmi:com:example:Thermostat;1");

deviceClient.Open();
```

Reporting DTDL Properties

Reporting these properties (which belong to the device twin) is supported. These are called desired properties and reported properties when sent from the device. Before opening the device client, the handler can be set up with `deviceClient.TwinUpdated += AzureTwinUpdated` and the handler. Assuming that we're interested in a hypothetical `ChlorineSetPoint` property, it could be something like this:

```
const string ChlorineSetPoint = "ChlorineSetPoint";

void AzureTwinUpdated(object sender, TwinUpdateEventArgs e)
{
    if (e.Twin.Contains(ChlorineSetPoint))
    {
        // We got an update for the Chlorine set point
        var target = e.Twin[ChlorineSetPoint];

        Debug.WriteLine($"Chlorine set point updated: {target}");
```

```
        PropertyAcknowledge targetReport = new() {
            Version = (int)e.Twin.Version,
            Status = PropertyStatus.Completed,
            Description = "All perfect", Value = target
        };

        TwinCollection twin = new TwinCollection();
        twin.Add(TargetTemperature, targetReport.BuildAcknowledge());
        azureIoT.UpdateReportedProperties(twin);
    }
}
```

To receive its update, we are subscribing to the twin update. After validating that the property is part of the update payload, we can grab the value through the e.Twin[ChlorineSetPoint]. The usage pattern requires that an acknowledge is sent back. Starts with creating a PropertyAcknowledge with the various fields properly set to build the acknowledge. Then create a TwinCollection, add the property name, and build the acknowledge. Please note that you can add as many properties are you need to the report. To send the acknowledgment, just call the UpdateReportedProperties() method.

Receiving Direct Method Commands

The handler for a DTDL command (direct method) is simply a method callback. As example, the method is called getMaxMinReport. Keep in mind that the name of the method in C# must be the same that will be used in the call. And that is case sensitive. To set this up, before opening the device client, it has to be declared with the following:

```
azureIoT.AddMethodCallback(getMaxMinReport);
```

And the handler can look like this:

```
string getMaxMinReport(int rid, string payload)
{
    TemperatureReporting reporting = new() {
         avgTemp = 20,
         maxTemp = 42,
         minTemp = 12.34,
```

```
        startTime = DateTime.UtcNow.AddDays(-10),
        endTime = DateTime.UtcNow
    };

    return JsonConvert.SerializeObject(reporting);
}
```

Sending Messages

To send any kind of message or telemetry to Azure IoT, simply call SendMessage().

```
var isReceived = deviceClient.SendMessage(
       $"{{\"Temperature\":42,\"Pressure\":1024}}",
      new CancellationTokenSource(5000).Token);
```

Cloud to Device Messages

You can register an event handler to receive cloud-to-device (C2D) messages:

```
azureIoT.CloudToDeviceMessage += CloudToDeviceMessageEvent;
```

For example purposes, take a look at the following handler that will list all the keys:

```
void CloudToDeviceMessageEvent(object sender, CloudToDeviceMessageEventArgs e)
{
        Debug.WriteLine($"Message arrived: {e.Message}");

        foreach (string key in e.Properties.Keys)
        {
            Debug.Write($"  Key: {key} = ");

            if (e.Properties[key] == null)
            {
                    Debug.WriteLine("null");
            }
            else
            {
                Debug.WriteLine((string)e.Properties[key]);
            }
        }
```

```
    // e.Message contains the message itself
    if(e.Message == "stop")
    {
        ShouldStop = true;
    }
}
```

Azure IoT Device Provisioning Service

The SDK also supports Azure Device Provisioning Service (DPS)—a zero-touch, scalable solution that links your IoT Hub to DPS and enables automatic device registrations. Once you've linked an IoT Hub to DPS and created either individual or group enrollments (using symmetric keys or X.509 certificates), a device can connect to DPS with its credentials. DPS authenticates the device, selects a linked IoT Hub, registers the device in that hub's registry, and then returns the proper connection details. Only after this handshake is complete can the device successfully connect and begin secure communication.

```
var provisioning = ProvisioningDeviceClient.Create(
                    DpsAddress, IdScope, RegistrationID, SasKey, azureCA);

var myDevice = provisioning.Register(new CancellationTokenSource(60000).
Token);

if(myDevice.Status != ProvisioningRegistrationStatusType.Assigned)
{
    Debug.WriteLine($"Registration is not assigned: {myDevice.Status},
    error message: {myDevice.ErrorMessage}");
    return;
}

// now create the device
var deviceClient = new DeviceClient(
       myDevice.AssignedHub,
       myDevice.DeviceId,
       Secrets.SasKey,
       nanoFramework.M2Mqtt.Messages.MqttQoSLevel.AtLeastOnce, azureCA
);

deviceClient.Open();
```

Amazon AWS IoT Core

Using Amazon's own words, AWS IoT provides the cloud services that connect IoT devices to other devices and AWS cloud services. AWS IoT provides device software that can help integrate IoT devices into AWS IoT-based solutions. It supports MQTT, HTTP, and WebSockets and is tightly integrated with AWS Lambda, S3, DynamoDB, and IoT Analytics.

The following are some features and highlights that are fully supported by nanoFramework APIs:

- Secure MQTT device connectivity
- Device shadow update/reporting
- Publish/subscribe messaging
- Certificate-based authentication

The AWS API was designed to be compatible, as much as possible, with the Azure SDK, thus allowing easier portability of the code between both cloud providers. Also note that the SDK is based in MQTT connection to AWS.

Practical Examples

Here are some examples.

Connecting a Client

As usual, simplicity and ease of use were top of mind when designing the API. To connect a client, a couple of lines is all it takes.

```
X509Certificate2 clientCert = new X509Certificate2(ClientRsaSha256Crt,
                              ClientRsaKey, "");
MqttConnectionClient awseIoT = new MqttConnectionClient(
                               IotBrokerAddress, ThingId, clientCert,
                               QoSLevel.AtLeastOnce, awsRootCACert);

 awseIoT.Open();
```

Operations with Device Shadows

You can request your shadow simply by calling the `GetShadow()` function.

```
var shadow = awsIoT.GetShadow(new CancellationTokenSource(20000).Token);

if (shadow == null)
{
    Debug.WriteLine($"Can't get the shadow");

    awsIoT.Close();
    return;
}

Debug.WriteLine($"Shadow ClientToken: {shadow.DeviceId}, #desired: {shadow.
status.desired}, #reported: {shadow.status.reported}");
```

Reporting a shadow is as simple as this:

```
ShadowCollection reported = new ShadowCollection();
reported.Add("firmware", "myNano");
reported.Add("sdk", 0.2);
awsIoT.UpdateReportedProperties(reported);
```

A handler can be set up to receive updates to shadow with `awsIoT.ShadowUpated += ShadowUpdatedEvent`.

Sending Messages

To send any kind of message or telemetry, there is the API SendMessage.

```
var isReceived = awsIoT.SendMessage($"{{\"Temperature\":42,\"Pressu
re\":1024}}", new CancellationTokenSource(5000).Token);
```

Cloud to Device Messages

A handler can be registered to receive cloud-to-device (C2D) messages, like this `awsIoT.CloudToDeviceMessage += CloudToDeviceMessageEvent`. And then the handler will look this:

```
void CloudToDeviceMessageEvent(object sender,
CloudToDeviceMessageEventArgs e)
{
    Debug.WriteLine($"Message arrived: {e.Message}");
    foreach (string key in e.Properties.Keys)
    {
        Debug.Write($"  Key: {key} = ");
        if (e.Properties[key] == null)
        {
            Debug.WriteLine("null");
        }
        else
        {
            Debug.WriteLine((string)e.Properties[key]);
        }
    }

    // e.Message contains the message itself
    if(e.Message == "stop")
    {
        ShoudIStop = true;
    }
}
```

Web Server on Embedded Devices

A web server is a software component that listens for HTTP requests on a network, processes them, and responds with data—often as web pages, files, or API payloads. For an embedded device to reliably serve as a web server, it must support basic network connectivity (Ethernet, Wi-Fi, or cellular), be capable of handling TCP/IP stack operations, and implement an HTTP parser and responder. This typically requires a device with sufficient RAM and flash storage, a multitasking-capable processor, and a secure execution environment. In many scenarios, supporting authentication mechanisms and secure (TLS/SSL) connections is essential to prevent unauthorized access.

Modern web servers on embedded devices are increasingly designed to provide RESTful APIs. Representational State Transfer (REST) is an architectural style for designing networked applications that use standard HTTP methods—GET, POST, PUT, DELETE—to operate on resources, usually encoded as JSON. REST APIs are stateless, easy to consume by web or mobile clients, and benefit from HTTP's broad compatibility. Compared to legacy approaches like Simple Object Access Protocol (SOAP), which relies on verbose XML and strict contract definitions, REST is lighter, simpler, and much more suitable for resource-constrained devices.

Use Cases for Embedded Web Servers

Embedded web servers are widely used for device configuration interfaces, allowing users to connect via a browser and set up Wi-Fi, view status, or initiate firmware updates. They're invaluable in industrial environments for monitoring and diagnostics—exposing sensor readings, logs, or performance metrics over a local network. Some devices offer web-based dashboards for real-time visualization. Another increasingly common use case is to expose a REST API for remote automation, allowing other systems to retrieve device state or send commands using simple HTTP calls. In the context of IoT, this enables seamless integration with home automation systems, cloud services, or mobile apps.

Practical HTTP Server Implementations

The `WebServer` API is quite complete and covers a variety of usage cases in embedded systems. We'll show examples with of the most common ones: serving web pages and handling REST APIs.

Serving Web Pages

Serving web pages is as straightforward as writing HTML content to the response object. For device UIs, you can embed static HTML, CSS, and even small JavaScript files within the firmware or a microSD card. The `nanoFramework.WebServer` library allows you to quickly spin up an HTTP server on your embedded device. Here's a minimal example for serving files from the internal storage:

```
using (WebServer server = new WebServer(80, HttpProtocol.Http))
{
    server.CommandReceived += ServerCommandReceived;
    server.Start();
    Thread.Sleep(Timeout.Infinite);
}

private static void ServerCommandReceived(object source,
WebServerEventArgs e)
{
    const string DirectoryPath = "I:\\"; // Internal storage
    var url = e.Context.Request.RawUrl;
    var fileName = url.Substring(1); // Remove leading '/'

    // Check if file exists and serve it
    string filePath = DirectoryPath + fileName;
    if (File.Exists(filePath))
    {
        WebServer.SendFileOverHTTP(e.Context.Response, filePath);
    }
    else
    {
        WebServer.OutputHttpCode(e.Context.Response, HttpStatusCode.
        NotFound);
    }
}
```

Handling REST APIs

REST APIs can be designed to expose device state, settings, or actions. For example, a POST endpoint can allow remote clients to set thresholds or trigger a pump. Registering a controller is matter of calling `RegisterController` and passing a class name.

```
server.RegisterController(typeof(PoolController));
```

You can add as many of those as you need. Here's how that class will look:

```
public class PoolController
{
   [Route("api/pool/status")]
   [Method("GET")]
   public void GetStatus(WebServerEventArgs e)
   {
       var status = new PoolStatus { pH = 7.2f, Chlorine = 1.5f,
       PumpActive = true };
       e.Context.Response.ContentType = "application/json";
       WebServer.OutPutStream(JsonConvert.SerializeObject(status));
   }

   [Route("api/pool/setpoint")]
   [Method("POST ")]
   public void SetSetpoint(WebServerEventArgs e)
   {
       var setpoint = new PoolSetpoint();
       JsonConvert.DeserializeObject(e.Context.Request.Data, setpoint);

       // Apply the new setpoint to the controller logic here

       var response = "{\"result\":\"ok\"}";

       e.Context.Response.ContentType = "application/json";
       WebServer.OutPutStream(e.Context.Response, response);
   }
}
```

This approach makes it easy to integrate the pool controller with mobile apps, dashboards, or automation scripts—while keeping the device logic simple and testable.

Security Best Practices for Embedded Web Servers

Security is crucial when exposing HTTP services on a device. Always require authentication for configuration and control endpoints, at least using basic auth or with token-based systems.

Adding a server certificate for an embedded device may not be that easy because of the difficulty of validating the device identity. Even for free services like Let's Encrypt. These services need to prove control over a publicly accessible domain name. This is the first obstacle as most embedded devices do not have a public domain name or are behind NAT/firewall.

Implement input validation to defend against injection attacks, and consider rate limiting to avoid a denial of service. Never expose debug endpoints or firmware update APIs to untrusted networks, and regularly update device firmware to patch vulnerabilities. Finally, audit all exposed API routes and keep the attack surface minimal—only enable features you truly need.

Wireless Technologies and Implementations

As we've mentioned before, .NET nanoFramework offers several API and implementations for a vast number of wireless technologies. It is beyond the scope of this book to dive into the tech details of each of the supported technologies. We'll assume the reader has a reasonable knowledge about the ones it's interested in. The following examples will focus on illustrating how they are implemented and the APIs available in nanoFramework context.

Wi-Fi Access Point (AP)

Many modern IoT devices allow first-time wireless configuration via a built-in "soft AP" (access point) mode. The device creates its own Wi-Fi network, and users connect via phone/laptop and then fill in the real Wi-Fi credentials through a simple web interface. Here's how to implement this pattern using nanoFramework.

Start by enabling Wi-Fi Soft AP mode, so the device creates its own hotspot. You'll specify the SSID and password.

```
using System.Device.Wi-Fi;

Wi-FiAdapter Wi-Fi = Wi-FiAdapter.FindAllAdapters()[0];

// Set up Soft AP (SSID and password)
Wi-Fi.SetAccessPointConfiguration(new AccessPointConfiguration()
```

```
{
    Ssid = "NanoConfigAP",
    Password = "nano1234"
});

// Start the AP
Wi-Fi.StartSoftAP();
```

After this, your device will broadcast a Wi-Fi network called NanoConfigAP. Users can connect using the password nano1234.

With the AP running, start a simple HTTP server that serves a configuration page and receives Wi-Fi credentials:

```
using nanoFramework.WebServer;

WebServer server = new WebServer(80, HttpProtocol.Http);

// Serve the HTML config page at root
server.Route("GET", "/", (ctx) =>
{
    ctx.Response.ContentType = "text/html";
    ctx.Response.Write(
        "<html><body><form method='post'>" +
        "SSID: <input name='ssid'/><br/>" +
        "Password: <input name='password' type='password'/><br/>" +
        "<input type='submit' value='Connect'/>" +
        "</form></body></html>");
});

// Handle the POST with Wi-Fi credentials
server.Route("POST", "/", (ctx) =>
{
    var form = ctx.Request.Data;
    string ssid = ExtractValue(form, "ssid");
    string pwd = ExtractValue(form, "password");

    // Here you would store these credentials securely (see below)
    ctx.Response.ContentType = "text/html";
```

```
    ctx.Response.Write("<html><body>Credentials received. Device will
    attempt to connect.<br/>You can close this page.</body></html>");

    // (Optionally) store and use the credentials to connect to real Wi-Fi
    // See step 4 below
});

server.Start();
```

Keep in mind that ExtractValue is a helper method to extract form values from the POST body. You may want to implement basic parsing for URL-encoded data. The previous example just shows the web flow; you should always store Wi-Fi credentials securely.

The user is instructed to connect their laptop or phone to the NanoConfigAP Wi-Fi, following which they have to open a browser and navigate to http://192.168.4.1 (the device's AP default address). The HTML form appears. They enter the target Wi-Fi SSID and password. Once credentials are submitted, use the nanoFramework Wi-Fi API to disconnect the AP, store the new network settings, and attempt to join the real Wi-Fi network:

```
// Stop the Soft AP
WirelessAP.Disable();

// Set station (client) mode and connect using received credentials
WifiNetworkHelper.ConnectDhcp(ssid, password,
WifiReconnectionKind.Automatic, true);
```

For security, always erase credentials after use or store them in a secure area (not plain text) or via NetworkHelper for persistence. As good practice, you can provide feedback on the device's display or through the web interface about the connection attempt result.

As improvement you can consider implementing a fallback: if the device fails to connect to Wi-Fi after reboot, it can revert to Soft AP mode for reconfiguration. Also, you extend the web server with additional diagnostics or troubleshooting info if the connection fails.

You'll find in the GitHub repository a complete sample of an application that performs all the above described operations and workflow.

Bluetooth Low Energy (BLE)

BLE is supported on .NET nanoFramework only for the ESP32 platform and requires a firmware image with BLE features enabled. You can identify these firmware packages by the inclusion of *ble* in their names, although there are exceptions (e.g., ESP32_BLE_REV3, ESP32_S3_BLE or LilygoTWatch2021). Be sure to select a compatible firmware for BLE development.

Advertising and Responding to Connections

Let's start with a simple scenario: making your device act as a BLE "peripheral," which means it will advertise itself and host a custom Generic Attribute Profile (GATT) service. Let's see how easy it is to advertise a custom service and handle client interactions. A GATT service is a collection of related data points called *characteristics*, each of which represents a single piece of data—like a configuration value, sensor reading, or control command—structured hierarchically under the service. The peripheral advertises itself so that central devices (e.g., phones or PCs) can discover and connect to it, at which point the GATT server exposes its services and characteristics for read, write, or notification operations.

First, add a reference to the Bluetooth NuGet `nanoFramework.Device.Bluetooth` and initialize a new `BluetoothLEServer` instance. Then you configure advertising parameters, define a service and its characteristic, and start advertising—making it easy to advertise a custom service and handle client interactions.

```
using nanoFramework.Device.Bluetooth;
using nanoFramework.Device.Bluetooth.GenericAttributeProfile;

BluetoothLEServer bleServer = new BluetoothLEServer();
GattServiceProviderResult serviceProviderResult = GattServiceProvider.
Create("12345678-1234-1234-1234-123456789abc", out var provider);

GattLocalCharacteristicParameters characteristicParameters = new
GattLocalCharacteristicParameters()
{
    CharacteristicProperties = GattCharacteristicProperties.Read |
    GattCharacteristicProperties.Write,
    ReadProtectionLevel = GattProtectionLevel.Plain,
```

```
    WriteProtectionLevel = GattProtectionLevel.Plain,
    UserDescription = "Sample characteristic"
};

provider.Service.CreateCharacteristic("abcdefab-1234-5678-9abc-
abcdefabcdef", characteristicParameters, out var characteristic);

provider.AdvertisementStatusChanged += (s, e) =>
{
    Debug.WriteLine($"Advertisement status changed: {e.Status}");
};

provider.StartAdvertising();
Debug.WriteLine("BLE Peripheral is now advertising!");
```

This code sets up a BLE peripheral that advertises a custom service (note the unique ID for the service through the GUID) and a characteristic that can be both be read and written by connected clients. When a BLE client connects, it can discover the service and interact with the characteristic to exchange data.

BLE Central: Pairing and Authentication

Now let's look at another scenario: the device as a *BLE central* that scans, discovers, pairs, and authenticates with a BLE peripheral.

Begin by setting up the central mode. You scan for devices, attempt to pair, and then authenticate before interacting with services.

```
using nanoFramework.Device.Bluetooth;

BluetoothLEClient client = new BluetoothLEClient();

client.DeviceDiscovered += (sender, e) =>
{
    Debug.WriteLine($"Discovered device: {e.DeviceAddress} - {e.DeviceName}");
    if (e.DeviceName == "TargetDeviceName")
    {
        client.StopScanning();
        Debug.WriteLine("Connecting...");
```

```
        client.Connect(e.DeviceAddress);
    }
};

client.DeviceConnected += (sender, e) =>
{
    Debug.WriteLine("Connected. Initiating pairing...");
    client.Pair(e.DeviceAddress, BluetoothLEPairingProtectionLevel.
    Encryption);
};

client.PairingCompleted += (sender, e) =>
{
    if (e.Status == BluetoothLEPairingStatus.Paired)
    {
        Debug.WriteLine("Pairing successful! Ready to authenticate and
        exchange data.");
        // Interact with services here
    }
    else
    {
        Debug.WriteLine($"Pairing failed: {e.Status}");
    }
};

Debug.WriteLine("Starting BLE scan...");
client.StartScanning();
```

This example demonstrates how to scan for nearby BLE devices, connect to a specific one by name, initiate pairing, and handle authentication events. Once pairing is successful, your application is ready to discover GATT services, read and write characteristics, or perform further communication.

LoRa and LoRaWAN

LoRa is a proprietary modulation scheme from Semtech optimized for long-range, low-power communication in sub-GHz ISM bands. The easiest path to use LoRa in nanoFramework is to leverage ready-made modules combining an ESP32 and a Semtech

SX1262 radio, exposing a simple SPI interface for radio control. The following examples use this hardware pattern to demonstrate both raw LoRa modulation tests (Ping-Pong) and LoRaWAN joining.

Assuming the radio is connected to the ESP32 using SPI (the most prevalent case in these modules), the first task is to configure the `SpiDevice`, like this:

```
using nanoFramework.Hardware.Esp32;
using Iot.Device.LoRa;
using System.Device.Spi;

SpiConnectionSettings settings = new SpiConnectionSettings(1, 18)
{
    ClockFrequency = 10000000,
    Mode = SpiMode.Mode0
};
SpiDevice spi = SpiDevice.Create(settings);
GpioController gpio = new GpioController();
LoRaRadio radio = new LoRaRadio(spi, gpio.OpenPin(5), gpio.OpenPin(4),
                  gpio.OpenPin(23));
```

Ping-Pong Example

The application can make device work as master or slave in Ping-Pong test. When starting up, it assumes to be a master and will send PING packets and receive PONG packets alternatively. When a PING packet received, the device switches itself to slave mode, then send PONG packets and expect to receive PING packets. In slave mode, if the device receive a non-PING packet, it will reset to master mode and start the previous process again.

```
using NFLora;
using NFSx126x;
using UnitsNet;
using System.Text;

Sx126xLoRa sx1262 = new Sx126xLoRa(
    2,
    chipSelectLine,
    dio1PinNumber,
    resetLine,
```

```
    busyLine,
    DeviceType.Sx1262,
    true,
    true,
    true);

// enable trace
Trace.TraceLevel = TraceLevel.Information;
Trace.TraceListener = WriteTrace;

// use LoRa library
Lora lora = new Lora(
    sx1262,
    LoraFrequencyBand.Band868);

// configure more radio details
lora.SetFrequency(Frequency.FromMegahertz(868.7));

lora.SetSpreadingsFactorAndBandWith(
    LoRaSpreadingFactor.Factor7,
    LoRaBandwidth.Bandwidth_125);

lora.SetTxPower(Level.FromDecibels(_txPower));
lora.SetMode(LoRaMode.HotStart);
```

The following LoRa configurations move to the packets to send:

```
// set the buffer to the ping message
Array.Copy(UTF8Encoding.UTF8.GetBytes(_pingMessage), _buffer, _pingMessage.
Length);
_buffer[_pingPongPrefixIndex] = 0;
_buffer[_iterationIndex] = _iteration;
_buffer[_payloadIndex] = _payloadIndex;
_buffer[_payloadIndex + 1] = _payloadIndex + 1;
```

We're ready to send the first PING:

```
// send the first ping
if (!lora.Send(_buffer, TimeSpan.FromMilliseconds(_pingPongDelay)))
{
    // failed to send
    Trace.WriteLine(TraceLevel.Error, "Failed to send message");
}
```

Following this, we'll enter a loop to process whatever is coming from the radio:

```
while (true)
{
    // wait for the pong
    LoRaReceivedFrame received = lora.ReceiveFrame(TimeSpan.
    FromMilliseconds(_pingPongDelay), default(DateTime), false);

    if (received != null)
    {
        // reset packets to sync
        _packetsToSync = 0;

        try
        {
            // get iteration from the packet
            _iteration = received.Frame[_iterationIndex];
            _iteration++;

            string message = Encoding.UTF8.GetString(received.Frame, 0,
            _pingPongPrefixIndex);

            if (_isMaster)
            {
                if (message.Equals(_pingMessage))
                {
                    // switch to slave
                    _isMaster = false;
```

```
            // set the buffer to the pong message
            Array.Copy(_pongMessage.ToCharArray(), _buffer,
            _pongMessage.Length);
        }
        else if (message.Equals(_pongMessage))
        {
            // unexpected message
            _packetsToSync++;
        }
        else
        {
            // really unexpected message
        }
    }
    else
    {
        if (!message.Equals(_pingMessage))
        {
            // unexpected message

            // switch to master
            _isMaster = true;

            // set the buffer to the ping message
            Array.Copy(_pingMessage.ToCharArray(), _buffer,
            _pingMessage.Length);
        }
        else
        {
            // really unexpected message
        }
    }

    // set the iteration
    _buffer[_iterationIndex] = _iteration;
```

```
                // send the next message
                if (!lora.Send(_buffer, TimeSpan.FromMilliseconds(
                _pingPongDelay)))
                {
                    // failed to send
                }
            }
            catch (Exception ex)
            {
            }
        }
        else
        {
            // no message received

            // bump packets to sync
            _packetsToSync++;

            if (_packetsToSync > _syncPacketsThreshold)
            {
                Trace.WriteLine(
                    TraceLevel.Warning,
                    "It looks like synchronisation is still not done, consider
                    resetting one of the boards");
            }
        }
    }
```

LoRaWAN OTAA Join and Sleep

In LoRaWAN, devices can join networks dynamically using over-the-air activation (OTAA). OTAA performs a secure handshake between the device and network server, negotiating session keys and assigning a device address.

Let's start with the initial configurations for the radio and OTAA credentials. If you're connecting to a comercial service, you need to get the authentication details from the service provider.

```
using NFSx126x;
using NFLora;
using Lora.LoraWanClient;
using UnitsNet;

var freqPlan = new FrequencyPlan(Region.EU868, true, 4, DataRate.Dr3);
OtaaAuthentication authentication = new OtaaAuthentication(new byte[] { 0,
1, 2, 3, 4, 5, 6, 7 }, new byte[8], new byte[] { 0, 1, 2, 3, 4, 5, 6, 7, 8,
9, 10, 11, 12, 13, 14, 15 });

Sx126xLoRa sx1262 = new Sx126xLoRa(2, chipSelectLine, dio1PinNumber,
resetLine, busyLine, DeviceType.Sx1262, true, true, true);

LoraWanClient loraWan = new LoraWanClient(sx1262, Region.custom,
authentication, channelConfig: freqPlan);
```

This checks for a successful join to the network and sends a dummy packet:

```
if (loraWan.Join())
{
    Debug.WriteLine("Join success");

    loraWan.SendReceive(new byte[] { 0x00, 0x01, 0x02 });
}
else
{
    Debug.WriteLine("Join failed");
}
```

The device is connected to the network, and we're ready to handle whatever simple or complex scenarios the application requires. The nanoFramework API includes management of low-power sleep and wake cycles, which allow coding both “sleepy” or “always on” devices. The following code demonstrates this:

```
loraWan.SetDeviceToSleepMode(true);

loraWan.WakeUpDevice();
```

OpenThread and Thread Networks

OpenThread brings IPv6-based mesh networking to embedded devices, enabling resilient, self-healing, low-power networks. To use it with .NET nanoFramework, you need hardware and firmware with IPv6/Thread support. As of this writing, supported platforms include `ESP32_C6_Thread`, `ESP32_H2_Thread`, and `ESP32_PSRAM_REV3_IPV6`, all shipping firmware builds with `Thread` enabled.

The nanoFramework `nanoFramework.Networking.Thread` library supports three device roles:

- **Router:** Forwards messages and maintains network topology
- **End Device:** Joins a Thread network and communicates through a router
- **Sleepy End Device:** Similar to End Device but spends most time in low-power sleep, polling for messages

The API exposes methods to initialize the Thread stack, set the device role, configure network parameters (PAN ID, channel, network key), and bring the interface up or down. Event callbacks inform you of status changes (Attached, Detached, Data Received).

This library supports both integrated 802.15.4 radios and external Radio Co-Processor (RCP) modules. You can attach to an existing Thread mesh using address discovery, or perform a secure network join via the Thread Commissioner API, which handles authentication and configuration with the network leader on your behalf.

OpenThread Server (Router)

In this example, the device acts as a Thread Router, forming or joining a network. We initialize the Thread stack, configure network settings, and start advertising as a router.

```
using nanoFramework.Networking.Thread;

var thread = new OpenThreadImplementation();
// Configure network parameters
thread.PanId = 0x1234;
thread.Channel = 15;
thread.NetworkKey = new byte[]{0x00,0x01,0x02,0x03,0x04,0x05,0x06,0x07,0x
08,0x09,0x0A,0x0B,0x0C,0x0D,0x0E,0x0F};
```

```
// Set role and start
thread.Role = DeviceRole.Router;
thread.Start();

thread.StatusChanged += (s, e) => Debug.WriteLine($"Thread status:
{e.NewState}");

Debug.WriteLine("Thread Router started.\n");
```

This code creates or attaches to a thread mesh as a router. The `StatusChanged` event reports when the device successfully attaches, at which point it can forward traffic and accept child devices.

OpenThread Client (End Device)

Here, the device performs as an end device. After joining the network, it sends a unicast message to the router's IPv6 address.

```
using nanoFramework.Networking.Thread;
using System.Net;
using System.Net.Sockets;

var thread = new OpenThreadImplementation()
{
    PanId = 0x1234,
    Channel = 15,
    NetworkKey = new byte[]{0x00,0x01,0x02,0x03,0x04,0x05,0x06,0x07,0x08,
    0x09,0x0A,0x0B,0x0C,0x0D,0x0E,0x0F},
    Role = DeviceRole.EndDevice
};

thread.Start();

thread.StatusChanged += (s, e) =>
{
    if (e.NewState == NetworkState.Attached)
    {
        Debug.WriteLine("Attached as End Device. Sending ping...");
```

```
        var socket = new Socket(AddressFamily.InterNetworkV6, SocketType.
        Dgram, ProtocolType.Udp);

        // Use mesh-local address or Router's address
        var routerAddr = IPAddress.Parse("fe80::1");

        socket.SendTo(Encoding.UTF8.GetBytes("Hello Thread Router!"), new
        IPEndPoint(routerAddr, 1234));
    }
};
```

This snippet shows joining the thread network as an end device and using a UDP socket to send a message. You have to replace *fe80::1* with the actual router's mesh-local IPv6.

Texas Instruments EasyLink

TI's EasyLink is a simple, low-power wireless API built on the CC13xx/CC26xx platform. To use it, flash your TI device (e.g., CC1310 or CC2650) with the nanoFramework firmware that includes EasyLink support. The `nanoFramework.TI.EasyLink` library exposes straightforward methods to configure radio parameters, send packets, and perform blocking receives with timeouts.

EasyLink Sender Example

The following configures the radio, composes a payload, and sends it in a loop:

```
using nanoFramework.TI.EasyLink;
using System.Text;

// Initialize and configure EasyLink
EasyLink.Init(EasyLinkModulation.LoraRfm, frequency: 915_000_000);
EasyLink.SetTxPower(14);
EasyLink.SetSyncWord(0x34);

while (true)
{
```

```
    string message = "Hello EasyLink!";
    byte[] payload = Encoding.UTF8.GetBytes(message);
    EasyLink.Send(payload);
    Debug.WriteLine($"Sent: {message}");
    Thread.Sleep(2000);
}
```

This is as simple as it can be. This snippet sets up EasyLink modulation at 915 MHz, TX power of 14 dBm, and a sync word. It then sends a UTF-8 encoded message every 2 seconds.

Note Mind the frequency bands in the region you're operating. These are different across the globe. Always make sure to follow local regulations.

EasyLink Receiver Example

Use the `Receive()` API to wait for packets and process them when they arrive. This call is blocking, so it won't return until a packet is received. Know that there is an overloaded method offering a timeout parameter. Typically you would implement this on a separate thread handling this. And then signal the application about the receive event. Learn more about this in Chapter 9.

```
using nanoFramework.TI.EasyLink;
using System.Text;

EasyLink.Init(EasyLinkModulation.LoraRfm, frequency: 915_000_000);
EasyLink.SetSyncWord(0x34);

while (true)
{
    if (EasyLink.Receive(out byte[] data, timeout: 5000))
    {
        string received = Encoding.UTF8.GetString(data);
        Debug.WriteLine($"Received: {received}");
    }
```

```
    else
    {
        Debug.WriteLine("Receive timeout, no packet.");
    }
}
```

The receiver initializes with matching parameters and calls `Receive()`, which blocks up to five seconds before returning false on timeout.

CAT-M and NB-IoT

If you need cellular connectivity for your project, nanoFramework has you covered. The platform provides a flexible and extensible IoT binding to connect to AT command-based modems through a standard serial (COM) port. Out of the box, the library supports several popular SIMCOM CAT-M and NB-IoT modem models, and it is designed for straightforward expansion to accommodate new devices by simply describing their AT command sets.

Working with cellular modems in nanoFramework is designed to be as simple as working with any other networking technology. The API handles common modem setup tasks, sending and receiving text messages, voice calls, and—most importantly for IoT—full-featured HTTP and MQTT communication. This means developers can reuse existing application logic with minimal adjustments.

For most modern embedded projects, HTTP(S) and MQTT(S) are the dominant cellular IoT use cases. Both protocols are fully supported and are designed for seamless integration with the generic `HttpClient` and `MqttClient` APIs in nanoFramework.

HTTP client example

Getting started with HTTPS is familiar to anyone who has used the nanoFramework `HttpClient` API. After initializing the modem and setting up the data connection, simply create an `HttpClient` as usual.

```
using nanoFramework.IoT.Device.AtModem;
using System.Net.Http;

SerialPort _serialPort;
```

```
_serialPort = new("COM3")
    {
        //Set parameters
        BaudRate = 115200,
    };

// Open the serial port
_serialPort.Open();

// Initialize and configure the modem (COM port, APN, etc.)
AtChannel atChannel = new AtChannel.Create(_serialPort);
Sim7080 modem = new(atChannel);

// Use HttpClient just as with Ethernet or Wi-Fi
var httpClient = modem.HttpClient;
var response = httpClient.Get("https://api.example.com/data");
var content = response.Content.ReadAsString();
Console.WriteLine("HTTP GET result: " + content);

response = httpClient.Post("https://api.example.com/data",
new StringContent("{\"title\":\"nano\",\"body\":\"Framework\",
"data\":998877}", System.Text.Encoding.UTF8, "application/json"));
Console.WriteLine($"Status should be OK 200: {response.StatusCode}");
Console.WriteLine($"HTTP POST: {response.Content?.ReadAsString()}");
```

Connecting to Azure IoT over CAT-M/NB-IoT

Likewise, MQTT support through the modem is API-compatible with the nanoFramework generic `MqttClient`, making it easy to connect to cloud brokers for telemetry or command/control. Just leverage the `MqttClient` property of the `AtChannel` and pass it to the `DeviceClient` constructor. Assuming you've already made the initial configuration of the COM port and `AtChannel` as shown, it will be as simple as this:

```
DeviceClient azureIoT = new DeviceClient(modem.MqttClient,
IotBrokerAddress, DeviceID, SasKey, azureCert: Resource.GetBytes(
Resource.BinaryResources.DigiCertGlobalRootG2));
```

Following this, you can use the Azure `DeviceClient` as you would if it was connected with Wi-Fi or Ethernet, as we've already shown.

Of course, you can use the `MqttClient` property as a regular MQTT client and perform the usual operations as already described in the section about MQTT API, like subscribing to topics, publish, and connect.

Certificates and Secure Communication

For secure HTTPS and MQTT over cellular, the modem API expects an X.509 certificate in DER format. Certificates can be provided to the modem in the respective constructor; if no certificate is passed, server validation will be bypassed (not recommended for production deployments). Both HTTPS and MQTTS use the same mechanism, ensuring consistent security behavior across protocols.

Security Best Practices

Security in embedded devices is not optional—modern threats make it essential to design for robust data confidentiality, integrity, and device identity right from the start. The .NET nanoFramework makes strong security accessible for resource-constrained targets, but it's up to the developer to use it effectively.

Whenever a device exchanges data—whether telemetry, control messages, or firmware updates—it risks interception, tampering, or impersonation if not properly protected. Attackers can monitor unencrypted traffic, alter messages in transit, or even impersonate a cloud service to issue malicious commands. Using secure protocols (TLS/SSL) is the foundation of trust and integrity in IoT systems, as it ensures only trusted endpoints can communicate and that data remains confidential and unchanged.

In .NET nanoFramework, all TLS/SSL operations are performed by *mbedTLS*, a highly respected embedded cryptographic library. This means that security protocols—such as HTTPS, MQTTS, and WSS—are as strong and standards-compliant as those found in desktop and cloud environments. You don't have to manage crypto primitives or protocol handshakes manually: nanoFramework networking stack and APIs abstract these details, letting you focus on correct usage.

Managing Root CA Certificates

TLS/SSL connections rely on trusted root certificate authorities (CAs) to validate the authenticity of servers. With nanoFramework, you have flexibility in how you store and manage root CAs:

- *Directly in code*: Embed a PEM string literal. This is simple but makes updating certificates cumbersome.
- *App resources*: Bundle one or more certificates as a resource file. This decouples certs from code, aiding maintainability.
- *Internal device storage*: This is the preferred option. Upload and manage certificates independently from app code, using the Visual Studio Device Explorer Network Config dialog. This allows for easy certificate rotation and updates without re-flashing firmware or having to update the application. (Figure 7-3)

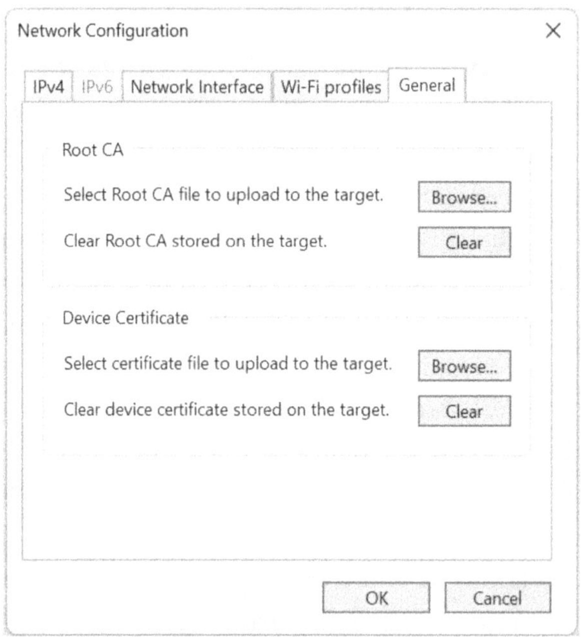

Figure 7-3. *Certificates storage management*

You can load multiple root CA certificates to trust several authorities. This is useful for devices that connect to services using certificates issued by different CAs, such as multiple cloud endpoints or third-party APIs.

Here's how it looks loading a root CA certificate in code:

```
// Loading a PEM-formatted root CA from code
string rootPem = @"
-----BEGIN CERTIFICATE-----
...certificate data...
-----END CERTIFICATE-----";
SslClientCertificates.AddRootCertificate(rootPem);

// Loading a CA cert from device storage
var rootCertBytes = File.ReadAllBytes("/Config/rootCA.pem");
SslClientCertificates.AddRootCertificate(rootCertBytes);
```

Storing root and device certificates in internal storage is strongly recommended for maintainability. This way, certificate rotation, renewal, or replacement is possible via remote updates or field service, without altering the application binary. Hard-coding credentials or certificates quickly becomes a liability as expiration or ecosystem changes occur.

By default, nanoFramework SSL APIs validate server certificates using the root CAs you've provided. The APIs also allow you to disable this check (e.g., for development or test environments) like this: `client.IgnoreCertificateErrors = true;`.

Warning Disabling certificate validation makes the device vulnerable to man-in-the-middle attacks and should never be used in production.

Some cloud services (Azure, AWS, enterprise APIs) require client certificates for mutual authentication. This is called mutual TLS.

Mutual TLS (mTLS) extends the standard TLS handshake by requiring *both* endpoints—client and server—to present and verify certificates. In traditional TLS, only the server provides a certificate, proving its identity to the client (so your device knows it's really talking to that cloud service, not a fake). With mTLS, the device also presents its own certificate to the server, and the server verifies it against a list of trusted client certificates or a trusted CA.

This two-way authentication is essential for many secure IoT deployments, particularly in industrial and commercial scenarios, where you must ensure that only genuine, authorized devices can connect and interact with cloud services. Each device gets a unique client certificate, typically issued by your company's own CA or the IoT provider and provisioned securely during manufacturing or setup.

These can be handled similarly to root CAs—either embedded or, preferably, provisioned into internal storage. Use the appropriate API to set both certificate and private key at runtime:

```
// Load device certificate and private key from secure storage
string certPem = File.ReadAllText("/Config/deviceCert.pem");
string keyPem = File.ReadAllText("/Config/deviceKey.pem");
SslClientCertificates.SetClientCertificate(certPem, keyPem);

// Optionally, load root CA(s) for server validation
string rootPem = File.ReadAllText("/Config/rootCA.pem");
SslClientCertificates.AddRootCertificate(rootPem);
```

With mTLS, device identity is not just based on a password or API key (which can be guessed or leaked) but on a cryptographic certificate that is extremely hard to fake or steal, especially when kept in protected storage. This approach also enables certificate revocation: if a device is compromised or decommissioned, you can revoke its certificate and block future access without affecting the rest of the fleet.

Data integrity is protected by TLS message authentication and encryption, which guarantees that transmitted data cannot be silently altered or forged. Device identity is assured by using unique client certificates and refusing to accept unauthenticated connections. These combined measures block spoofing, replay, and impersonation attacks.

Best Practices and Recommendations

The following are the best practices and recommendations for your embedded projects. They are based on industry recognized guidelines and personal experience.

- *Never store passwords, API keys, or secrets in plain source code.* Use secure provisioning, or encrypted storage.
- *Keep device firmware and networking libraries up-to-date,* to patch vulnerabilities as soon as they're discovered.
- *Always use secure network transports* (e.g., HTTPS, MQTTS, WSS), even for internal or testing deployments. Small projects often become production systems over time.

- *Disable certificate validation checks only for debug builds or lab tests*—never in real deployments.
- *Limit network exposure:* Only open the strictly necessary ports, and close all unused interfaces.
- *Audit and rotate certificates periodically* to reduce risk from leaked or expired keys.
- *Log authentication failures and unusual connection attempts* for monitoring and threat detection.

Summary

Selecting the right connectivity protocol for an embedded project is a balancing act between application requirements and available resources. Developers should match protocols to use cases—for example, using Wi-Fi or Ethernet for high-bandwidth device control, LoRa or EasyLink for long-range low-power sensing, BLE for local peripherals, and Thread or OpenThread for scalable mesh networks. Scalability and maintainability are best achieved by building on standardized technologies, using robust patterns like publish/subscribe or REST APIs, and leveraging platform support for secure communication. Commercial cloud platforms, such as Azure IoT and AWS IoT Core, simplify large-scale deployments and provide security and monitoring out of the box but come with cost and integration considerations. In contrast, rolling your own solution can maximize flexibility but often increases the burden of long-term maintenance and security.

For deployment, it is essential to ensure reliable network provisioning, to keep credentials out of code, and to rely on trusted certificate management practices. Devices should always use encrypted channels, validate server and client identities, and be designed with updatable firmware to respond to emerging threats. Common pitfalls include overlooking resource constraints, hard-coding secrets, or ignoring power management implications when using persistent protocols like WebSockets.

As embedded connectivity continues to evolve, trends such as seamless device provisioning, mutual TLS authentication, integration of mesh protocols like Thread, and adoption of efficient binary serialization formats (such as MessagePack) are reshaping how even the smallest devices interact with the wider world. By understanding the strengths and trade-offs of each technology covered in this chapter, developers can design scalable, secure, and future-ready networked solutions using .NET nanoFramework.

Additional Resources

Learn more at the following locations:

MQTT: `https://mqtt.org/`

AMQP 1.0: `https://www.oasis-open.org/committees/amqp/`

WebSockets: `https://developer.mozilla.org/en-US/docs/Web/API/WebSockets_API`

SignalR: `https://learn.microsoft.com/en-us/aspnet/core/signalr/introduction`

Bluetooth LE Overview: `https://www.bluetooth.com/learn-about-bluetooth/bluetooth-technology/bluetooth-low-energy/`

Semtech LoRa Technology: `https://www.semtech.com/lora`

LoRaWAN Specifications: `https://lora-alliance.org/resource_hub/lorawan-specification/`

OpenThread: `https://openthread.io/`

Microsoft Azure IoT: `https://learn.microsoft.com/en-us/azure/iot-fundamentals/`

AWS IoT Core: `https://docs.aws.amazon.com/iot/latest/developerguide/what-is-aws-iot.html`

MessagePack: `https://github.com/msgpack/msgpack/blob/master/spec.md`

CHAPTER 8

Testing for Embedded Success

Test and validation are fundamental tools for any serious development platform. .NET nanoFramework is not an exception.

When building embedded applications, reliability is everything. You want to make sure your code behaves as expected, especially when your project is running on a small microcontroller and deployed in the field, far from easy debugging tools. That's where the .NET nanoFramework Test Framework comes in: helping you catching bugs early and gain confidence as you make progress and introduce changes in your code.

Overview

In this chapter, you'll explore how to create and run unit tests using the .NET nanoFramework Test Framework. We'll start with a hands-on tutorial: setting up a unit test project, writing test classes and methods, and using various assertion methods.

You'll then learn how to execute tests using Visual Studio Test Explorer and how to interpret the results. Next, we'll discuss the available options to control and configure test execution through the `.runsettings` file and cover test result analysis and debugging strategies. Finally, we'll dive into the architecture and inner workings of the test framework, uncovering how the test runner discovers and executes tests and how it integrates with Visual Studio test platform.

J. Simões, *Embedded Systems with .NET nanoFramework*, https://doi.org/10.1007/979-8-8688-2096-0_8

Setting Up Your First nanoFramework Unit Test Project

Getting started with unit testing on .NET nanoFramework is pretty straightforward by use the built-in Visual Studio project template. This creates a dedicated test project (typically a class library) that contains your test code and references the code you want to test.

Assuming that you have .NET nanoFramework extension installed in Visual Studio 2022 and that you have a Solution loaded, please follow these steps:

1. Right-click the Solution in Solution Explorer and choose Add > New Project. In the Add New Project window, select the nanoFramework Unit Test template from the available project templates.

2. Choose the location and name for the unit test project.

3. This template sets up a blank unit test project with all the necessary bits preconfigured. It will automatically add the `nanoFramework.TestFramework` NuGet package and include a default `.runsettings` file with the required settings, as well as ensure the assembly is named NFUnitTest.

4. In the unit test project, make sure to add a reference to the project or library that contains the code you want to test. This allows your test code to instantiate classes and call methods from the target project. You can do this by right-clicking the test project in Solution Explorer, choosing Add > Project Reference, and selecting the project that contains the code to test.

5. After adding the reference, you should add `using` for the target project's namespaces in your test classes and call its public methods just as you would from any other code.

By now you should have something similar to this in VS Solution Explorer view. See Figure 8-1.

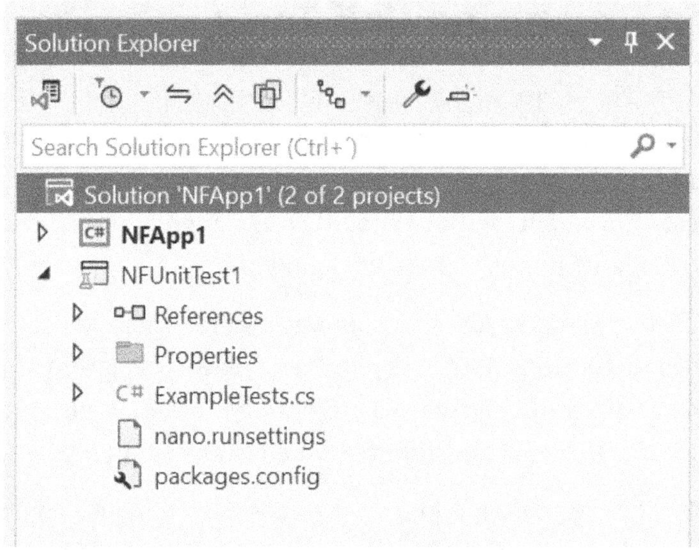

***Figure 8-1.** Solution Explorer with Unit Test project*

The unit test project can contain as many test classes and methods as you need. It's often convenient to mirror the structure of your main code. For example, if you have a class `Calculator` in your app, you might have a `CalculatorTests` class in your test project to group tests related to that class. One important limitation as of now is that all test assemblies must be named `NFUnitTest` (which is already the default name provided by the project template). This is a temporary restriction in the framework's design: the test runner on the device looks specifically for an assembly by that name when executing tests. So, if you happen to create a custom test project manually, ensure you set the assembly name to `NFUnitTest` (in the project's properties) to avoid any discovery issues. As already mentioned, the template takes care of this for you automatically.

Keep in mind that this restriction applies to the assembly name only. You're free to name the test project as you feel like.

Also worth mentioning that you can have as many test project in the same solutions as you want. Therefore, feel free to organize and group the tests by projects and test classes in such a manner that it's tidy and suits your work organization.

After these steps, you should have a test project ready to go. Now it's time to write some tests!

Writing and Organizing Unit Tests

With the unit test project set up, let's create our first tests. In nanoFramework test framework (much like other .NET test frameworks), tests are organized into classes and methods marked with special attributes. These attributes signal to the test runner which classes contain tests and which methods should be executed as tests (or setup/cleanup routines). The available attributes include the following:

- `[TestClass]`: Marks a class that contains unit test methods. If a class isn't decorated with `[TestClass]`, the test engine will ignore it. You can have as many test classes in a project as you want. Usually it's a good practice that each one groups related tests together.
- `[TestMethod]`: Marks a method as a test case. Each method with this attribute will be executed by the test runner (unless it's skipped or filtered out). There's no limit to how many `[TestMethod]`s you can have in a class (or in total).
- `[Setup]`: Marks a method to be run *before* any test in the class. Typically, you use a `Setup` method to initialize any common resources or state needed by the tests (for example, setting up hardware peripherals, initializing variables, etc.). Although technically you could have multiple `[Setup]` methods in a class, it's recommended to have at most one per class for clarity.
- `[Cleanup]`: Marks a method to be run after all the test methods in its class have run. This is useful for tearing down or releasing resources that were used during testing (like disposing objects, resetting hardware state, etc.). Like `[Setup]`, it's best to have only one `[Cleanup]` method per class, which will execute after all tests in the class have finished.

All of these special methods (`Setup`, `Cleanup`, and the tests themselves) must be `public` and return `void`. They also cannot take any parameters. If a method is not `public void` (for example, if you accidentally make a test method `private` or give it a return type), the test framework will not discover or run it. So be sure your test signatures are correct. The only exception to this is when a test method is decorated with `[DataRow]` attributes, which will see how it works in a moment.

Let's walk through a simple example of a test class to see how these pieces fit together. Suppose we're testing a piece of code that involves some simple data manipulation; we'll use a trivial scenario here for demonstration. Let's create a test class that uses a global counter and an array, just to illustrate state being set up and verified. (In a real scenario, these would likely be replaced by calls into your application's methods or classes.)

```
using nanoFramework.TestFramework;
using System;
using System.Diagnostics;

[TestClass]
public class ExampleTests
{
    // Some sample data to use in tests
    private static int _globalCounter;
    private static int[] _numbers;

    [Setup]
    public void Initialize()
    {
        // This runs before the first test (once for this class).
        OutputHelper.WriteLine("Running setup...");

        _globalCounter = 42;
        _numbers = new int[] { 1, 4, 9 };
    }

    [Cleanup]
    public void Cleanup()
    {
        // This runs after all tests in this class have executed.
        OutputHelper.WriteLine("Running cleanup...");

        // For example, ensure that our array still has elements and then
        clean up:
        CollectionAssert.NotEmpty(_numbers);
        _numbers = null;
```

```
        Assert.IsNull(_numbers);
    }

    [TestMethod]
    public void TestCounterAndArrayValues()
    {
        // This is a test method that will be executed by the test runner.
        OutputHelper.WriteLine("TestCounterAndArrayValues starting");

        // The Setup method should have set _globalCounter to 42
        Assert.AreNotEqual(0, _globalCounter);
        // _globalCounter should equal 42 (initialized in Setup)
        Assert.AreEqual(42, _globalCounter);
        // The Setup method should have initialized _numbers array
        // The array should have 3 elements
        Assert.AreEqual(3, _numbers.Length);
        Assert.AreEqual(1, _numbers[0], "First element should be 1");
        Assert.AreEqual(4, _numbers[1]; "Second element should be 4");
        Assert.AreEqual(9, _numbers[2], "Third element should be 9");
    }

    [TestMethod]
    public void TestStringUtilities()
    {
        OutputHelper.WriteLine("TestStringUtilities starting");
        string phrase = "nanoFramework is great";

        // Check some string conditions:
        Assert.Contains("nano", phrase);
        Assert.StartsWith("nanoFramework", phrase);
        Assert.EndsWith("great", phrase);
        // Also demonstrate the DoesNotContains assertion:
        Assert.DoesNotContains("XYZ", phrase);
    }

    [TestMethod]
    public void ThisTestIsToBeSkipped()
```

```
{
    // This test will be skipped by the test runner.
    OutputHelper.Write("ThisTestIsToBeSkipped starting");
    Assert.SkipTest("Skipping test for demonstration.");
}

[TestMethod]
public void TestExceptionThrowing()
{
    OutputHelper.WriteLine("TestExceptionThrowing starting");

    // Example: verify that a certain action throws an exception as
    expected.
    Assert.ThrowsException(typeof(ArgumentNullException), ThrowNull);
    // The above will pass if calling ThrowNull() throws an
    ArgumentNullException.
    // We can also use a lambda for convenience:
    Assert.ThrowsException(typeof(InvalidOperationException), () =>
    {
        // This code should throw InvalidOperationException to satisfy
        the test
        OutputHelper.WriteLine("Throwing InvalidOperationException as
        expected");
        throw new InvalidOperationException("Testing exception");
    });
}

// A helper method for the test above:
private void ThrowNull()
{
    OutputHelper.WriteLine("About to throw ArgumentNullException");
    throw new ArgumentNullException();
}

[TestMethod]
public void ThisTestWillFail()
```

```
    {
        // An example of a test that fails (to illustrate failure output)
        Assert.IsTrue(false, "This is a deliberate failure for
        demonstration");
    }
}
```

In the previous code, a variety of scenarios were demonstrated. Let's review them.

- The `[Setup]` method `Initialize()` sets up some static fields and even uses an `Assert` to verify that setup was correct. (If an assertion fails in setup, it will abort the tests in that class; we'll discuss skipping and failures shortly.)
- The `[Cleanup]` method `Cleanup()` checks the state after tests run and then cleans up (in this case, ensuring the array is not empty during cleanup and then nullifying it and checking that it's null).
- `TestCounterAndArrayValues` uses `Assert.AreEqual` and `Assert.AreNotEqual` to check that the `_globalCounter` and `_numbers` were properly set by `Initialize()`. It also shows that `Assert.AreEqual` works on simple values. For array and collections there are specific assert methods inside `CollectionAssert`, for example, to evaluate lengths and contents.
- `TestStringUtilities` demonstrates string-specific assertions like `Assert.Contains`, `Assert.StartsWith`, `Assert.EndsWith`, and `Assert.DoesNotContains` to validate string content.
- `TestExceptionThrowing` shows how to use `Assert.ThrowsException` by either providing a named method (in our example, `ThrowNull()` which throws an `ArgumentNullException`) or an inline lambda that throws the expected exception. This test will pass only if the specified exception type is thrown during the call.
- `ThisTestWillFail` is a contrived test that uses `Assert.IsTrue(false, "message")` to produce a failure on purpose, illustrating how a failing test is reported. In real usage, you wouldn't write a test that deliberately fails, but we include it here to see the

outcome when a test does not meet expectations. An exception to this would be, for example, when you're debugging a Unit Test and want to cause a failure on purpose at a specific point of the code.

Here are a few things to note about the previous example:

- We used `OutputHelper.WriteLine()` instead of the most common `Debug.WriteLine()` within tests. The test framework provides this `OutputHelper` class with `OutputHelper.WriteLine`, which works similarly and is specifically meant for test output. This is required to ensure that the output is properly captured by the test logger and added to the test log output. It can be helpful for diagnosing or documenting what a test is doing. Under the hood it's like using `Debug`, but it's there for convenience and clarity. Of course, you can still use `Debug.WriteLine` in case you need to output something to Visual Studio output pane with test debug messages.
- The `Assert` class provides a variety of static methods to verify conditions. If an assertion fails, it will throw an exception (like `AssertionFailedException`), which causes the test method to abort and be marked as failed. The nanoFramework test framework's philosophy is that any unhandled exception in a test method means the test failed. This is consistent with other test frameworks: tests pass if they complete without throwing an exception, and they fail if they throw an exception (except in the case of `Assert.ThrowsException`, where throwing the expected exception is actually a success).
- We showed a static field `_globalCounter` and `_numbers array`. Fields to be accessed by test methods have to be static; otherwise, the content will be "lost" as the methods are executed by the runner using reflection and invoking them, which will see in more detail in the section about the framework architecture. The test runner will instantiate your test class (if needed) and call methods on that instance. In our example, since we didn't create any object of `ExampleTests` manually, the reflection-based test runner will handle it. Behind the scenes, the test launcher uses reflection to find all `[TestClass]` types and then invokes their methods. Test methods are static, so assume each `[TestClass]` is handled in isolation.

The nanoFramework `Assert` class includes a rich set of assertion methods to cover common testing needs. We've already used several in the example. Here's a quick overview of key assertions and what they do:

- `Assert.IsTrue(condition)` and `Assert.IsFalse(condition)`: Verify a boolean condition is true or false, respectively. Use these for simple true/false checks.
- `Assert.AreEqual(expected, actual)` and `Assert.AreNotEqual(expected, actual)`: Check that two values are equal or not equal. These are heavily overloaded to support all the primitive value types (int, double, etc.), as well as objects and arrays. For reference types, `Assert.AreEqual` will check if the two references point to equal values or objects (for arrays the `CollectionAssert.AreEqual` should be used, and it will iterate through elements to compare each element). For `Assert.AreNotEqual`, of course, the logic is inverted: it passes if the values differ in any way.
- `Assert.IsNull(object)` and `Assert.IsNotNull(object)`: Validate that an object is `null` or not `null`. This is straightforward and useful for checking whether something was properly initialized or cleaned up.
- `Assert.IsType(expectedType, object)` and `Assert.IsNotType(expectedType, object)`: Verify the runtime type of an object. For example, `Assert.IsType(typeof(int), someVar)` will pass if `someVar.GetType() == typeof(int)`. This can be useful when your code returns a base class or interface and you want to ensure the actual implementation type is what you expect. The "not type" variant ensures an object is not of a given type.
- `Assert.AreSame(expectedObject, actualObject)` and `Assert.AreNotSame(expectedObject, actualObject)`: Check object identity. `Assert.AreSame` passes only if the two references refer to the exact same object instance. `Assert.AreNotSame` passes if they are different instances. This is useful when you want to ensure that something hasn't accidentally created a new object when it was supposed to reuse an existing one (or vice versa).

- `CollectionAssert.Empty(collection)` and `CollectionAssert.NotEmpty(collection)`: Verify that a collection is empty or not empty. For example, `CollectionAssert.Empty(myList)` would fail if `myList.Count > 0`. In our cleanup method, we used `CollectionAssert.NotEmpty(_numbers)` to ensure our array still had elements before we nullified it. This is a quick way to check collection length without explicitly comparing to 0. (Under the hood, the framework checks for properties like `Count` or `Length` on the object. If the object is a string, `Empty` means `string.Length == 0`; for arrays, `Length == 0`; for other collections that have a `Count` property, `Count == 0`.

There are a bunch of convenience methods for strings. Let's review them.

- `Assert.Contains(substring, string)`: Checks that the given substring occurs within the string
- `Assert.DoesNotContains(substring, string)`: Checks that the substring does not appear in the string
- `Assert.StartsWith(prefix, string)`: Checks that the string starts with the specified prefix
- `Assert.EndsWith(suffix, string)`: Checks that the string ends with the specified suffix

These were showcased in `TestStringUtilities`. They help make tests more readable compared to using general methods like `string.IndexOf` or `string.StartsWith` and then asserting on the result. For example, `Assert.Contains("abc", someText)` expresses intent clearly: "ensure *abc* exists somewhere in *someText*."

The following are the last two ones that are very useful in specific situations:

- `Assert.ThrowsException(exceptionType, action)`: As shown, this asserts that executing a given piece of code throws a specific type of exception. One provides the expected exception Type (for example, `typeof(ArgumentException)`) and a delegate (in practice, often a lambda `() => {...}`) that runs the code. If the code throws an exception of the expected type, the assertion passes (the test continues); if no exception is thrown, or if an exception of a different type is thrown, the assertion fails. This is essential for testing error-handling logic: e.g., if you want to ensure a method throws `ArgumentNullException` when passed a null argument, you can write the following:

```
Assert.ThrowsException(
    typeof(ArgumentNullException),
    () => MyMethod(null));
```

- `Assert.SkipTest(message)`: This is a special one that allows you to skip a test under certain conditions. When you call `Assert.SkipTest("reason")`, the framework will essentially mark the test as skipped (not passed or failed, just not executed due to a condition). One typical use is in a `[Setup]` method: you might detect that the hardware or environment isn't suitable for the tests in that class and decide to skip them. For example, if a set of tests require a double-precision floating point unit and the current device doesn't support it, you could call `Assert.SkipTest("Double floating point not supported, skipping...")` in the `Setup`. The effect is that all tests in that class will be skipped. Skipping is preferable to failing in such a scenario because it communicates that the test wasn't run due to environment constraints, rather than because the code under test is wrong. In Test Explorer, skipped tests are shown with a different icon (a yellow warning icon) and not counted as failures.

All assertion methods can take an optional final parameter for a custom message. We used this in `Assert.IsTrue(false, "This is a deliberate failure...")`. If you provide a custom message, it will be included in the test output to help explain the failure. If you don't, the framework often provides a default message (e.g., for `Assert.AreEqual(expected, actual)`, it might output something like "Expected X but got Y" automatically, as shown in the failure output later). Custom messages are useful to add context, but they're optional. By leveraging these asserts, you can validate just about any condition in your code. The test framework is designed to mirror the familiar assertions of frameworks like MSTest, so seasoned developers will find the names and behaviors intuitive, while beginners can rely on these straightforward checks to ensure code works as expected.

Another attribute extremely useful is [DataRow()]. It also exists in other test platforms, and the usage is quite similar. This attribute allows you to pass test parameters to a unit test. Why is this useful? Well, with just one attribute, which you can add multiple times to a test method, basically you can multiply the test cases without adding more code. This is powerful and convenient.

The following is an example from the nanoFramework System.IO.Hashing library.

```
static ArrayList _testData = new()
{
    new byte[] { },
    new byte[] { 0x01 },
    new byte[] { 0x31, 0x32, 0x33, 0x34, 0x35, 0x36, 0x37, 0x38, 0x39,
    0x26, 0x39, 0xF4, 0xCB },
    Encoding.UTF8.GetBytes("The quick brown fox jumps over the lazy dog")
};

[DataRow("Empty", 0, 0u)]
[DataRow("One", 1, 0xA505DF1Bu)]
[DataRow("Self-test inverse residue", 5, 0xFFFFFFFFu)]
[DataRow("String message digest", 8, 0x414FA339u)]
[TestMethod]
public void TestByteArrayHashing_00(
    string testName,
    int dataIndex,
    uint hash)
{
    OutputHelper.WriteLine($"Test: {testName}");

    var crc32 = new Crc32();

    crc32.Append((byte[])_testData[dataIndex]);
    Assert.AreEqual(hash, crc32.GetCurrentHashAsUInt32());
}
```

Now that you've seen an example, let's dig in more details on the [DataRow()] attribute. For starters it's very flexible in the sense that you can add any number of elements to it. You just have to use the same amount of elements on all of the ones in the same method. Next, each element can be of any type. You just can't involve any constructors or instantiations; like for example `new MyClass()` or `int[] { 0, 1, 2}` aren't valid. As one would expect, the types of the elements should match on all rows. Lastly, and this is the already mentioned exception, the test method declaration, instead of being empty, has to have a parameter list that matches in count and type whatever is in the `[DataRow()]` attributes for that method.

In the method body, you use the parameters as usual as you see fit.

What happens when the tests actually are run? Well, the test runner will notice that a test method is decorated with those `[DataRow()]` attributes and will call the test method for as many entries and will pass the content of the `[DataRow()]` to the test as parameters. It is incredibly simple but hugely effective, isn't it?

Running Tests with Visual Studio Test Explorer

Once you have written your tests, running them is the fun part; this is where you see the red/green (fail/pass) feedback and can verify that your code behaves as expected. The nanoFramework testing tools integrate with Visual Studio's Test Explorer, making the experience similar to running regular .NET unit tests.

Test Discovery

First, build your solution. After a successful build, Visual Studio should automatically discover your nanoFramework tests. Open the Test Explorer window (in Visual Studio, go to Test > Test Explorer if it's not already visible). You should see a list of your tests appear, organized by assembly and class name. For example, if you followed along with the sample `ExampleTests` class shown earlier, you might see an entry for the `NFUnitTest` assembly, under it a node for `ExampleTests`, and within that nodes for each test method (and setup/cleanup) that it found. Figure 8-2 shows how it might look in Test Explorer immediately after build (before running any tests).

In Figure 8-2, notice a few things:

- The project `NFUnitTest1` is listed (with the nanoFramework logo icon), and under it our test class `ExampleTests` appears. Test Explorer nests tests by class for easy navigation.

- All our [TestMethod]s are listed (e.g., TestCounterAndArrayValues, TestStringUtilities, etc.), and interestingly, the [Setup] and [Cleanup] methods are also listed as individual test entries (likely with a category or trait indicating they are setup/cleanup). The nanoFramework Test Adapter treats setup and cleanup methods as distinct test cases in the listing. This is a bit unusual compared to other test frameworks (where setup/teardown aren't shown as separate tests), but it makes sense here because the nanoFramework runner will report their execution and outcomes. If a Setup method fails (throws an exception or calls Skip), it will be marked accordingly in the results, so showing it in the UI is useful to pinpoint issues in initialization or cleanup.
- At this stage (just after build), none of the tests has run yet, so they might all appear in a neutral or not-run state. You may see a gray dash or no icon next to them initially.

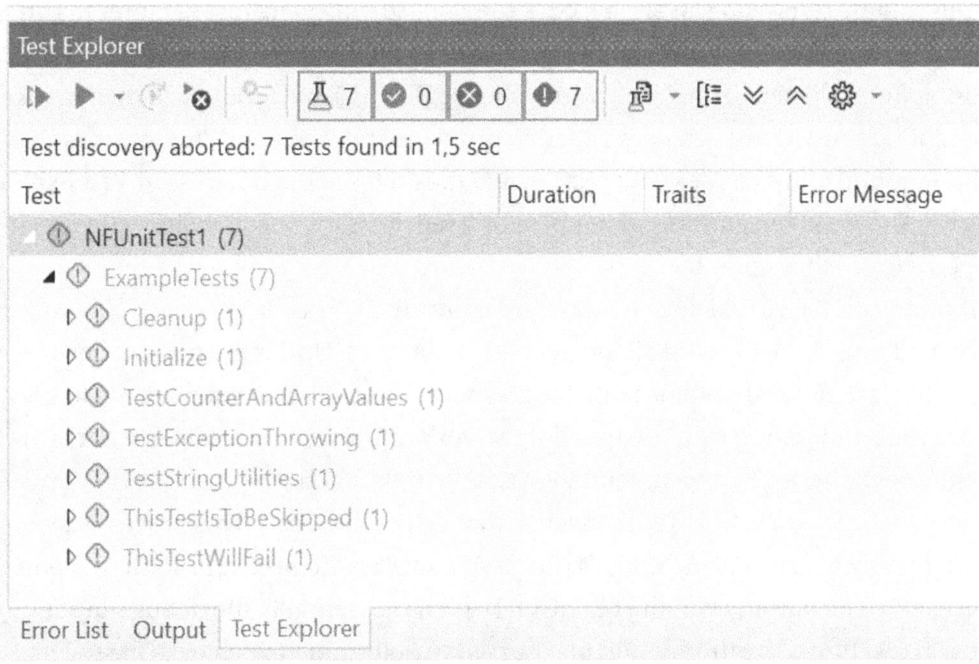

Figure 8-2. *Test Explorer with tests discovered*

If your tests do not appear in Test Explorer at this point, double-check that you have the `.runsettings` file present in the solution (at the root or in the same directory as the test project) with the proper content (especially the `<TargetFrameworkVersion>net48 </TargetFrameworkVersion>` entry). This setting is what triggers the Visual Studio test discovery mechanism to treat the assembly as containing tests, via a bit of a hack in the adapter. Also ensure your project's output name is `NFUnitTest.dll` (as already mentioned, this is a requirement by design) and that the nanoFramework extension and test adapter are correctly installed. If all this is set up, a rebuild of the solution can force test discovery to run again. Occasionally, it may require closing Visual Studio and manually deleting the `bin`, `obj`, and `.vs` folders. After reopening the solutions, restoring NuGets and rebuilding will cause the test discovery to eventually succeed.

Running Tests on the Virtual Device

By default, the tests will run on the virtual nanoCLR, which is effectively a "virtual device," provided as a .NET tool hosting a working version of the nanoFramework CLR. To run the tests, you can simply click the Run All button in Test Explorer to run everything, or you can run individual test classes or methods by selecting them and choosing Run Selected (or right-click and choose Run). Visual Studio will then invoke the nanoFramework Test Adapter, which in turn launches the nanoFramework's CLR in the background and executes your tests inside it. You'll see the progress in Test Explorer. Tests will show a green checkmark for pass or a red cross for fail, or a blue icon for skipped, etc., as they complete.

Running on the virtual device is fast and convenient. The virtual nanoCLR process is spawned automatically with all the needed assemblies. Under the hood, what's happening is that the adapter is launching a process and loading your test assembly (`NFUnitTest.dll`) along with the nanoFramework runtime libraries (like `mscorlib`) and the test framework's own assemblies (`nanoFramework.TestFramework.dll` and a special `nanoFramework.UnitTestLauncher` that drives the tests). This process executes independently of your Visual Studio's process; Visual Studio just waits for it to report back results. The output from the nanoCLR (which is essentially the debug output from the tests) is captured by the adapter and parsed to determine which tests passed or failed. We'll talk more about that in the architecture section, but suffice it to say that clicking Run in Test Explorer abstracts all these details. To you, it just looks like tests are running.

When the tests finish, you'll get the results in Test Explorer. Figure 8-3 shows an example after running all tests in our `ExampleTests` class.

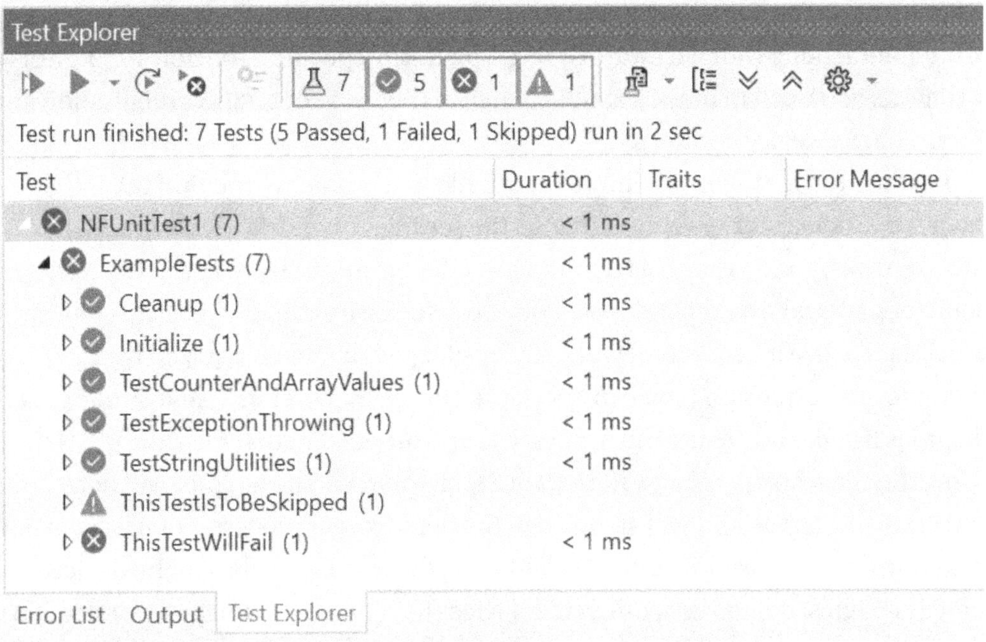

***Figure 8-3.** Test Explorer after running tests*

In Figure 8-3, we see the outcome of running tests. Five out of seven tests passed (green). The test `ThisTestWillFail` indeed failed, as expected, and is marked with a red X. The failure message "This is a deliberate failure for demonstration" (which we provided in the `Assert.IsTrue` call) is displayed as part of the test result. Additionally, if there were any stack trace or exception details, those would appear as well. One test is shown with a yellow warning icon indicating it was skipped. Skipped tests are neither red nor green; they're simply noted as not executed due to the conditions given. In our example, for demonstration purposes, we've just simply added an `Assert.SkipTest("Skipping test for demonstration");`. In practice, you would skip based on a particular situation, like hardware or configuration conditions.

Running Tests on Real Hardware

One of the powerful features of nanoFramework test platform is that you can run the very same tests on an actual microcontroller device. This is great for verifying not just logic but interactions with hardware or other platform-specific behavior. To run tests on a real device, you need to make a small change in the `.runsettings` configuration and, of course, have a device connected.

Open the `.runsettings` file (more on this file in a moment) and find the `<nanoFrameworkAdapter>` section. Change the setting `<IsRealHardware>false </IsRealHardware>` to `true`. This tells the test adapter that when you run the tests, it should deploy and execute them on a physical device instead of the virtual device. Make sure you have a nanoFramework device plugged in and recognized by the nanoFramework extension (you can check the Device Explorer in Visual Studio to see if the board is listed, and ensure the firmware is up-to-date for good measure).

Now run the tests again (e.g., *Run All* in Test Explorer). The adapter will detect that `IsRealHardware` is true and will go through the deployment process. You'll see Visual Studio's output or status indicating it's deploying the test assemblies to the device. Behind the scenes, it finds the connected device (usually via a serial port connection), reboots it into a mode ready for deployment, erases the previous app on the device, and uploads the required assemblies (your test assembly and the framework assemblies). The device then runs the `nanoFramework.UnitTestLauncher`, which in turn runs your tests on the device. The test output (those `OutputHelper.WriteLine` and assertion results) are captured via the device's debug channel (over the serial/USB connection). The Visual Studio adapter listens to that output and parses it just as it would for the emulator case.

From the user perspective, running on hardware doesn't look much different in Test Explorer. You still get pass/fail results in the UI. It might be a tad slower than the virtual device depending on the device speed and number of tests, but it's usually quite manageable. You'll see the same icons for tests passed, failed, and skipped. The key difference is simply that the code actually executed on your microcontroller, so you've validated the behavior and execution on real hardware. This is invaluable for tests that involve hardware-specific functionality (timing, peripherals, etc.) that the virtual device might not support or simulate. For instance, currently the virtual device doesn't support networking and APIs that access hardware like GPIOs, SPI/I^{2}C busses, and such.

You can switch back and forth between virtual device and hardware runs by toggling that `IsRealHardware` flag. Typically, while writing tests, you might use the emulator for quick cycles (especially if your tests are purely logic-based and don't need actual I/O) and then periodically run on the hardware to ensure everything works end to end. In continuous integration or automated testing, you might even set up separate runs; some projects run the fast logic tests on an emulator as part of every build and perhaps run a nightly suite on actual hardware for deeper validation.

Interpreting Test Results

The Test Explorer UI gives you a high-level view: green for passed tests, red for failures, yellow for skipped, etc. You can click any test in the list to see details. For example, clicking a failed test will show the exception message or assertion message that caused the failure and possibly a stack trace. In nanoFramework's case, because tests are executed remotely, you might not get a full traditional .NET stack trace, but the framework does output the exception message. In our failing test shown earlier, the message "This is a deliberate failure for demonstration" was shown because we provided it. If an assertion failed without a custom message, the framework might output something like "Expected X but got Y" or whatever is appropriate.

Because of limitations in the platform, unlike what happens in test projects for other platforms, Visual Studio won't be able to mark the tested code in the editor nor show the test pass/fail annotation near the test method name. But you'll get full mapping between the test explorer and the code view, meaning that if you double-click a test in the test tree view, Visual Studio will take the cursor to the corresponding method in the source code view.

Test Timing and Performance

Next to each test, you'll also see the time it took to run, usually in milliseconds. The test framework measures the execution time for each test method and reports it in the output. This is useful for identifying any slow tests. Keep in mind that on a microcontroller, even a few milliseconds might indicate a fair amount of work, and if using the virtual device, times will generally be faster.

Skipping Tests Outcome

If a test was skipped via `Assert.SkipTest`, Test Explorer will show it as skipped. It won't be green or red; it'll typically have an yellow warning icon. The reason provided in `SkipTest` (the message string) will be displayed so you know why it was skipped (e.g., "Double floating point not supported, skipping the test"). If a `[Setup]` method calls `SkipTest`, you'll see that the Setup is marked as skipped, and all the test methods in that class will be automatically skipped as well. The framework does this to avoid running tests that likely depend on that setup. In Test Explorer, you'd see every test in that class marked as skipped in one go.

Troubleshooting Discovery and Execution

If tests aren't showing up or running properly, check the Visual Studio Output window in the "Tests" section. The adapter may log some information there (especially if you increase logging verbosity in *.runsettings*, which we'll cover next). Common issues include:

- Misplaced or missing `.runsettings` file (remember to put it in the solution folder or the same folder as the test project so VS picks it up automatically).
- Incorrect assembly name (not `NFUnitTest`). Note that the assembly name usually matches the filename. And also that you can adjust the assembly name in the project properties view.
- Device connection issues (if running on hardware, ensure only one device is connected to avoid ambiguity or that the intended device is stated in `.runsettings`).
- Out-of-date nanoFramework extension or test adapter. Make sure you have the latest version for compatibility with your VS version.
- nanoCLR image (or firmware) with a mismatch or lacking an assembly that's being deployed as part of the test run.

For the most part, though, once configured, running tests is a smooth process.

Customizing Test Execution with .runsettings

Earlier, we mentioned the `.runsettings` file that is required for the nanoFramework tests to work. This file is not unique to nanoFramework. `.runsettings` is a general mechanism in Visual Studio to configure test runs, but it's absolutely critical here because the nanoFramework adapter uses it to know how to handle your tests. Let's examine what's in this file and what settings are supported.

A typical nanoFramework test `.runsettings` file looks like this:

```
<?xml version="1.0" encoding="utf-8"?>
<RunSettings>
   <!-- Configurations that affect the Test Framework -->
   <RunConfiguration>
       <MaxCpuCount>1</MaxCpuCount>
       <ResultsDirectory>.\TestResults</ResultsDirectory>
       <!-- Path relative to solution directory -->
       <TestSessionTimeout>120000</TestSessionTimeout>
       <!-- Milliseconds -->
       <TargetFrameworkVersion>Framework48</TargetFrameworkVersion>
   </RunConfiguration>
   <nanoFrameworkAdapter>
       <Logging>None</Logging>
       <IsRealHardware>false</IsRealHardware>
   </nanoFrameworkAdapter>
</RunSettings>
```

Let's break down the important settings here:

- `TargetFrameworkVersion`: This is required for test discovery. Do not change this! Leave it as `net48` even though your project is not actually targeting this .NET framework.
- `TargetPlatform`: This is also required for test discovery and run. Do not change this! Leave it as x64 even though your project might run in a microcontroller.

- `TestSessionTimeout:` This sets an upper limit (in milliseconds) for a test run session. In the previous snippet, it's 120000 which is 120 seconds. This means if the test run hasn't completed in 2 minutes, the adapter will consider it timed out and likely abort the run. This is a safety mechanism. For example, if your device crashes or hangs during a test, you don't want Visual Studio waiting forever. You can increase this if you have tests that legitimately take longer (for example, long-running integration tests or stress tests). If you find your tests being cut off, consider raising the timeout. But generally, unit tests should be quick, so two minutes should be more than sufficient for most scenarios.
- `ResultsDirectory:` This is where Test results (like the TRX file, if you export results, and any diagnostic data) will be stored. The default `.\TestResults` relative path is fine; you can customize it if needed. It doesn't affect the outcome of tests, just where logs go.

The following settings are specific to nanoFramework.

- `Logging:` This controls the verbosity of logs from the nanoFramework test adapter itself. In the previous file, it's set to `None`, meaning the adapter will not produce extra logging. If you're troubleshooting, you might change this to a higher level. Setting it to `Verbose` might cause the adapter to output detailed information about what it's doing (e.g., device discovery, deployment steps, raw output from device) to the Test output or Visual Studio's output window. Use `None` for normal usage to avoid clutter, and a higher level when diagnosing issues. Supported values are `None`, `Normal`, or `Verbose`.
- `IsRealHardware:` This boolean controls whether tests run on the virtual device or on a real device. `False` means use the virtual device; `True` means use the first real hardware device found. Take a look at the next setting to control this. This is the only thing you need to toggle to switch the execution target; everything else in your tests stays the same. Keep in mind, if requested to run on an hardware device and if no device is connected, the test run will fail. Now if you set to `false` and you intended to test on hardware, you might wonder why your hardware LED isn't blinking; it's because the tests actually ran on your PC. So double-check this flag when you switch contexts.

- `RealHardwarePort`: This setting is only honored in case `IsRealHardware` is set to `true`. Here you specify the hardware port of the nano device that will run the tests, for example `COM3`. If none is specified, a device detection is performed, and the first available one will be used.
- `CLRVersion`: Specify the nanoCLR version to use for the virtual device. If not specified, the latest available one will be used. This is meant to be used in situations where a specific nanoCLR is required like testing a new feature in development. In the virtual device setup stage, the test framework will try to download the specified version and will run the tests using it.
- `PathToLocalCLRInstance`: Specify the path to a local nanoCLR instance. If not specified, the default one installed with nanoclr CLR will be used. This is again useful when it's necessary to use a specific version of the nanoCLR that is not available for download in the cloud repository.
- `UsePreviewClr`: If set to `True` when updating the virtual device, the latest preview version will be used.
- `RunnerExtraArguments`: Extra arguments to pass to the test runner, which, in turn, will use when launching the virtual device. These are added to the ones that the test runner composes to start the virtual device.

For Visual Studio to automatically use these settings, the file should be placed at the solution level or in the same directory as the test project file (the `.nfproj` for the Unit Test project). Typically, the nanoFramework test template puts it in the test project folder. Visual Studio will find it there by convention. If you have multiple `.runsettings` files (not common and not recommended, unless you really have to have different test run configurations), you can explicitly select one in Visual Studio's Test menu (Test > Configure Run Settings).

Customizing for CI/Pipeline

If you run tests via command line (`vstest.console.exe`) or in a CI pipeline (like Azure DevOps), you can specify the path to the `.runsettings` file in the command arguments, for example, `vstest.console NFUnitTest.dll /Settings:nanoFramework.runsettings`. In Azure DevOps YAML, if you are using the `VSTest@3` task, you can use a task parameter point to the intended `.runsettings` file. This ensures the adapter knows whether to use real hardware or not, what timeout to apply, etc., even when running automated. Typically, in a CI scenario, you'll run on the virtual device (since the build agent likely doesn't have a device attached). That's fine, and it will catch a good portion of issues.

As an example, here's a snippet of a YAML file for Azure DevOps illustrating the described usage:

```
- task: VisualStudioTestPlatformInstaller@1
  displayName: 'Visual Studio Test Platform Installer'
  inputs:
    versionSelector: latestStable

- task: VSTest@2
  displayName: 'Running Unit Tests'
  inputs:
    testSelector: 'testAssemblies'
    testAssemblyVer2: |
      **\NFUnitTest.dll
      **\*Tests*.dll
      !**\obj\**
      !**\TestAdapter\**
      !**\NFUnitTest_DummyAdapter\**
      !**\nanoFramework.TestFramework\**
    searchFolder: '$(System.DefaultWorkingDirectory)'
    platform: '$(BuildPlatform)'
    configuration: '$(BuildConfiguration)'
    diagnosticsEnabled: true
    vsTestVersion: toolsInstaller
    runSettingsFile: '${{ parameters.unitTestRunsettings }}'
```

The first task installs the Visual Studio Test platform (required for running the vstest), and the second task is running the tests. There are various parameters to configure all sorts of details. Most of those in the previous snippet are coming from variables or parameters. Notice the entry to configure `.runsettings`.

Beyond traditional unit tests, there are also integration tests that touch the hardware aspects deeply. There is an experimental version of a nanoFramework build agent for Azure DevOps that a pipeline can connect to, which acts as proxy to a real device. The agent has a manifest of the devices capabilities, and the pipeline can query that and deploy specific tests and/or test configuration accordingly. This opens up the possibility to install entire test rigs with several connected nano devices. As one can imagine, this is a powerful feature that allows virtually infinite test possibilities and can cover the most complex test and validation scenarios.

Analyzing Test Results and Debugging Tests

After running your tests, you'll spend time analysing the results, especially if some tests failed. The nanoFramework test framework outputs information that can help you understand failures, but debugging on an embedded device has some unique aspects. In this section, we'll cover how to read test results, interpret common issues, and how you can debug your tests or the code under test, given the platform's constraints.

Reading Test Output

When a test fails, the test runner will output a line indicating the failure, the test method name, and the reason (typically the exception message). For example, if an assertion fails because two values were not equal, you might see something like this:

```
Test failed: ThisTestWillFail, This is a deliberate failure for
demonstration or if no custom message was given, maybe:
```

```
Test failed: CalculateSumTest, Expected 5 but got 7
```

The exact wording depends on the assert. In our earlier failing example, we purposely provided a message, so it used that. If an unexpected exception occurs in your code (say a `NullReferenceException` or something not caught), the message might just be that exception's message or type. All such output is captured by the adapter and usually displayed in the Test Explorer's result details view.

If a test passes, the framework also outputs a line:

```
Test passed: TestCounterAndArrayValues, <ticks>
```

The <ticks> is a number representing the time it took, in CPU ticks (which at 10,000 ticks per millisecond for .NET DateTime ticks, corresponds to the execution time). Visual Studio might not show this raw output line unless you go looking in diagnostic logs, but it uses it to show the timing. For skipped tests, the output line contains *"Test skipped"* (or the skip reason as an exception message).

Now, Visual Studio's Test Explorer UI is user-friendly, but sometimes you want to see the raw output as well (especially for debugging). You can enable Verbose logging as mentioned earlier via .runsettings, which will cause all the device debug output to be logged. Then, you can check the Output window (under Tests) or any log files to see the sequence of events. For instance, you'd see the OutputHelper.WriteLine messages from your tests in the output, not just the final pass/fail lines. This can be incredibly helpful if a test is failing and you're not sure why. By sprinkling a few OutputHelper.WriteLine calls in your test or even in the code under test, you can trace what's happening when running through the Test Explorer.

The nature of failures in nanoFramework tests will largely mirror those in unit tests of similar test frameworks, with a few differences:

- *Assertion failures:* If an Assert.X fails, it throws an exception internally (like AssertionFailedException). The test framework catches that and marks the test as failed, outputting the message. The exception type isn't always exposed to you, but the message is. So you'll typically rely on the message to know what went wrong (expected vs actual, etc.). If you provided a custom message, that's what you'll see; if not, the framework's default message should give enough clue. In some cases, if the default message isn't helpful, you might re-run the test with additional logging to investigate (more on debugging soon).
- *Unhandled exceptions:* If your code under test throws an exception that wasn't caught inside the test method (or by an Assert), it will bubble up and also cause the test to fail. The output will say something like "Test failed: MethodName, <exception message>." The type of exception might be discernible from the message if it's included (e.g., "Object reference not set to an instance of an object"

implies a `NullReferenceException`). Since nanoFramework is a subset of .NET, the exception messages can be slightly different or less detailed, but generally you'll know what happened. In such cases, you'd need to fix the code under test (or adjust the test if the exception was actually expected and you didn't use `Assert.ThrowsException`).

- *Setup or cleanup failures:* If a `[Setup]` method fails (throws an exception or fails an assert), none of the tests in that class will run. The Test Explorer will show the Setup as failed. Because our adapter lists Setup as a test, you'll directly see it. If Setup fails, effectively all tests might be marked as skipped or not run (since the framework can't safely execute them). Similarly, if a `[Cleanup]` fails at the end, the tests might have run (so you'll see their results, possibly all passed), but then the cleanup failure will also be reported. This situation is a bit unusual (tests passed but cleanup failed; you'd consider that an overall failure or at least something to fix, because it indicates your test didn't tidy up correctly or some condition at the end was wrong).
- *Skipped tests:* If you see tests marked as skipped, read the skip reason. It's likely something intentional, like a hardware capability not present. This is by design to let you know "we didn't even run this test because it doesn't apply." If you see an unexpected skip (i.e., you didn't call `SkipTest` anywhere, yet a test was skipped), that would be odd and usually an indication of some failure in the platform or failure to launch the virtual device for some reason. So, this is pretty much under your control.

Debugging Strategies

Debugging nanoFramework tests is a bit different from debugging regular .NET tests due to the remote execution. In a typical .NET Core unit test, for example, you can right-click a test and choose Debug, and it will run that test under the debugger, allowing you to step through the test code. In the nanoFramework case, when you click Run, it's actually launching an external process (nanoCLR) or using a device. The code isn't running under the Visual Studio managed debugger. So, the usual interactive debugging (setting breakpoints, stepping line by line) is not available when running tests through Test Explorer.

However, this doesn't mean you cannot debug your code; you just have to do it differently.

Creating a Debug Test Harness

For debugging complex logic, you might create a separate project for a nanoFramework application (not a unit test one) for which you add a reference to the unit test project or simply link the test classes code files. Essentially, in `Program.Main()` call the test(s) method that you want to debug, set breakpoints, and debug on the device as usual. This is more ad hoc but can be effective if you really need step-by-step debugging on hardware for something that's hard to diagnose via logs. After solving the issue, you can remove that harness.

Using Logging and Output

Often, straightforward print debugging is sufficient. As suggested, scatter `OutputHelper.WriteLine` statements to trace values and execution flow and then run the tests (without a debugger, just normal run) and inspect the output. Because the output is captured (probably better to adjust that setting to `Verbose`), you can infer where things went wrong. This is especially useful when debugging on the actual device, where attaching a debugger might interfere with real-time behavior or isn't feasible at all.

Platform Caveats and Limitations

When debugging nanoFramework tests, keep in mind the following:

- If running on hardware, you're subject to the device's limitations. For example, if an infinite loop occurs, the device might need a hard reset. The `TestSessionTimeout` will eventually abort the run on the PC side, but your device might still be stuck. You'll have to reset it manually. So be careful with long loops or blocking waits in tests.
- The device's resources are limited. If you allocate a lot of memory in tests or have memory leaks, you could hit out-of-memory issues, which manifest as test failures or device reboots. If a device

spontaneously reboots (you might notice test run aborts abruptly), check if the test might have caused a crash (e.g., invalid pointer in native code, or an assertion in native code). These are harder to debug; you may need to simplify and isolate such tests.

- The virtual device is a great testing ground, but it's not a perfect emulator of hardware. Some APIs are not implemented (like networking as already mentioned, or even GPIO) or timing might be slightly differ. These are another reasons to occasionally run on real hardware for confidence.
- Visual Studio doesn't allow mix-and-match debugging: you can't simultaneously use the nanoFramework device debugger and the Test Explorer's runner easily. It's one or the other at a time. So plan whether you're in "test run mode" or "interactive debug mode."
- There is no real code coverage data. This is because of platform limitations that make it overcomplicated and expensive to track and compute coverage.

Under the Hood: How the nanoFramework Unit Test Platform Works

So, how does nanoFramework's test runner actually find your tests, run them on a device or emulator, and report the results to Visual Studio? In this section, we'll explore the architecture and sequence of operations that occur when you build and run nanoFramework unit tests. This is the "juicy details" part for those who want a deeper understanding. Feel free to skip this on a first read and come back later, but if you're curious, let's dive in.

Visual Studio Test Adapter

The integration with Visual Studio is achieved via a custom Test Adapter (`nanoFramework.TestAdapter`) that plugs into the Visual Studio Test Platform (also used by MSTest, xUnit, and others). This adapter implements interfaces for test discovery and execution defined by the VS test framework (namely `ITestDiscoverer` and `ITestExecutor`). When you build a project, Visual Studio invokes all registered test adapters to see if any tests are present. The nanoFramework adapter is triggered for any assemblies that match certain criteria, specifically, as we discussed, if the assembly's target framework is marked as `net48` and it's likely an output of a `.nfproj`. There's no official nanoFramework test project type known to VS, so the adapter uses that `TargetFrameworkVersion` trick to know it should inspect the assembly.

Test Discovery Phase

During the discovery phase, the adapter needs to identify what tests exist so it can list them in Test Explorer. For regular .NET frameworks, you might load the assembly via reflection and look for attributes. Interestingly, the nanoFramework adapter takes a two-pronged approach:

- It tries to treat the nanoFramework test assembly as a .NET assembly (because, at the end of the day, it actually is a .NET IL assembly, just with a different BCL). The adapter can load it using reflection in the context of the VS process and look for types with the `[TestClass]` attribute, methods with `[TestMethod]`, and so on. Since the attribute classes (`TestClassAttribute`, etc.) are defined in the `nanoFramework.TestFramework` (which is also a .NET assembly), the adapter has to be careful. It likely doesn't want to fully execute anything, just inspect metadata. It compares attribute names or uses the `.FullName` property to avoid needing the actual attribute types loaded in the adapter process. Essentially, it's scanning for anything that looks like a test attribute by name.
- Additionally (this is unique), the adapter searches for the `.nfproj` project file on disk and then parses the C# source files to map test method names to file names and line numbers. Why? Because nanoFramework PDBs (which are in a special PDBX format) might not be trivially readable by VS for source info. By scanning the source code, the adapter can find, say, that `ExampleTests.cs` contains a method `TestCounterAndArrayValues` and thus maps that method to a filename and line. This allows it to supply Visual Studio with the exact location of each test method. That's why when you double-click

a test in Test Explorer, it can open the right source file and highlight the method, even though the test is for an embedded project. This is a clever solution to ensure a smooth and friendly developer experience.

- The adapter uses certain conventions to simplify its job: it assumes the test assembly is named `NFUnitTest` and that the output directory is a subfolder of the project (which is typically true). It then finds the `.nfproj` file in the parent directories and reads all `.cs` files from it. These conventions avoid the need for complex project system integration.

Once the adapter collects all test cases, it creates a list of `TestCase` objects (each includes the name, source assembly, and the identifier of the executor to use) and returns them to Visual Studio. Visual Studio then populates the Test Explorer UI with these test cases. At this point, the tests are just identified, not run yet. This corresponds to what we saw in one of the first sections of this chapter. Tests are populated in Test Explorer only after the Solution build is successful.

Test Execution Phase

When you actually run tests (via Test Explorer or vstest console), the VS test framework calls the adapter's executor with the list of tests to run. The nanoFramework adapter's `ITestExecutor` implementation then orchestrates running those tests either on the emulator or on hardware, depending on settings.

What happens for each context is described next.

Running on the Virtual Device

The adapter will determine if the `nanoclr` .NET tool is installed. If not, it will install it. Next it will ensure that the latest nanoCLR is installed by querying the cloud repository. If it's not, it will update it. This is the moment where those settings related to the usage of preview version and specific version come into play. The adapter will look for these are will honor the requested settings.

Following this introductory ceremony, it needs to supply the nanoCLR with all the assemblies. For nanoFramework, code runs from special `.pe` files (which are compiled, compact IL binaries as we've seen in a previous chapter). The adapter gathers the necessary .pe files: NFUnitTest.pe, nanoFramework.TestFramework.pe (containing the Assert and attribute implementations), nanoFramework.UnitTestLauncher.pe (the test runner that lives on the device side), and any other libraries (plus mscorlib.pe). It then launches the nanoCLR process with these .pe files passed as command-line arguments. The nanoCLR, when it starts up, will load those assemblies and begin executing the one marked as startup (which is the UnitTestLauncher). The adapter uses the .NET Process class to start the nanoclr tool and redirects its standard output and error streams. This way, any OutputHelper.WriteLine from the nanoFramework (which goes to debug console, but in the tool appears on stdout) will be captured. The adapter waits for the process to exit or for the timeout to elapse. If the process runs longer than TestSessionTimeout, the adapter will kill it (that's why that setting is important: to avoid hung processes).

Running on Real Hardware

The adapter communicates with the device through the nanoFramework debugging engine (which is part of the extension). It will first find an attached device. Then it essentially performs a deploy: erases the existing program on the device and writes the new assemblies to it. Once deployment is done, the adapter instructs the device to execute. The UnitTestLauncher on the device then runs the tests. As the device executes, it sends Debug messages over the wire. The adapter subscribes to these messages via the DebugEngine events. It accumulates the output in a buffer until it sees a special marker indicating the tests are done (in the current implementation, after finishing, the UnitTestLauncher writes "Finished."). While the device is running tests, Visual Studio might show tests as "Running..." in the explorer. When done, or on timeout, the adapter will disconnect.

Despite these differences, the output format of test results is the same in both cases, because it's produced by the UnitTestLauncher logic. The test launcher prints lines like Test passed: <Name>, <Ticks> or Test failed: <Name>, <ExceptionMessage> for each test (including setups and cleanups). It's also worth noting that the launcher runs tests in a specific order: for each [TestClass], it invokes all [Setup] methods, then all [TestMethod]s, and then all [Cleanup] methods. This means if you have multiple setup methods, they *all* run before any test, though as mentioned we typically only use one. It's the same for cleanup. Also, it does this per class; it creates a new instance of the test class (or uses static methods directly) for each test class.

Parsing Results

Once the adapter has the output from the nanoCLR or device, it parses it. It looks for each line that starts with "Test passed:" and "Test failed:" and "Test skipped:." It then correlates that with the test cases it discovered earlier. For example, if it sees `Test failed: ThisTestWillFail, This is a deliberate failure for demonstration`, it knows that corresponds to the test case with name `ExampleTests.ThisTestWillFail`. It then marks that test as failed in the results, attaches the "This is a deliberate failure for demonstration" message as the error message, and if possible, sets the duration from the tick count that was also in the output. If there's an exception type or stack trace info (not much beyond message usually), it would include that. For passed tests, it logs the duration. For skipped tests, it would mark them as skipped (the adapter might treat a "skip" as a special outcome or possibly as a passed test with a special trait indicating skip).

The adapter treats Setup and Cleanup a bit specially: since they show up as test cases, their pass/fail will be reported. If a Setup fails, the adapter automatically marks the dependent `TestMethod` cases as skipped because they never ran.

After parsing, the adapter passes the results to Visual Studio's test framework, which in turn updates the UI (and any log files, etc.). This completes the cycle.

In Figure 8-4, we can see a high-level representation of the test framework architecture showing the pieces: on one side Visual Studio and vstest, on the other side the nanoCLR (either the virtual device or hardware) running the tests, with the adapter as the bridge. The key point is that the nanoFramework Unit Test Platform is layered on top of the existing VS test infrastructure. This is a rather complex orchestration of several software blocks. Fortunately, as far as developers are concerned, all these pieces are conveniently packaged in a NuGet, ready to consume and with all the complexity largely invisible.

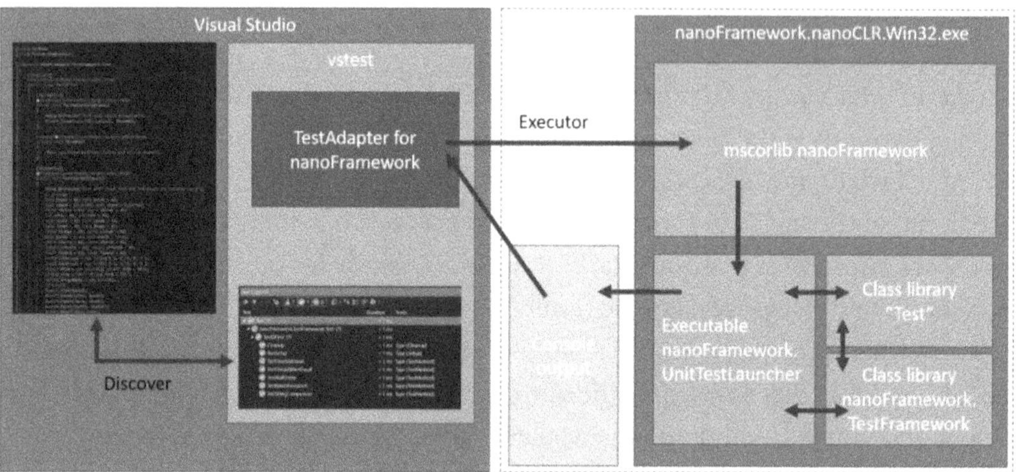

Figure 8-4. *Test framework architecture*

Known Limitations

Given this architecture, there are a few limitations or things to be aware of (some we have already touched):

- *Assembly Naming*: As noted, a test assembly must be named `NFUnitTest`. This is because the `UnitTestLauncher` in the device explicitly does `Assembly.Load("NFUnitTest")` to load a test assembly.
- *Deployment Folders:* The test adapter expects the compiled `.pe` files to be in the default output location (like `bin\Debug`). You shouldn't move or change the output path of the test project; just use the standard project structure so the adapter can locate the files.
- *virtual nanoCLR vs Hardware Differences:* The virtual device is super useful, but it doesn't implement everything a real device might have. For example, networking is limited. If your tests try to open a socket or connect to WiFi, those won't work on the virtual device. You'd need to run on actual hardware for those. Also, timing might differ, as the PC is a much faster machine.

- *Visual Studio Compatibility:* The test framework works with Visual Studio 2019 and 2022. It's not supported in VS2017. Therefore, the recommendation it to always use the latest VS for best results. Also, ensure you have the nanoFramework VS extension installed; it provides the project system and device debug engine that the adapter leverages.
- *Execution Order and Selection:* Currently, if you run a single test from the Test Explorer (say you right-click one test and choose Run), the adapter doesn't actually have a way to execute just that one test on the device. The `UnitTestLauncher`, as implemented, runs all tests in the assembly. The adapter, knowing which one you wanted, will parse results and report only that one (and maybe mark others as not run or ignored). From the user perspective, it seems to run just that test, but in reality, the whole suite ran under the hood. This isn't usually a problem (the tests are fast), but it's a nuance. There's no efficient way yet to run a subset of tests on the device because the device side just runs them all. If you have side-effect tests, keep this in mind (they'll run, even if you didn't explicitly choose them, as soon as you run any test in the same assembly).
- *Assertion Implementation:* The Assert methods in nanoFramework are implemented to throw exceptions when conditions fail. This is a simple and effective strategy. However, one must remember that because of this, if you put multiple `Assert.X` calls in one test, the test will stop at the first failing assert (since it throws). Any subsequent asserts in that method won't execute. So sometimes it's better to structure tests as one logical assertion per test method for clarity. Or if you do have multiple asserts, know that you might only see the first failure. This is standard in unit testing but worth mentioning.
- *Test Class Instances:* Test methods are invoked as static. In our example, we didn't use instance fields (we used static fields). If you prefer instance fields (nonstatic), ensure your test methods aren't static. The framework creates an object of your test class for you. If something isn't working with state between setup and test, try using static fields as a workaround. This can sometimes circumvent any scoping issues with how the reflection invokes methods.

Lifecycle Summary

To put it all together, here's the typical lifecycle when you run tests:

1. **Build**: You build the solution. The nanoFramework test project compiles your tests into IL, and then the nanoFramework tooling post-processes it into a `.pe` file (plus `.pdbx` for symbols). The NuGet ensures the test adapter and nanoCLR tool are available.

2. **Discovery**: Visual Studio calls the nanoFramework adapter to find tests in the output dll (which it thinks is .NET Framework 4.8 due to the `.runsettings` hack). The adapter loads the assembly metadata, finds test classes and methods (via attributes), uses the `.nfproj` and source code to get file info, and returns the list of tests to VS. Now you see tests in Test Explorer.

3. **Execution (virtual device)**: You initiate a run (all or some tests). The adapter prepares the nanoCLR process and required assemblies, starts the process, and feeds it the assemblies.

4. **Execution (Device)**: The adapter tries to find the requested nano device (or performs a general search and attaches to the first one), deploys the assemblies, and starts execution via the nanoFramework debugging engine.

5. **Testing**: On the target (virtual or real device), the `UnitTestLauncher` loads `NFUnitTest` assembly, and for each class with `[TestClass]` it runs setup(s), then each test method, and then cleanup(s). It catches any exceptions from tests to determine pass/fail and prints results via `Debug.WriteLine`.

6. **Collection**: The adapter collects the output. For emulator, it reads stdout of the process. For hardware, it captures debug messages from the device.

7. **Result Processing**: The adapter parses the output lines, matches them to test cases, and creates `TestResult` objects. It signals back to VS which tests passed, failed, or were skipped, along with messages and durations.

8. **Display**: Visual Studio updates the Test Explorer UI, and the developer sees the outcomes.

9. **Cleanup**: The adapter stops the nanoCLR process or, in the case of hardware, leaves the device in whatever state the tests left it (often the program just ends, and the device may restart or await further commands). If you run tests again, it will redeploy fresh.

This process happens very quickly, typically within seconds for a handful of tests. The architecture is robust enough that you can integrate it into automated build pipelines. As shown in the references, you can run vstest.console.exe on a build agent with the nanoFramework adapter, and the tests will run (virtual device on the agent) and produce standard TRX test results. This means that nanoFramework projects can have continuous integration and unit test checks just like any other .NET project, which is a big win for quality in embedded development.

Finally, to circle back to a higher level, the creation of this unit test framework for nanoFramework involved tackling many challenges. The end result is a system where, as a developer, you get a familiar and streamlined experience (write tests in C#, run them, get green/red feedback), even though under the hood it's running on tiny microcontrollers or a simulated environment. This is a testament to the power of .NET and Visual Studio, along with the effort of the nanoFramework community to bring modern development practices to embedded development.

Summary

In this chapter, you learned how to use the nanoFramework Test Framework to write and run unit tests for embedded C# projects. Testing in nanoFramework isn't just for perfectionists; it's a great way to save time and headaches, especially when you start making changes or adding new features to your firmware or C# projects. Even with the somewhat reduced feature set, the ability to quickly check that your code still works as intended is invaluable. And since the syntax and concepts mirror what you find in the bigger .NET world, it's easy to get started if you've done any kind of C# development before.

We covered setting up a test project via the provided template, writing test classes with the appropriate attributes and using a wide range of assertion methods to validate behaviour. We then saw how to execute tests using Visual Studio's Test Explorer, whether on the virtual device or on actual hardware devices, and how to interpret the results, from reading pass/fail outcomes and assertion messages to leveraging code highlight and output logs to diagnose issues. We also discussed strategies for debugging tests given the unique constraints of running code on microcontrollers.

The final section peeled back the covers on the test framework's architecture, explaining how test discovery and execution are implemented. We now understand that when we click Run, a lot is happening behind the scenes.

With this knowledge, you're now well-equipped to create a comprehensive suite of unit tests for your nanoFramework projects. Writing tests will not only improve the reliability of your code but also speed up your development; you can catch regressions quickly by running tests after each change and confidently refactor knowing your test harness will alert you if something breaks. Even on resource-constrained devices, nanoFramework makes modern testing practices possible.

Additional Resources

Learn more at the following locations:

GitHub repo: `https://github.com/nanoframework/nanoFramework.TestFramework`

MSTest: `https://learn.microsoft.com/en-us/dotnet/core/testing/unit-testing-csharp-with-mstest`

Visual Studio Test Platform: `https://github.com/microsoft/vstest`

Azure DevOps VSTest task: `https://learn.microsoft.com/en-us/azure/devops/pipelines/tasks/reference/vstest-v3?view=azure-pipelines`

CHAPTER 9

Advanced Coding Topics

Ready to take your embedded .NET nanoFramework projects to the next level? In this chapter, you'll unlock advanced coding techniques tailored for resource-constrained devices—mastering memory management, resource cleanup, threading and synchronization, execution constraints, and dependency injection. Dive in, experiment with these strategies, and see how they can transform your firmware into efficient, reliable, and maintainable solutions for real-world embedded challenges.

Advanced Memory and GC Optimization

.NET nanoFramework uses a lightweight mark-and-sweep garbage collection mechanism. As covered in Chapter 2, when a GC cycle starts, it briefly pauses all executing threads and then proceeds in two phases:

- **Mark Phase:** The collector starts at root references—static variables and thread stacks—to trace and mark which objects are still reachable.
- **Sweep Phase:** It scans the entire managed heap, freeing memory occupied by objects that were not marked as live. Optionally, the collector can compact the heap by relocating live objects to eliminate fragmentation, which you can do by passing true to `GC.Run()`.

This approach is simple and efficient for constrained devices, but as fragmentation builds up over time, and depending on the complexity and memory usage your code does, the execution can face inefficient memory use and, possibly, unpredictable pauses.

Fragmentation happens when multiple freed memory blocks lie between active objects. Even if total free memory is sufficient, you might still encounter allocation failures because there's no single contiguous block large enough for the request allocation. This fragmentation is common in mark-and-sweep collectors unless compaction is used. With microcontrollers that have smaller RAM, this may trigger frequent and unpredictable GC cycles.

J. Simões, *Embedded Systems with .NET nanoFramework*, https://doi.org/10.1007/979-8-8688-2096-0_9

It's important to understand and clarify that this is not a flaw; rather, it's a feature of mark-and-sweep GC. And, this will only have a negative impact on applications with high performance demands, in which case the GC kicks in. Code-sensitive parts can have a negative impact on performance in the sense that in that particular run, the overall execution time will be extended with *that* extra time for the GC run. If that's not the case, then you're good, and you won't even notice that GC is there and doing its job.

Strategies to Reduce Fragmentation and Preserve Predictability

Being aware of all this, let's discuss strategies to reduce fragmentation and preserve predictability on GC runs.

One of the most obvious ones is using shared buffers and object pooling. This consists on pre-allocating reusable objects and reclaiming them manually instead of creating and discarding them dynamically. For instance, if your application uses buffers extensively, you can create a large enough byte array in the class constructor and store it in a class field. In your code, just use that readily available buffer wherever you need instead of creating buffers again and again, which is (CPU and execution-wise) expensive and will eventually cause GC runs. Remember that you can access `byte[]` using the index and that most APIs that take `byte[]` as a parameter have an overload that allows you to specify the start index and length.

The same is true for other variables that are used throughout a class or an application. Consider instantiating them once and reusing them where needed. A typical example would be a variable that you use inside an event handler to perform a certain comparison. Instead of declaring it in the event handler, do it beforehand and just use it. Mind the scope as the field has to be reachable. That will not only make the execution slightly faster (because there is no "wasted" time spent on creating that variable) but will also prevent the heap to be left with "holes" for the various instances of that variable, which contributes to fragmentation and eventually a GC run and compaction.

The key takeaway to this strategy is that you should be mindful of how this works and the implications. This doesn't necessarily mean you have to be paranoid about this and start declaring every object up front. That will disfigure your code, possibly making you lose the benefits from object context and other C# features. Be aware of it, and weigh the advantages of pre-allocating. Then keep coding as you usually do.

Another strategy is controlling GC invocation. This could be something you can do, for example, during development to take the pulse of how the application execution behaves and the impact from GC runs, if any.

During development, you can activate GC logging with `GC.EnableGCMessages(true)` and call `GC.Run(true)` in strategic places to force a compacting collection. This would be called in a location where there is nothing performance critical happening and at a time that the system has no penalty to having the GC take its time to run. Looking at the output of the GC messages lets you inspect fragmentation trends in real time and fine-tune memory usage patterns, if needed. Controlling when the GC runs removes the potential downsides of random and—possibly—unwanted executions.

No matter how well-designed the app is, if you don't measure memory behavior, you're flying blind. This is particularly relevant during development as a quality metric. Plus, looking at this gives you invaluable insight into fragmentation patterns and can point out memory leaks or unwanted behavior.

Here's some code capturing the previous ideas:

```
GC.EnableGCMessages(true);
uint freeAfter = GC.Run(true);
Debug.WriteLine($"After compact GC, free = {freeAfter} bytes");
```

The ESP32 platform includes an API that gives you insights on the native memory heap (the one reserved for the C/C++ IDF code). The previous could be adapted to an improved version like this:

```
NativeMemory.GetMemoryInfo(
    NativeMemory.MemoryType.Internal,
    out uint total,
    out uint free,
    out uint largestFree);

Debug.WriteLine(
   $"NativeMem total={total} free={free} largest={largestFree}");

Debug.WriteLine($"Managed free={GC.Run(false)}");
```

You should implement the `IDisposable` interface and the `Dispose` pattern when your class holds onto unmanaged resources (such as file handles, sockets, or memory obtained via native code) or it owns other managed objects that themselves implement

IDisposable. By doing so, you enable deterministic cleanup—freeing resources promptly rather than waiting for the finalizer or, worse, never.

If your class only uses managed resources and has no unmanaged resources, you don't need a finalizer. If it's sealed (noninheritable), you can simply implement Dispose() to dispose of its fields. However, if you aim for extensibility, you should implement the full Dispose pattern with an overload of Dispose(bool) to allow derived classes to clean up properly.

The following is an example of a class that manages a SpiDevice to show proper resource cleanup using the Dispose pattern. For readability and focus, only the relevant methods are fully listed.

```
public class SpiSensorManager : IDisposable
{
    private bool _disposed = false;
    private SpiDevice? _spi;
    private readonly SpiConnectionSettings _settings;

    public SpiSensorManager(int busId, int chipSelectLine)
    {
        // create SpiConnectionSettings
        // instanciate SpiDevice
        // other code
    }

    public byte ReadRegister(byte register)
    {
        if (_disposed)
        {
            throw new ObjectDisposedException();
        }
        // perform SPI operation
    }

    protected virtual void Dispose(bool disposing)
    {
        if (_disposed)
        {
```

```
            return;
        }

        if (disposing)
        {
            // Dispose managed resources
            _spi?.Dispose();
            _spi = null;
        }

        // No unmanaged resources to clean up in this example

        _disposed = true;
    }

    public void Dispose()
    {
        Dispose(true);
        GC.SuppressFinalize(this);
    }

    ~SpiSensorManager()
    {
        Dispose(false);
    }
}
```

Let's go through the code and the relevant details. The class `SpiSensorManager` encapsulates an `SpiDevice`, which itself implements `IDisposable` and holds unmanaged, platform-specific resources (hardware handles for the SPI microcontroller peripheral and possibly RAM buffers for DMA transfers). Therefore, we need to clean it up explicitly to avoid resource leaks.

The constructor stores `SpiConnectionSettings` and invokes `SpiDevice.Create()` to initialize the SPI interface. This is where unmanaged resources are obtained and must eventually be released.

The method `ReadRegister()` checks whether the object has already been disposed, throwing `ObjectDisposedException` if so. This prevents invalid usage after cleanup, aligning with best practices.

The main thing with the pattern Dispose(bool disposing) is that when disposing is true, we are executing deterministic cleanup via Dispose(). We call _spi.Dispose() to clean up managed and unmanaged resources held by the SPI device. Since SpiDevice.Dispose() handles unmanaged cleanup internally, we do not need extra code in the false execution path of the finalizer.

For safety, the finalizer ~SpiSensorManager() ensures that unmanaged resources are not leaked if Dispose() is never called by the code that was using the SpiSensorManager class. It calls Dispose(false) to clean up unmanaged resources without touching managed ones (which may already be finalized).

Lastly, we are suppressing the finalizer in Dispose(). After calling Dispose(true), we invoke GC.SuppressFinalize(this). The goal is to prevent the finalizer from running later, to optimize GC performance, and avoid redundant cleanup.

Here's a summary recapping what will happen on all possible situations:

- *Not disposed manually:* Finalizer ensures cleanup in the background.
- *Disposed early:* Dispose() cleans resources deterministically and suppresses the finalizer.
- *Disposed repeatedly:* Safe, subsequent calls detect disposal via _disposed, and no further operations are performed.

This pattern ensures that your classes manage both managed and unmanaged resources properly—even on resource-constrained embedded devices where cleanups like these are crucial for stability and reliability.

As a final note on the Dispose pattern usage, recall that you can take advantage of a handy C# feature that was designed to take care of resource cleanup *automagically*: the using statement. When you wrap your SpiSensorManager in a using, it guarantees that Dispose() is called at the end of the block—even if an exception is thrown!

Here's how you use the concise C# using declaration syntax:

```
public void DemoSpiUsage()
{
    using var manager = new SpiSensorManager(1, 12);
    byte value = manager.ReadRegister(0x10);
    Debug.WriteLine($"Read via SPI: 0x{value:X2}");
}
```

The call to Dispose() will happen automatically when exiting the method scope. Curious on how this is implemented under the hood? The compiler recognizes the usage of the concise using pattern and wraps the relevant code in a try/finally block. That's why this makes sure Dispose() is called even if an exception is thrown. And it makes the code very clean and much easier to read.

```
SpiSensorManager manager = null;
try
{
    manager = new SpiSensorManager(1, 12);
    // use it...
}
finally
{
    manager?.Dispose();
}
```

A Robust Memory Strategy in Practice

To manage memory reliably in a long-running embedded nanoFramework application, begin your system startup by pre-allocating all needed object pools and shared buffers. By using static arrays or a pooling mechanism, you eliminate the need for repeated allocations during runtime, which prevents heap fragmentation from ever starting.

Once the main application loop begins, always retrieve reusable objects from your pools or shared buffers instead of creating new ones. This keeps your heap usage predictable and avoids triggering the garbage collector unnecessarily.

During idle times, you can force a garbage collection with compaction by calling GC.Run(true). Doing this when the system is not busy helps defragment the heap and consolidate available memory into larger contiguous blocks.

While your application runs, periodically log memory metrics using diagnostic calls such as NativeMemory.GetMemoryInfo() and GC.Run(false). These calls report how much managed and native heap memory remains, allowing you to detect any creeping fragmentation or memory exhaustion before it causes critical failures.

By simulating peak workloads during development, you can run these memory and GC diagnostics to observe how the heap behaves under stress. If you notice that fragmentation grows over time, consider adjusting pool sizes or frequency of compaction cycles until the heap stabilizes.

Additionally, integrate the `Dispose` pattern into any class that wraps native or shared resources. Make use of the `using` statement to deal with disposable classes.

Putting all these elements together gives you a robust lifecycle: start with pre-allocation, runtime reuse, idle-time compaction, continuous diagnostics, and deterministic resource cleanup. By following this disciplined approach, your embedded firmware can achieve stable, predictable behavior—even after days or weeks of operation on resource-constrained hardware.

It's important to keep in mind that for most of the applications, you don't have to bother with garbage collection at all. It's there on the background, quietly doing what is meant to do. You're not even supposed to notice that it is there. You have to pay attention to it only if you want to profile memory usage as part of QA or your project requires it. Or if you're seeing GC messages or unexpected delays in some code execution paths that could be caused by GC running. Otherwise, again, you don't have to worry about this at all.

Scheduling, Synchronization, and Execution Control

In embedded systems, especially when written in C# with .NET nanoFramework, using threads allows you to separate well-defined tasks—such as polling sensors, handling communication, or managing power modes—so each piece runs independently. To illustrate, imagine the application for the pool controller we've developed in Chapter 5: one thread handles sensor readings periodically, while another manages user input. By putting these in separate threads, each task can execute at its own pace without blocking the others, ensuring responsive system behavior even under load.

As we've seen in Chapter 2, under the hood the execution engine is responsible for running all threads in a round-robin fashion, with 20 milliseconds time slice per thread.

Threads and Events

Threads in nanoFramework are created using the familiar .NET Thread API. You can pass in a method:

```
Thread sensorThread = new Thread(SensorLoop);
sensorThread.Start();
```

Or you can spin up a thread inline with a lambda:

```
new Thread(() =>
{
    Debug.WriteLine("Worker thread is alive");
    Thread.Sleep(5000);
    Debug.WriteLine("Worker thread has completed");
}).Start();
```

Even though only one thread runs at any given moment, this model gives your system modularity and clarity—tasks are logically separated and independently controlled.

Occasionally it is required to pass parameters to a working thread. The simplest way to do this is using a class to hold the parameters and have the thread method get the parameters from the class. Like this:

```
// Supply the state information required by the task.
ThreadWithState tws = new ThreadWithState(
    "This report displays the number", 42);

// Create a thread to execute the task, and then...

Thread t = new Thread(new ThreadStart(tws.ThreadProc));


// ...start the thread
t.Start();
```

This is a mock-up for the ThreadWithState class:

```
public class ThreadWithState
{
    private readonly string _messageTemplate;
    private readonly int _numberValue;

    public ThreadWithState(string messageTemplate, int numberValue)
    {
        _messageTemplate = messageTemplate;
        _numberValue = numberValue;
    }

    public void ThreadProc()
    {
        // Format the message using the stored template and number
        Console.WriteLine($"{_messageTemplate}: {_numberValue]");
    }
}
```

Another common situation is needing to access data that results from a thread execution, like a sensor reading that arrives upon a pooled access to a bus. In this case, setting up a callback that gets executed by the thread before leaving its execution is a very convenient way of dealing with this.

```
// Supply the state information required by the task.
ThreadWithState tws = new ThreadWithState(
    "This report displays the number",
    42,
    new ExampleCallback(ResultCallback)
);

Thread t = new Thread(new ThreadStart(tws.ThreadProc));
t.Start();
```

For this to work, the class `ThreadWithState` must be adjusted to include the parameter and delegate:

```
// Delegate that defines the signature for the callback method.
public delegate void ExampleCallback(int lineCount);

public class ThreadWithState
{
    private readonly string _messageTemplate;
    private readonly int _numberValue;
    private readonly ExampleCallback _callback;

    public ThreadWithState(string messageTemplate, int numberValue,
    ExampleCallback callback)
    {
        _messageTemplate = messageTemplate;
        _numberValue = numberValue;
        _callback = callback;
    }

    public void ThreadProc()
    {
        // Execute the main work
        Console.WriteLine(_messageTemplate, _numberValue);

        // After finishing, invoke the callback with a sample result (e.g.,
        number of lines printed)
        _callback?.Invoke(1);
    }
}
```

You should also be aware that thread execution can be controlled by means of the thread API that allows starting, suspending, and aborting a thread's execution. In embedded systems, properly controlling a thread's lifecycle—starting, pausing, and terminating it—is essential for managing limited CPU, memory, and peripheral resources. Nevertheless, be aware that a cooperative coding approach (between threads) is recommended.

> **Note** Although .NET officially recommends avoiding the use of `Abort()` and `Suspend()`, the nanoFramework implementation of these methods does not exhibit the same issues found in the full .NET framework. As a result, their use remains acceptable in nano projects.

When aborting (or ending) a thread, make sure to provide a exit execution path at a safe points, ensuring resources like file handles, peripherals, or memory are properly released. This is crucial in embedded environments where improper cleanup can lead to deadlocks, memory exhaustion, or hardware faults. This is an example of how to use those APIs:

```
// create and start a thread
var sleepingThread1 = new Thread(RunIndefinitely);
sleepingThread1.Start();

Thread.Sleep(2000);

// suspend 1st thread
sleepingThread1.Suspend();

Thread.Sleep(1000);

// create and start 2nd thread
var sleepingThread2 = new Thread(RunIndefinitely);
sleepingThread2.Start();

Thread.Sleep(2000);

// abort 2nd thread
sleepingThread2.Abort();

// abort 1st thread
sleepingThread1.Abort();
```

To avoid CPU-consuming busy loops, it's better to use synchronization primitives such as `AutoResetEvent` or `ManualResetEvent`. This lets your thread block efficiently until work is available, rather than continuously polling and wasting CPU cycles. For example, suppose you need to process user input from key presses, update an LCD menu, and adjust settings: instead of constantly polling the key state in a loop, you set up a thread that waits until a key press occurs before executing UI processing. Take a look at the following code snippet:

```
AutoResetEvent triggerUIProcessing = new AutoResetEvent(false);

Thread sensor = new Thread(() =>
{
    // Loop keeps the thread alive for multiple inputs
    while (true)
    {
        // Blocks here until a key is pressed
        triggerUIProcessing.WaitOne();

        // Safely process the input
        ProcessUI();
    }
});
```

Here is the code that handles the key presses:

```
// Signal waiting thread
void OnButtonPressed() => triggerUIProcessing.Set();
```

Here's what happens: while the thread contains a `while()` loop, it doesn't consume CPU—because it blocks at `WaitOne()` until the `OnButtonPressed()` method signals it. This pattern ensures the thread runs only when needed, preserving CPU cycles and improving overall responsiveness. Blocking calls like `WaitOne()` are nonbusy waits and far more efficient than polling or sleeping loops.

If you need a thread to run until a specific reset condition occurs—like continuous logging—you'd use a `ManualResetEvent` instead, on which the code has to specifically reset the event. The following example demonstrates this:

```
public class Logger
{
    // ManualResetEvent acts like a gate: stays open until Reset()
    is called.
    private readonly ManualResetEvent _continueLogging = new
    ManualResetEvent(true);
    private bool _running = true;
```

```
public void Run()
{
    Console.WriteLine("Logger thread started.");

    while (_running)
    {
        // Blocks here if the gate is closed
        _continueLogging.WaitOne();

        // Perform logging work
        LogData();

        // simulate periodic logging
        Thread.Sleep(1000);
    }

    Console.WriteLine("Logger thread exiting.");
}

public void PauseLogging()
{
    Console.WriteLine("Logger paused.");

    // Close the gate, blocking the logger thread
    _continueLogging.Reset();
}

public void ResumeLogging()
{
    Console.WriteLine("Logger resumed.");

    // Open the gate, allowing the thread to continue
    _continueLogging.Set();
}

public void Stop()
{
    _running = false;
```

```
        // Ensure thread can exit WaitOne loop
        _continueLogging.Set();
    }

    private void LogData()
    {
        // Insert log collection or sensor reading logic here
        Console.WriteLine($"Logged at {DateTime.UtcNow}");
    }
}
```

And here is an usage example:

```
var logger = new Logger();
var thread = new Thread(logger.Run);
thread.Start();

// ...later when conditions require pausing:
logger.PauseLogging();

// ...and when ready to resume:
logger.ResumeLogging();

// ...when finished:
logger.Stop();
thread.Join();
```

Here, the logger thread loops indefinitely, but it blocks at `WaitOne()` whenever `PauseLogging()` is called—conserving CPU and power by not entering busy-wait. This "gate" stays open when `Set()` is called, allowing continuous operation until a reset is triggered. A `ManualResetEvent`, when signaled, remains in that state until manually reset, and all threads waiting on it will pass through.

This pattern is ideal for embedded tasks like periodic logging, sensor polling, or system maintenance—where pausing and resuming work based on system states helps manage power consumption and responsiveness.

Protecting Shared Resources

When threads share resources—say, performing a sequence of operations to an `I2cDevice` that can't be interrupted—you must avoid concurrency issues so that the operation is not interrupted with bus traffic from another thread. You can accomplish this by using C#'s built-in `lock` construct:

```
private readonly object _sync = new object();

void WriteShared(byte[] data)
{
    lock (_sync)
    {
        I2cDevice.WriteByte(_unlockConfigState);
        I2cDevice.Write(newConfig);
        I2cDevice.WriteByte(_lockConfigState);
    }
}
```

Another example would be accessing a shared buffer; otherwise, data in the buffer could become garbled as one thread is reading from the buffer and another one is writing to it at the same time. If the buffer `_readings` is a `byte[]`, it implements the API from the base class `Array`, which includes the property `SyncRoot` to be used to synchronize access to the array. In this case, the usage pattern would be as follows:

```
public void TransmitAll()
{
    Debug.WriteLine("Sending sensor log:");

    lock (_readings.SyncRoot)
    {
       TransmitBuffer();
    }
}
```

The `lock` keyword wraps the `Monitor.Enter` and `Monitor.Exit` calls with exception safety. Internally, the first thread that reaches the `lock` statement acquires a mutual exclusion lock on `_sync` object. Any other thread encountering the same lock will be blocked—not consuming CPU in a busy loop—but waiting until the lock is released by the first thread. Once the original thread exits the lock block (no matter whether by reaching the end of the block or due to an exception), the next waiting thread is unblocked, acquires the lock, and proceeds.

Enforcing Execution Time with Constraints

Critical operations like real-time sensor reads should complete within an allotted time interval. .NET nanoFramework provides `ExecutionConstraint`, allowing you to set a timeout (500 milliseconds in this case) and a priority:

```
try
{
    ExecutionConstraint.Install(500, Thread.MaxPriority);
    PerformReadOperation();
}
catch (ConstraintException)
{
    Debug.WriteLine("Read operation timed out");
}
finally
{
    // remove constraint
    ExecutionConstraint.Install(Timeout.Infinite, 0);
}
```

The last call to `ExecutionConstraint` performs two essential actions:

- By passing `Timeout.Infinite`, basically you're removing the timing constraint—meaning the thread is no longer monitored for overrunning the previously specified 500 milliseconds window. In other words, no timeout will be enforced after this call.
- Resetting the thread priority back to 0 restores it to its normal baseline level. You're effectively undoing the elevated priority set with `Thread.MaxPriority` during the critical operation.

Together, this “cleanup” call ensures that after the potentially time-sensitive operation completes—or times out—the thread returns to its default, unconstrained state and standard scheduling priority. That way, only the critical section benefits from tighter controls, and overall system scheduling remains balanced.

This should be used whenever there are operations that depend on external components and can, somehow misbehave and lock the system in an endless state waiting for the call to return. Not implementing this safety mechanism would mean that the thread executing this code would be locked forever, leaving the system unresponsive or not being able to perform normally.

Managing Device Reboots Safely

For planned reboots, you can call `Power.RebootDevice()`. This exists to not only execute the requested reboot of the CLR but to also provide a mechanism to ensure graceful shutdown events. There is even `OnRebootEvent`, which can be subscribed to by as many handlers as you need. For example:

```
Power.OnRebootEvent += (s, e) =>
{
    Debug.WriteLine("Saving state...");
    SaveSettings();
};

Power.OnRebootEvent += (s, e) =>
{
    Debug.WriteLine("Clearing LCD and disabling backlight...");

    lcd.Clear();
    lcd.SetBacklightEnabled(false);
};
```

The first handler saves the system settings, and the second one clears the LCD and shuts down the backlight. Now, when this call is performed:

```
Power.RebootDevice(500, RebootOption.NormalReboot);
```

Both handlers are invoked automatically. If handlers exceed the 500 milliseconds constraint, the CLR aborts them and proceeds with the reboot—preventing hangs during shutdown.

This model ensures your embedded system performs a graceful and reliable reboot, by doing whatever is required for that to happen by using a clean simple API and mechanism perfectly common in .NET style.

Deep Sleep for Ultra-Low Power

On devices like the ESP32, STM32 series, TI CC1352, and Silicon Labs Giant Gecko, nanoFramework offers deep sleep modes to significantly cut power consumption—whether you're running from battery or energy harvesting. These modes disable most of the system while allowing select peripherals to stay active, effectively pausing your firmware until a wake-up event occurs.

There are NuGets specific for each platform to expose and take advantage of what each platform has to offer in these matters.

For ESP32-based boards, there is the `Sleep` class in `nanoFramework.Hardware.Esp32`. You enable wake-up sources—like timer, GPIO, or touch pad—then call `StartDeepSleep()`. When sleep is triggered, execution stops immediately; on wake-up, the MCU essentially undergoes a reset, and execution resumes from the `Main()` method.

```
Sleep.EnableWakeupByTimer(TimeSpan.FromMinutes(15));

// example: wake on button press
Sleep.EnableWakeupByPin(GpioPin.GPIO_NUM_0, 0);

// never returns execution—device resets when awake
Sleep.StartDeepSleep();
```

You can also use `StartLightSleep()` to maintain context, but this mode works only if Wi-Fi/Bluetooth hardware blocks are idle—it won't work during active network use and offers slightly higher power draw.

On wake-up, the API provides insight into what triggered the reset through `Sleep.GetWakeupCause()`, like this:

```
var cause = Sleep.GetWakeupCause();
Debug.WriteLine($"Awoke from: {cause}");
```

Possible causes include `WakeupCause.Timer`, `Ext0`, or `Ext1` (GPIO triggers via RTC), `TouchPad`, `ULP` (for ESP32's ultra-low-power coprocessor), among others.

STM32 devices support RTC alarms and offer data persistence across reboots with RAM backup for small amounts of data via nanoFramework.Hardware.Stm32, enabling you to use low-power RTCs to wake up the system in a timed fashion.

TI CC13xx/CC26xx chips feature low-power timers and deep-sleep modes accessible through nanoFramework.Hardware.TI.

Silicon Labs Giant Gecko series offer similar RTC, low-energy timer, and RAM retention modes via nanoFramework.Hardware.GiantGecko.

Although these platforms share a common API shape, each diverges in terms of power domains, retained memory, and wake-up sources.

Since deep sleep acts like a reset, you need robust startup logic to inspect the wake-up cause and restore the previous state. Here's an example of how that could be done:

```
public static void Main()
{
    var cause = Sleep.GetWakeupCause();

    if (cause == WakeupCause.Undefined)
    {
        // first run
        InitializeFullSystem();
    }
    else
    {
        RecoverFromSleep(cause);
    }

    RunMainFunctionality();
}
```

State that must survive sleep—such as sensor cache or counters—has to be stored in a way that it can accessed after the next wake-up. It will depend on the type and amount of data: either persistent storage (if available in the hardware) or in a more temporary storage that depends on the power being kept during the sleep period like RTC memory or backup registers/RAM. No matter what storage approach is used, after waking, you restore just enough context to resume normal operation without reinitializing everything.

Using deep sleep dramatically reduces power consumption—from tens of milliamps during active run to microamps while sleeping. This enables devices to operate for years on battery. By carefully configuring wake-up sources, preserving just-enough state, and correctly structuring your boot logic, you can build reliable, ultra-low-power embedded systems across platforms—all using familiar C# code and APIs.

Dependency Injection (IoC Architecture)

Inversion of control (IoC) is a design principle that inverts the traditional flow of control by moving object creation and binding out of application code and into an external container. In practice, this means classes declare their dependencies (often via constructor parameters) rather than instantiating them directly. A dependency injection (DI) container implements IoC by resolving and supplying those dependencies at runtime. In other words, the container becomes "an engine that resolves and manages object graphs" by using reflection to examine requested classes and automatically injecting the required services. This decouples components (making them easier to test and extend) and centralizes configuration.

Common DI patterns include constructor injection (providing dependencies via constructor parameters), property/setter injection (setting public properties), and method injection (passing dependencies as method arguments). These all follow IoC by moving the responsibility of creating objects out of the dependent class. Some alternatives, like the Service Locator pattern, are less favored because they hide dependencies (the container must be accessed inside classes).

Coding in IoC architecture is not mandatory, and not every developer likes the style. There are both pros and cons on using this approach.

- *Pros:* DI promotes loose coupling, easier unit testing (mocks can replace real services), and flexible composition of functionality at runtime.
- *Cons:* It adds complexity and indirection, can increase memory/performance overhead (particularly relevant in constrained devices usage, due to dependency on reflection and service storage), and can make code less explicit (dependency chains may be hidden).

The trade-offs should be considered. For many embedded IoT scenarios, the clear structure and testability often outweigh the costs.

nanoFramework Dependency Injection and Hosting

.NET nanoFramework provides a dependency injection library that closely mirrors the Microsoft Microsoft.Extensions.DependencyInjection API. This is on purpose like most of the other APIs to ease portability and promote code reuse along with leveraging on existing developers' know-how and learned skills. The nanoFramework DI library supplies the familiar ServiceCollection/ServiceProvider classes for registering and resolving services. For example, you create a ServiceCollection, call AddSingleton AddScoped AddTransient to register types with specific lifetimes, and then call BuildServiceProvider() to get an IServiceProvider. This allows nanoFramework applications to use the same IoC patterns as full .NET applications.

Additionally, the nanoFramework.Hosting library implements the Generic Host model familiar from ASP.NET Core. The Generic Host bootstraps a DI container and manages the application lifetime. When the host starts, it automatically runs all registered IHostedService instances (e.g., background tasks). The Generic Host provides convenience methods for creating DI application containers with preconfigured defaults, again mirroring the official .NET Generic Host API. For example, a typical nanoFramework program, IoC style, would look like this:

```
IHost host = Host.CreateDefaultBuilder()
    .ConfigureServices(services =>
    {
        services.AddSingleton(typeof(BackgroundQueue));
        services.AddHostedService(typeof(SensorService));
        services.AddHostedService(typeof(DisplayService));
    })
    .Build();

host.Run();
```

Here the host builds a DI container, and then starts each registered IHostedService, by calling their Start() or ExecuteAsync() to run the application. It should be clear that those services implement the IHostedService interface for this to be possible. That includes BackgroundQueue, SensorService, and DisplayService. This aligns with .NET's patterns, making nanoFramework apps easier to write for developers familiar with .NET Core/ASP.NET Core.

ServiceCollection, Service Lifetimes, and ActivatorUtilities

The ServiceCollection is central to setting up DI. You register each service type and its lifetime and then build a ServiceProvider. For example:

```
var serviceProvider = new ServiceCollection()
    .AddSingleton(typeof(ServiceObject))
    .AddSingleton(typeof(RootObject))
    .BuildServiceProvider();
```

This code creates a DI container and registers ServiceObject and RootObject as singleton services. Once built, you can retrieve services from the provider:

```
var root = (RootObject)serviceProvider.GetService(typeof(RootObject));
```

The container will automatically construct the object graph (RootObject and its ServiceObject dependency) at resolve time.

Service lifetimes control how instances are reused:

- *Singleton* (AddSingleton): One shared instance for the lifetime of the container. Every request for that service gets the same object.
- *Scoped* (AddScoped): One instance per *scope*. A scope is created with serviceProvider.CreateScope(). Each scope gets its own instancebut resolves within the scope will reuse that instance. This is typically used for per-request services.
- *Transient* (AddTransient): A new instance is created every time the service is requested.

For example, to use a scoped service, use this:

```
var provider = new ServiceCollection()
    .AddScoped(typeof(MyService))
    .BuildServiceProvider();

using (var scope = provider.CreateScope())
{
    // Within this scope, MyService will be one instance
    var svc1 = scope.ServiceProvider.GetService(typeof(MyService));
    var svc2 = scope.ServiceProvider.GetService(typeof(MyService));
}
```

Note that svc1 and svc2 are the same object within this scope. And also that disposing scope cleans up scoped instances. In nanoFramework you typically dispose scopes with a using block. A check (implemented with ValidateScopes) ensures scoped services are not resolved from the root provider to avoid misuses.

The ActivatorUtilities class offers a way to manually create instances using the DI container, even if the type wasn't registered. It invokes the constructor with dependency parameters resolved by the container. Like this:

```
// Create a RootObject instance, passing extra constructor args 1 and "2":
var instance = (RootObject)ActivatorUtilities.CreateInstance(
    serviceProvider, typeof(RootObject), 1, "2"
);

Console.WriteLine($"One: {instance.One}, Two: {instance.Two}");
```

This will use the ServiceObject from the container and pass the literal 1 and 2 for the other parameters. ActivatorUtilities is useful for creating objects on the fly without needing to register them first.

Usage Example

What follows now are some example patterns to illustrate IoC in nanoFramework.

In the following example, a DI container is used to wire up an application that blinks an LED and logs status. The program defines an Application class that takes an IHardwareService and an ILoggerFactory in its constructor. In Main(), these services are registered and built:

```
ServiceProvider services = new ServiceCollection()
    .AddSingleton(typeof(Application))
    .AddSingleton(typeof(IHardwareService), typeof(HardwareService))
    .AddSingleton(typeof(ILoggerFactory), typeof(DebugLoggerFactory))
    .BuildServiceProvider();

var app = (Application)services.GetRequiredService(typeof(Application));
app.Run();
```

The HardwareService class (registered as IHardwareService) manages a GpioController and a thread that toggles an LED pin, logging "on" and "off" via the provided ILogger. Because of DI, the Application class doesn't know how HardwareService or DebugLoggerFactory are constructed—it just receives them. This decouples the logic and cleanly combines hardware and logging via DI. All the boilerplate for creating GPIO controllers and threads is hidden inside HardwareService, while the main program simply starts blinking.

To demonstrate scoped lifetimes, imagine a service that should live for only a short-lived operation. You create a scope from the root provider:

```
var provider = new ServiceCollection()
    .AddScoped(typeof(ProcessingService))
    .BuildServiceProvider();

using (var scope = provider.CreateScope())
{
    // Each time we request ProcessingService inside this scope,
    // we get the *same* instance.
    var proc1 = scope.ServiceProvider.GetService(typeof(Processing
    Service));
    var proc2 = scope.ServiceProvider.GetService(typeof(Processing
    Service));
    // proc1 == proc2, but outside this using-block it will be disposed.
}
```

This pattern is useful in server-like scenarios (each request can get a fresh scope) or any situation where you want to group a set of resolutions. The IServiceScope returned by CreateScope() has its own ServiceProvider, so disposing of the scope will also dispose of any scoped or transient services created within it.

For controllers and services, let's code a web server to integrate DI with the nanoFramework HTTP server. Instead of using the default WebServer constructor, it defines a subclass that accepts an IServiceProvider. In the overridden InvokeRoute method, it uses ActivatorUtilities to create the controller instance with injected services. Like this:

```
internal class WebServerDi : WebServer
{
    private readonly IServiceProvider _sp;
    public WebServerDi(int port, HttpProtocol protocol, Type[] controllers,
    IServiceProvider sp)
        : base(port, protocol, controllers)
    {
        _sp = sp;
    }

    protected override void InvokeRoute(CallbackRoutes route,
    HttpListenerContext ctx)
    {
        // Create controller instance via DI container:
        object controller = ActivatorUtilities.CreateInstance(_sp, route.
        Callback.DeclaringType);
        route.Callback.Invoke(controller, new object[]{ new
        WebServerEventArgs(ctx) });
    }
}
```

Now, when creating the server, you build a service provider with your dependencies and pass it in:

```
var sp = new ServiceCollection()
    .AddTransient(typeof(ITextService), typeof(TextService))
    .AddSingleton(typeof(ITextServiceSingleton), typeof(TextService))
    .BuildServiceProvider();

using (var server = new WebServerDi(80, HttpProtocol.Http, new Type[]{
typeof(ControllerTest) }, sp))
{
    server.Start();
    Thread.Sleep(Timeout.Infinite);
}
```

In this setup, the `ControllerTest` constructor can take `ITextService` and `ITextServiceSingleton`, and the container will inject them. Each HTTP request causes `InvokeRoute` to run, which uses `ActivatorUtilities.CreateInstance()` to instantiate the controller with its dependencies. As a result, `ControllerTest` methods can use injected services, and even a singleton service will maintain a consistent instance across requests (one GUID remains constant) while transient services can vary per call.

Summary

Effective memory management in embedded systems ensures efficient use of limited RAM, significantly improving system stability and responsiveness by reducing wasted memory and minimizing allocation delays. It helps prevent fragmentation, which occurs when available memory becomes scattered into unusable pieces over time—a problem that can trigger unexpected failures even though the total free space seems sufficient. Proper allocation strategies like pooling and compacting not only maintain performance but also help satisfy real-time requirements by avoiding unpredictable delays in memory allocation. Garbage collector is not evil! It's a fine tool and an intrinsic part of how .NET works. It's one of the features that sets it apart from traditional C/C++ manual memory allocation and deallocation. In other words, it is a productivity booster for embedded developers. Finally, disciplined memory usage reduces the risk of leaks or dangling references that, in long-duration deployments, can result in crashes or degraded battery life due to higher CPU usage as the system struggles with inefficient memory.

Modern embedded applications running on .NET nanoFramework benefit greatly from using threads to separate responsibilities. We've looked on how to start threads, pass parameters, read processing results, synchronize them, and control thread flow. Next, we've went through primitives for thread signaling and protecting shared results.

You also learned about adding reliability and predictability by using `ExecutionConstrain`, which sets explicit execution time limits. This is mandatory for operations that can misbehave. It fails fast, preventing deadlocks or performance degradation. Finally, controlled firmware restarts `Power.RebootDevice()` and uses the `OnRebootEvent` callback mechanism to enable graceful shutdown routines.

Bringing DI into embedded firmware introduces modularity, testability, and clear separation of concerns. We've covered nanoFramework `DependencyInjection` and `Hosting` libraries, which mirror standard .NET IoC patterns, allowing C# native construction of object graphs through `ServiceCollection` and controlled service lifetimes. You learned how to register services as singletons, scoped, or transient to match the desired lifecycle of your application and use `ActivatorUtilities` to construct types on demand even without explicit registration The Slow Blink example demonstrated how hardware and logging services can be injected cleanly, while the WebServer example highlighted how controllers can receive services like text providers or hardware interfaces via constructor injection at runtime. Overall, this pattern brings structured, maintainable firmware design with embedded-class modularity, without sacrificing performance—especially when dependencies are lean and limited in number. If IoC is your thing, you have a clean, robust, and standard API to use in your applications.

Additional Resources

You can learn more at the following locations:

Using threads and threading: `https://learn.microsoft.com/en-us/dotnet/standard/threading/using-threads-and-threading`

The lock statement: `https://learn.microsoft.com/en-us/dotnet/csharp/language-reference/statements/lock`

using statement: `https://learn.microsoft.com/en-us/dotnet/csharp/language-reference/statements/using`

Implement a Dispose method: `https://learn.microsoft.com/en-us/dotnet/standard/garbage-collection/implementing-dispose`

.NET dependency injection: `https://learn.microsoft.com/en-us/dotnet/core/extensions/dependency-injection`

.NET Generic Host: `https://learn.microsoft.com/en-us/dotnet/core/extensions/generic-host`

CHAPTER 10

Beyond Connectivity: MCP in Embedded Devices

In this final chapter, we'll explore how embedding a Model Context Protocol (MCP) server within your nanoFramework-powered device marks a transformative shift, from mere connectivity to intelligent autonomy across the industrial IoT landscape.

At its core, MCP is an open, standardized protocol—often compared to the "USB-C port for AI"—that enables any IoT device to expose its capabilities, answer queries, and execute instructions issued by large language models (LLMs) or external systems. Rather than building custom connectors for each tool or API, MCP establishes a universal interface enabling LLM-driven agents to dynamically discover, invoke, and collaborate with embedded hardware.

Imagine industrial sensors and actuators not only streaming data but also responding to runtime queries ("What's the current pressure threshold?"), executing commands ("Recalibrate valve 12"), and even collaborating with cloud-based LLMs to generate automated maintenance logs or optimize process control. MCP makes all of this possible with minimal overhead. It is a simple lightweight server running on the device, exposing structured tools, prompts, and resources to intelligently orchestrate behavior.

In an industrial context, MCP-based microcontrollers evolve into intelligent agents on the edge. They provide real-time, context-aware functionality: predictive maintenance, automated anomaly handling, adaptive control loops, and transparent integration with enterprise information systems. With nanoFramework hosting the MCP server, C# developers can readily expose device APIs, sensor reads, and command endpoints alongside industrial-grade communication protocols—all aligned under one standard interface (see Figure 10-1).

J. Simões, *Embedded Systems with .NET nanoFramework*, https://doi.org/10.1007/979-8-8688-2096-0_10

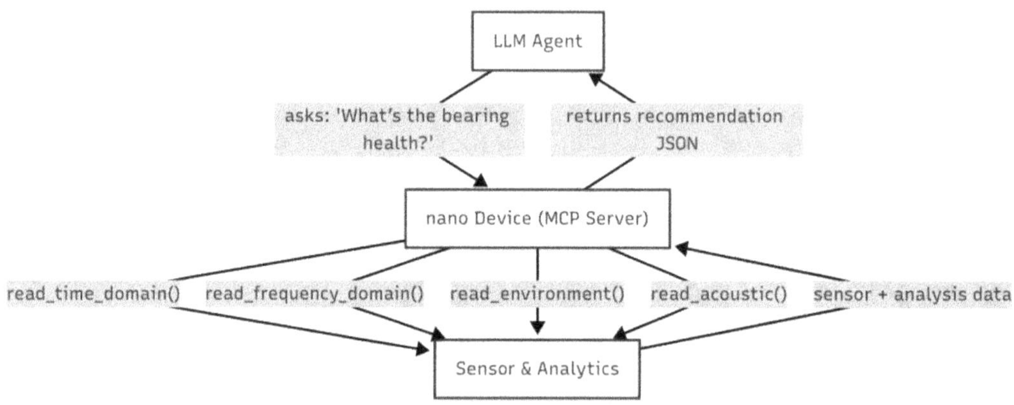

Figure 10-1. *Principal schema with agent interacting with MCP server on nano device*

By the end of this chapter, you'll see how a .NET nanoFramework MCP implementation allows you to empower your embedded systems projects to step beyond connectivity and into a future where intelligent things collaborate, reason, and act within an IoT ecosystem to become the next generation of factory automation, smart infrastructure, and industrial intelligence.

As with previous chapters, the code for the examples provided is made available in the companion GitHub repository. Some of the examples are heavy on code. For the sake of readability and not wasting space with mere code listing, we are including only the relevant snippets in the chapter.

MCP 101: Principles and Industrial Relevance

MCP is an open standard, first introduced by Anthropic in November 2024, that establishes a universal interface for connecting AI systems—especially LLMs—to external tools, data sources, and services. At its heart, MCP answers the question: How can we make any AI assistant discover and use external capabilities in a consistent, structured way?

Overview of the Model Context Protocol

MCP is often referred as the "USB-C port for AI integrations" because it offers a universal connector between models and capabilities. By standardizing discovery, invocation, and data exchange, it dramatically reduces complexity and accelerates intelligent, composable systems for industrial IoT and beyond.

MCP organizes communication using JSON-RPC 2.0, a lightweight, transport-agnostic format for remote procedure calls. This enables three primary message types—requests, responses, and notifications—to flow between an MCP client (an LLM or AI agent) and an MCP server (a service exposing tools or data). For instance, a client may send a *tools/list* request to discover available capabilities and then invoke *tools/call* to execute a function—such as reading sensor data—from the server.

Before MCP, each AI model (let's call it **N**) needed separate custom logic to communicate with each external service (referred as **M**)—databases, SaaS APIs, internal systems—resulting in a combinatorial explosion of integrations. This **N × M** problem forced developers to constantly build and maintain one-off connectors, leading to fragmented implementations and high maintenance.

MCP elegantly addresses this by defining a standardized protocol. Once a system exposes its capabilities through MCP, any compliant AI client can access it—without additional glue code. For example, whether you're using Claude, ChatGPT, Gemini, or Copilot, you can leverage a single MCP server to discover and invoke tools across repositories like GitHub, cloud databases, or—you guessed it—industrial sensor nodes.

Let's look at the core features that make MCP so powerful:

- *Discovery and Tool Invocation:* Every MCP server exposes a list of tools, with method names, parameter definitions, input schemas, and human-readable descriptions. An AI agent can query this catalog at runtime and dynamically decide which tool to call.
- *Consistent Format Across Systems:* Communication always uses JSON-RPC, so agents don't need custom parsers. The same mechanism retrieves data from a GitHub repo or a pressure sensor.
- *Support for Rich Data Types:* MCP tools can accept and return complex JSON objects—nested structures, arrays, strings—enabling powerful use cases like fetching FFT arrays from an accelerometer or structured database records.
- *Prompt Templates:* Servers can offer reusable "prompts," which are prewritten instruction sets or workflows (like "analyze current vibration data and produce a health summary") that AI agents can invoke, speeding up intelligent behavior without crafting context from scratch.

- *Transport Flexibility and Security:* MCP can run over HTTP, standard IO pipes, SSE, or custom transports. While JSON-based communication is the norm, higher-performance encoding (like binary) is possible. Servers implement authentication mechanisms to ensure only authorized clients can invoke sensitive tools and access resources.

MCP is perceived as a game changer, which is why it has swiftly earned support from major AI providers—OpenAI, Microsoft, Google DeepMind, and Anthropic itself—who have integrated it into tools like Claude Desktop, the OpenAI Agents SDK, and Gemini and Copilot. This broad adoption clearly illustrates its value in enabling interoperability, modularity, and efficiency in building AI-powered systems.

MCP in Industrial and Embedded Contexts

In the context of industrial embedded systems, at the time of this writing, there are no significant offers from any major vendor. However, there is a growing number of proof of concepts in the industrial context. This is paving the way to agentic AI across the industrial space. MCP empowers a factory-grade edge gateway to expose sensor and actuator capabilities as discoverable tools. An LLM can then autonomously query motor vibration levels, configure thresholds, request diagnostics, or send logs to MES, all without custom coding per model or per sensor. Essentially, MCP transforms static sensors into active, intelligent participants in an automated ecosystem. This can transform LLMs into intelligent field agents capable of direct interaction with devices—no custom API wiring required. It also enables plug-and-play interoperability: add any MCP-enabled device or system, and agents can discover and invoke its tools dynamically. Further, it reduces the integration effort from an N×M problem to one standardized protocol, accelerating deployments and maintaining flexibility.

At a first glance, one might see MCP as a competitor to other standards that try to "fix" that N×M problem, like OPC UA. OPC UA is a device-level communication standard, designed to enable secure, platform-independent data acquisition and control across diverse industrial assets. It defines rich information models for sensors, PLCs, and controllers; supports both client-server and pub/sub architectures; and is backed by a mature ecosystem supporting binary, XML, and MQTT mappings.

In contrast, MCP operates at a higher layer as an AI-native protocol. Its purpose is to expose external tools, services, and data sources—including OPC UA nodes—as discoverable capabilities (tools) that AI models can dynamically query and interact with via JSON-RPC. MCP focuses on providing contextual knowledge and tool metadata to LLMs, enabling intelligent workflows. See Figure 10-2.

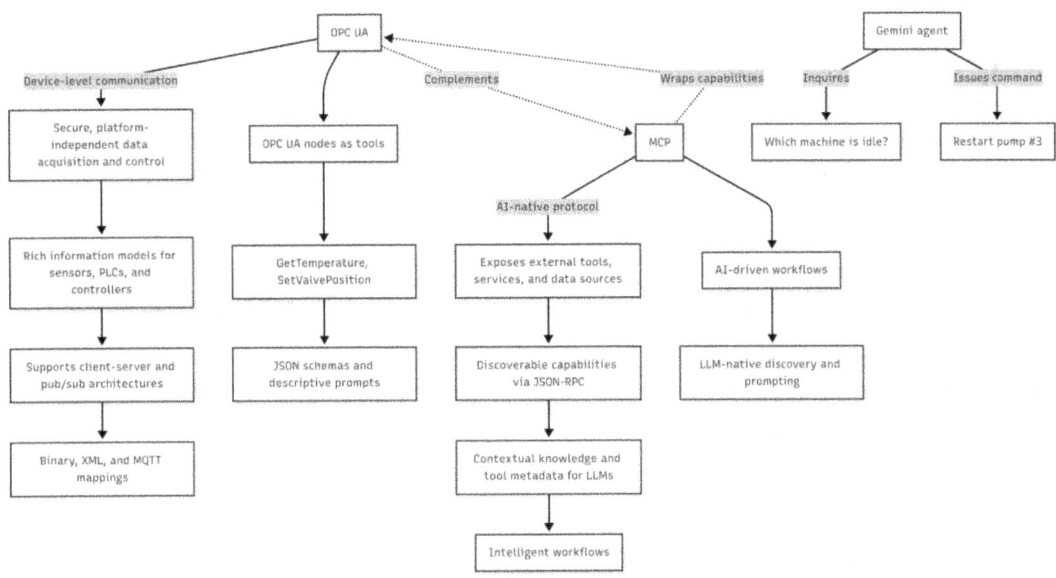

Figure 10-2. *MCP and OPC UA interaction flow*

With OPC UA, clients can methodically browse an address space, read/write variables, subscribe to events, and control devices. MCP, by comparison, doesn't define how data is acquired—that remains to OPC UA, MQTT, Modbus, etc. Instead, MCP standardizes how the capabilities of these sources are exposed to AI. For example, an MCP server could wrap OPC UA nodes as `GetTemperature()` or `SetValvePosition()` tools, complete with JSON schemas and descriptive prompts.

Rather than replacing OPC UA, MCP complements it. MCP enables LLMs to interact with field devices via AI-driven workflows—using LLM-native discovery and prompting—while OPC UA continues to manage secure and standardized data acquisition from sensors and actuators. Ultimately this brings to reality a scenario on which a Gemini agent can inquire "Which machine is idle?" or issue the command "Restart pump #3."

To summarize, OPC UA and MCP aren't competitors—they're partners in building next-generation industrial systems. OPC UA ensures that shop-floor devices are safely discoverable and controllable. MCP wraps those capabilities with semantic descriptions and tool interfaces that AI agents can understand, enabling reasoning, diagnostics, and automated workflows seamlessly.

Integration with an MES

A manufacturing execution system (MES) is a vital software platform used in industrial environments to monitor, control, and document manufacturing operations on the shop floor in real time. It acts as a bridge between high-level planning tools (like ERP systems) and the actual factory floor processes, enabling seamless communication and data exchange. One of its tasks is to provide integration capabilities by connecting with sensors, machines, SCADA systems, ERPs, and analytics platforms to optimize plant-floor execution. A tight integration in an MES allows closed-loop automation, and a device doesn't just feed data—it becomes an integral, intelligent component of the digital factory.

By now it should have become somewhat obvious that an MES plays a relevant role in the connected shop-floor scenario we've been describing. And along with MCP and LLMs, it enables next-gen industrial automation and operational excellence.

To summarize, this pattern transforms traditional automation chains into AI-driven, interoperable agents—the future of Industry 4.0.

System Architecture

To guide you through the technologies being discussed, we'll assemble an industrial device that instruments an electrical motor using an array of sensors and exposes them through an MCP server and connection to MES system. We'll focus on the features and details relevant to these matters, skipping the rest of the implementation details that have already discussed in previous chapters or that you can implement as complementary exercise.

Regarding the system architecture, the core block of the system is the ST Microelectronics STEVAL-BFA001V2B (1 in Figure 10-3), a predictive maintenance kit with sensors and IO-Link capability.

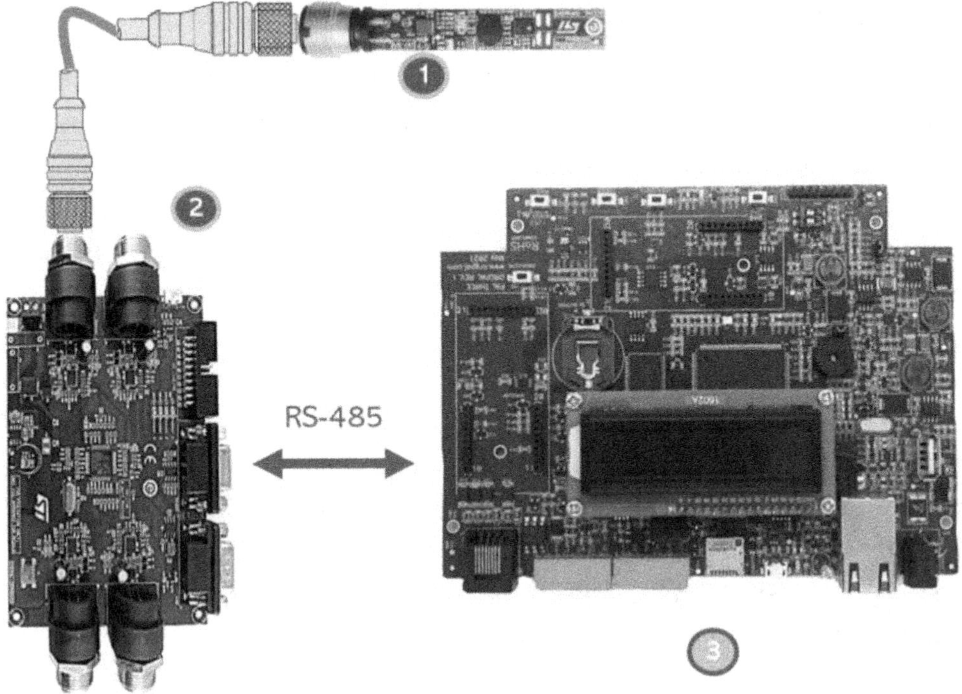

Figure 10-3. *System components*

This device connects to a STEVAL-IDP004V2 IO-Link master (2 in Figure 10-3) that acts as a bridge between the IO-Link sensor node and the RS-485 industrial bus. The processing unit and networking are handled by an Orgpal PALTHREE board (3 in Figure 10-3), the same used in the pool controller project in Chapter 6. Industrial-grade board and network modules are perfectly suited to factory environments. It supports .NET nanoFramework out of the box, enabling single-board hosting of all required features, including network connectivity for the MCP server and HTTP client, and also capable of handling the RS-485 interface. As a side note, know that the minimum required specs for nanoFramework to run the MCP server is network connectivity and a recommended 500kB of RAM. The requirements beyond that are related to the complexity of the sensors and actuators that the device will have to handle. The bottom line is that the requirements are very low.

Setting Up the System

As a first prerequisite, we'll assume that you have a STEVAL BFA001V2B flashed with the latest version of the `Predictive_Maintenance_IOL` demonstration binary from the software package provided by ST Microelectronics. The package runs on the STM32F469AI microcontroller (fitted in the BFA001V2B board), includes drivers for the various sensor devices, and integrates complete middleware with algorithms for accelerometer data signal processing in time and frequency domains and the audio library to perform acoustic emission analysis.

Next, you should have the BFA001V2B connected to the STEVAL-IDP004V2 board (required to assemble the IO-Link cable to the M12 industrial connector). You need to flash the STEVAL-IDP004V2 with the predictive maintenance evaluation kit firmware, following the instructions provided by ST. As there is plenty of guidance from the manufacturer about setting up these two boards, we'll assume you have this covered.

The last prerequisite is an PALTHREE board flashed with the latest .NET nanoFramework firmware. This will be connecting to the IO-Link master board through the RS-485 connector.

Hardware Context

The STEVAL-BFA001V2B includes the following sensors:

- Ultra-wide bandwidth, low-noise, three-axis digital vibration sensor (IIS3DWB)
- Piezoresistive absolute pressure sensor (LPS22HB)
- Relative humidity and temperature sensor (HTS221)
- Digital microphone sensor (IMP34DT05)

The connection to the outside world is done through an industrial IO-Link PHY (L6362A). See Figure 10-4.

***Figure 10-4.** The STEVAL-BFA001V2B*

Software Context

Let's look at what can be extracted from the data provided by the various sensors in the STEVAL-BFA001V2B board.

The board is equipped with a powerful set of sensors, perfect for industrial predictive maintenance applications. At its core is an advanced three-axis digital accelerometer (IIS3DWB), providing vibration data with a broad bandwidth of up to 6kHz, an absolute pressure sensor (LPS22HB), a humidity and temperature sensor (HTS221), and a digital omnidirectional microphone (IMP34DT05) ideal for acoustic monitoring.

Leveraging the provided ST software—particularly the STM32 Motion Signal Processing (referred to as *MotionSP*) middleware—we have access to several high-level signal-processing primitives exposed via IO-Link communication. From the accelerometer data, the library offers rich analysis tools such as the calculation of root mean square (RMS) values for acceleration, useful for detecting vibration intensity and general equipment condition. It also provides comprehensive frequency analysis through Fast Fourier Transform (FFT), enabling detailed investigation into the spectral content of vibrations.

FFT analysis is particularly valuable for monitoring industrial motors and rotating equipment, as it transforms raw acceleration data from the time domain—where data points represent vibration intensity over time—into the frequency domain. Here, it becomes possible to precisely identify specific vibration frequencies that correlate with different mechanical phenomena, such as unbalanced rotors, misalignments, or bearing failures. By regularly examining changes in these frequency patterns, predictive maintenance strategies can accurately detect and diagnose mechanical issues before critical failures occur.

Configurable parameters available within the *MotionSP* middleware allow fine-tuning of the FFT analysis. Users can choose from several windowing methods—Rectangular, Hanning, Hamming, or Flat Top—to suit different analytical scenarios. Windowing helps mitigate spectral leakage and ensures accurate frequency identification, enhancing diagnostic accuracy.

In addition, the middleware provides configurable options for Time Domain Analysis. Engineers can monitor acceleration or speed RMS moving averages, individually or simultaneously, with customizable averaging windows. This functionality enables effective tracking of motor speed and vibrations over time, facilitating both condition monitoring and predictive diagnostics.

Through IO-Link queries via the STEVAL-IDP004V1, the ORGPAL3 can access these primitives directly, encapsulate them as MCP-exposed tools, and seamlessly integrate them into intelligent, AI-driven workflows.

The acoustic analysis provided by the digital omnidirectional microphone IMP34DT05 is supported by ST's Acoustic dB SPL library. This middleware providing primitives for sound pressure level (SPL) calculations, enabling effective acoustic monitoring of machinery. Acoustic monitoring is increasingly recognized for its utility in predictive maintenance, where deviations in expected acoustic patterns often precede mechanical issues such as misalignment, friction, or bearing degradation. By continuously monitoring SPL and acoustic patterns, maintenance teams can proactively detect anomalies and address problems before they become critical. Despite this being available the `Predictive_Maintenance_IOL` demonstration firmware that we're using doesn't expose this. Only the *AcousticAnalysis* one. You can take this as an exercise and implement an MCP server targeting the acoustic analysis monitoring.

MCP Server

Moving on to the C# solution, we start an empty nanoFramework application project in Visual Studio and add a reference to the `nanoFramework.WebServer.Mcp` NuGet package.

The minimal code to get an MCP server running is as simple as this:

```
// Discover and register tools
McpToolRegistry.DiscoverTools(new Type[] { typeof(PredictiveMaintenanceMcp
Tools) });

// Start MCP server
using (var server = new WebServer(80, HttpProtocol.Http, new Type[] {
typeof(McpServerController) }))
{
    server.Start();
    Console.WriteLine("MCP server running on port 80");
    Thread.Sleep(Timeout.Infinite);
}
```

Note that we're exposing the server through regular HTTP port 80. It's perfectly alright, as this will be consumed by a tool/proxy sitting in the local network. If it was exposed to external access or more strict security policies, we could have instantiated the web server with HTTPS at port 443, setting the SSL protocol and passing a certificated for the server.

Defining Tools

As you would expect, we're following as much as possible the API from the official C# SDK for Model Context Protocol servers. To have a class method exposed as a tool, you decorate it with the `McpServerTool` attribute and add a name for the tool and a description to it. Tool methods can—optionally—accept one parameter, which can be of any type. If it's not a primitive type, it will be deserialized. Let's look at an initial version of the tools for our MCP server:

```
namespace PredictiveMaintenance
{
    public class PredictiveMaintenanceMcpTools
    {
        private readonly PmController _controller = new PmController();

        [McpServerTool("read_time_domain", "Read time-domain vibration data
        and RMS values.")]
        public TimeDomainResult ReadTimeDomain() =>
                                    _controller.GetTimeDomainData();

        [McpServerTool("read_frequency_domain", "Read frequency-domain FFT
        spectrum and subrange maxima.")]
        public FftResult ReadFrequencyDomain() =>
                              _controller.GetFftData();

        [McpServerTool("read_environment", "Get current temperature,
        humidity, and pressure data.")]
        public EnvironmentalData ReadEnvironment() =>
                                      _controller.GetEnvironment();

        [McpServerTool("read_acoustic", "Get current sound pressure level
        from onboard microphone.")]
```

```
        public AcousticData ReadAcoustic() =>
                                _controller.GetAcoustic();

        [McpServerTool("configure_pm", "Configure predictive maintenance,
        sensor, FFT, and accelerometer settings.")]
        public void Configure(PmConfiguration cfg)
        {
            _controller.ApplyConfiguration(cfg);
        }
    }
}
```

The PmController class will implement the methods to handle those calls relying on the primitives available in the ST firmware, which we can treat as an API. The following is a possible implementation:

```
public class PmController
{
    public TimeDomainResult GetTimeDomainData()
    {
        // Firmware primitives via IO-Link
        float speedRms = FirmwareApi.ReadSpeedRms();
        float accelPeak = FirmwareApi.ReadAccelPeak();
        return new TimeDomainResult
        {
            Timestamp = DateTime.UtcNow,
            SpeedRMS = speedRms,
            AccelerationPeak = accelPeak
        };
    }

    public FftResult GetFftData()
    {
        // BLOB or array via IO-Link
        double[] spectrum = FirmwareApi.ReadFftSpectrum();
        double maxWithinSubranges = FirmwareApi.ReadFftSubrangeMax();
        return new FftResult
```

```
    {
        Timestamp = DateTime.UtcNow,
        Spectrum = spectrum,
        SubrangeMax = maxWithinSubranges
    };
}

public EnvironmentalData GetEnvironment()
{
    return new EnvironmentalData
    {
        Timestamp = DateTime.UtcNow,
        TemperatureC = FirmwareApi.ReadTemperature(),
        Humidity = FirmwareApi.ReadHumidity(),
        PressurehPa = FirmwareApi.ReadPressure()
    };
}

public AcousticData GetAcoustic()
{
    return new AcousticData
    {
        Timestamp = DateTime.UtcNow,
        SoundPressureLevelDb = FirmwareApi.ReadSPL()
    };
}

public void ApplyConfiguration(PmConfiguration cfg)
{
    FirmwareApi.SetFftSize(cfg.MotionSp.FftSize);
    FirmwareApi.SetFftOverlapPercent(cfg.MotionSp.FftOverlapPercent);
    FirmwareApi.SetFftWindow(cfg.MotionSp.FftWindow.ToFirmware());
    FirmwareApi.SetTimeDomainType(cfg.MotionSp.TimeDomainType.
    ToFirmware());
    FirmwareApi.SetSubrangeCount(cfg.MotionSp.SubrangeCount);
    FirmwareApi.SetSpeedRmsTau(cfg.MotionSp.RmsTauMs);
```

```
        FirmwareApi.SetAccFullScale(cfg.Accelerometer.FullScaleG);
        FirmwareApi.SetAccHighPassDivider(cfg.Accelerometer.
        HighPassFilterDivider);
    }
}
```

The supporting classes for configuration can benefit from being decorated with the `Description` attribute. You can notice that nested classes are perfectly handled as the JSON deserialization can handle those nice and smoothly.

```
using System.ComponentModel;

public class PmConfiguration
{
    [Description("Configuration parameters for the onboard
    accelerometer.")]
    public AccelerometerConfig Accelerometer { get; set; }

    [Description("Signal processing and FFT parameters for vibration
    analysis.")]
    public MotionSpConfig MotionSp { get; set; }
}

public class AccelerometerConfig
{
    [Description("Accelerometer full-scale range in g (2, 4, 8, 16).")]
    public int FullScaleG { get; set; }

    [Description("Accelerometer high-pass filter divider setting.")]
    public int HighPassFilterDivider { get; set; }
}

public class MotionSpConfig
{
    [Description("FFT size (e.g., 256, 512, 1024, 2048).")]
    public int FftSize { get; set; }

    [Description("FFT overlap percentage (5 to 75%).")]
    public int FftOverlapPercent { get; set; }
```

```
    [Description("FFT window type.")]
    public FftWindowType FftWindow { get; set; }

    [Description("Time-domain type to return (Speed, Acceleration, or 
    Both).")]
    public TimeDomainType TimeDomainType { get; set; }

    [Description("Number of frequency subranges for max detection.")]
    public int SubrangeCount { get; set; }

    [Description("RMS integration time constant in ms.")]
    public int RmsTauMs { get; set; }
}

public enum FftWindowType
{
    Rectangular,
    Hanning,
    Hamming,
    FlatTop
}

public enum TimeDomainType
{
    SpeedRMSOnly,
    AccelRMSOnly,
    SpeedAndAccelRMS
}
```

The same goes for the data model classes that will be the payload for the acquisition readings.

```
public class TimeDomainResult
{
    [Description("Timestamp (UTC) of the reading.")]
    public DateTime Timestamp { get; set; }

    [Description("Root Mean Square of vibration speed.")]
    public float SpeedRMS { get; set; }
```

```
    [Description("Peak vibration acceleration.")]
    public float AccelerationPeak { get; set; }
}

public class FftResult
{
    [Description("Timestamp (UTC) of the reading.")]
    public DateTime Timestamp { get; set; }

    [Description("Frequency spectrum data array.")]
    public double[] Spectrum { get; set; }

    [Description("Maximum magnitude in each frequency subrange.")]
    public double[] SubrangeMax { get; set; }
}

public class EnvironmentalData
{
    [Description("Timestamp (UTC) of the reading.")]
    public DateTime Timestamp { get; set; }

    [Description("Ambient temperature in Celsius.")]
    public float TemperatureC { get; set; }

    [Description("Relative humidity percentage.")]
    public float Humidity { get; set; }

    [Description("Barometric pressure in hPa.")]
    public float PressurehPa { get; set; }
}

public class AcousticData
{
    [Description("Timestamp (UTC) of the reading.")]
    public DateTime Timestamp { get; set; }

    [Description("Sound pressure level in decibels.")]
    public float SoundPressureLevelDb { get; set; }
}
```

With the Description annotations applied across all components, our MCP server will expose detailed, self-describing schemas via JSON-RPC discovery, greatly enhancing usability for AI agents or external systems.

Defining Prompts

Prompt definition follows a similar pattern to tools. Also here, we're following the official C# SDK style. To have a class method exposed as a prompt, you decorate it with the McpServerPrompt attribute, add a name for the prompt, and add a description to it. Prompt methods can—optionally—accept string parameters. Each of those that you want to see listed in the prompt listing requires a McpPromptParameter attribute with the details of the parameter. They should match the order of the method parameters and the parameter name.

Regarding the parameter body, it's composed of an array of PromptMessage objects with the prompt text. The prompt text can contain replacement tokens that will be replaced by the parameters content when the prompt text is generated. Let's look at an initial version of the prompts for our predictive maintenance MCP server:

```
namespace PredictiveMaintenance
{
    public class PredictiveMaintenanceMcpPrompts
    {
        [McpServerPrompt(
            "diagnose_motor_bearing",
            "Evaluate motor bearing health using vibration RMS and FFT
            data, and recommend maintenance actions.")]
        public static PromptMessage[] DiagnoseMotorBearing()
        {
            return new PromptMessage[]
            {
                new PromptMessage(
                    "You are an expert diagnostic assistant. First call
                    ‘read_time_domain()’ " +
                    "and ‘read_frequency_domain()’. Then analyze SpeedRMS
                    using industry thresholds " +
```

```
                "and inspect FFT spectrum for 1× and 2× RPM peaks and
                high-frequency anomalies. " +
                "Return a structured JSON report with:\r\n{\r\n" +
                "  \"diagnosis\": \"normal|imbalance|misalignment|bearing
                Wear\",\r\n" +
                "  \"SpeedRMS\": <value>,\r\n" +
                "  \"PeakFrequencies\": [ ... ],\r\n" +
                "  \"RecommendedAction\": \"...\"\r\n}")
        };
    }

    [McpServerPrompt(
        "check_environment_and_acoustic",
        "Monitor environmental and acoustic conditions and alert if
        limits are exceeded.")]
    public static PromptMessage[] CheckEnvironmentAndAcoustic()
    {`
        return new PromptMessage[]
        {
            new PromptMessage(
                "Please call `read_environment() and `read_acoustic()`.
                Then check if " +
                "temperature > 40 °C, humidity > 70 %, or sound
                pressure levels > 85 dB. " +
                "Respond with JSON:\r\n{\r\n" +
                "  \"environmentStatus\": \"OK|Warning\",\r\n" +
                "  \"temperatureC\": <value>,\r\n" +
                "  \"humidity\": <value>,\r\n" +
                "  \"soundPressureLevelDb\": <value>,\r\n" +
                "  \"Alert\": \"true|false\",\r\n" +
                "  \"Recommendation\": \"...\"\r\n}")
        };
    }
  }
}
```

This pattern allows construction of dynamic prompts and also multistep workflows that help formalize complex workflows. Here's an example of such a prompt:

```
[McpServerPrompt("multi_step_motor_diagnostics", "Run full diagnostics:
vibration, environment, and MES logging workflow.")]
public static PromptMessage[] MultiStepMotorDiagnostics()
{
    return new[]
    {
        new PromptMessage("Step 1: Call `read_time_domain()` and capture
        SpeedRMS and AccelerationPeak.") ,
        new PromptMessage("Step 2: Call `read_frequency_domain()` and
        obtain Spectrum and SubrangeMax."){ Role = Role.Assistant },
        new PromptMessage(
    "Step 3: Call `read_environment()` and `read_acoustic()`, then analyze
    all collected data. " +
    "Format your output as a JSON object matching the structure:\r\n" +
            "{" +
            "  \"TimestampUtc\": \"<ISO-8601 timestamp>\"," +
            "  \"SpeedRMS\": <value>," +
            "  \"FftSubrangeMax\": [ ... ]" +
            "  \"TemperatureC\":<value>, " +
            "  \"AlarmActive\": <true|false>, " +
            "  \"WorkOrderId\": \"<optional-work-order>\", " +
            "  \"Diagnostic\": \"normal|imbalance|misalignment|bearingWe
               ar\"," +
            "  \"SuggestedAction\": \"...\"," +
            "  \"RecommendationId\": \"<LLM-generated message ID>\"" +
            "}"
        ){ Role = Role.Assistant },
        new PromptMessage("Step 4: If your diagnosis is critical or
        requires action, call `log_recommendation()` with the structured
        JSON report to notify MES."){ Role = Role.Assistant },
    };
}
```

Authentication

It is worth mentioning that authentication is available out of the box. In the WebServer configuration, considering that this is running on a local network and therefore trusted, there is no need to set this up. The supported options are basic authentication with a NetworkCredential (user and password) or API key authentication.

Let's see how simple it is to add this to the configuration. Suppose we want to set up an API key; we would have to pass it in the ApiKey property—before the server is started—like this:

```
using (var server = new WebServer(80, HttpProtocol.Http, new Type[] {
typeof(McpServerController) }))
{
    // Set API key
    server.ApiKey = "my-secret-key-1234abcd778899";

    server.Start();
    Console.WriteLine("MCP server running on port 80");
    Thread.Sleep(Timeout.Infinite);
}
```

The call from a client will have to include the expected authentication, in this case, an HTTP header named *ApiKey*. For the previous, a CURL command would look like this:

```
curl -X POST [URL] \
-H "ApiKey: my-secret-key-1234abcd778899" \
-H "Content-Type: application/json" \
-d '{"jsonrpc":"2.0","method":"tools/list","id":1}'
```

Custom Server Information

You can add details about the MCP server for asset management and provide extra details to AI agents. Again, this is done by setting properties in the McpServerController. At a convenient location in the code and before the server is started, add the following:

```
// server information
McpServerController.ServerName = "ACME-CNC3-M01 Predictive Maintenance
Gateway";
McpServerController.ServerVersion = "1.1.0";

// information and instructions for AI agents
McpServerController.Instructions =
  "This MCP endpoint exposes vibration, acoustic, " +
  "and environmental diagnostics tools for the STEVAL-BFA001V2B sensor via
IO-Link and RS-485. " +
  "Use 'read_time_domain', 'read_frequency_domain', 'read_environment', " +
  "'read_acoustic', and 'configure_pm' to interact." +
  "Please send requests one at a time and wait for responses.";
```

This context helps LLMs understand the purpose and capabilities of the connection, enabling them to choose the right tools for diagnostics, threshold tuning, or data logging tasks.

Note The last sentence on the instructions is there on purpose to let the LLM know that it shouldn't send cascading requests to this server. The reason is that the operations we're providing require execution time, and the AI agent is usually expecting immediate replies.

This is how clients see it when listing the tools:

```
{
  "server": "nanoFramework Predictive Maintenance Gateway",
  "instructions": "This MCP endpoint exposes vibration, acoustic, ...",
  "tools": [
    { "name": "read_time_domain", ... },
    ...
  ]
}
```

Integrating with MES

A key advantage of MCP-enabled gateways like the one we're building is their ability to bridge local intelligence with enterprise systems—specifically MESs. This "intelligent edge-to-enterprise" integration allows real-time information from sensor nodes to flow into high-level production systems, enabling immediate action, traceability, and decision-making.

Why should we integrate with MES? An MES acts as the factory's digital nerve center: logging sensor events, annotating work orders, triggering quality control, and orchestrating workflows. When our gateway detects anomalies—like vibration peaks or environmental drifts—it can generate structured JSON payloads and push them to MES endpoints (e.g., `/mes/log`), where they are validated, enriched, and acted upon in real time. This integration creates a closed-loop system: edge detection leads to MES-triggered actions such as work orders, alerts, maintenance requests, or process adjustments.

Each MES will have its own interface and ceremony. For the purpose of our example, we'll assume that it is exposed as an HTTP with API key authentication, accepting JSON payloads. A simplistic `MesLogger` class could be implemented such as this:

```
public class MesLogger
{
    private static readonly HttpClient _httpClient = new HttpClient();

    public MesLogger(string baseUrl, string apiKey = null)
    {
        _httpClient.BaseAddress = new Uri(baseUrl);

        if (!string.IsNullOrEmpty(apiKey))
        {
            _httpClient.DefaultRequestHeaders.Add("Authorization", $"Bearer
            {apiKey}");
        }
    }

    public bool LogMaintenanceEvent(MaintenanceLog log)
    {
        // Serialize object to JSON string
        string json = JsonConvert.SerializeObject(log);
```

```
        using var content = new StringContent(json, Encoding.UTF8,
        "application/json");

        try
        {
            HttpResponseMessage response = _httpClient.Post("/mes/log",
                 content);

            if (!response.IsSuccessStatusCode)
            {
                Console.WriteLine($"MES log failed: {response.
                StatusCode}");
                return false;
            }
        }
        catch (Exception ex)
        {
            Console.WriteLine($"MES log exception: {ex.Message}");
            return false;
        }

        return true;
    }
}
```

At some point during application boot the `MesLogger` would be initialized with this call:

```
var logger = new MesLogger("https://mes.company.com", "my-secret-api-key");
```

And, when the time comes, a maintenance log event is sent to the MES:

```
var success = logger.LogMaintenanceEvent(new MaintenanceLog {
    DeviceId = "ACME-CNC3-M01",
    TimestampUtc = DateTime.UtcNow.ToString("o"),
    SpeedRMS = 1.35f,
    FftSubrangeMax = new double[]{0.45, 0.80, 0.55},
    TemperatureC = 24.6f,
```

```
    AlarmActive = true,
    WorkOrderId = "WO-1234",
    Diagnostic = "...",
    SuggestedAction = "...",
    RecommendationId = " b1a4fc8a-6e4a-4e99-9e50-4d2a2b123abc "
});
```

Sample Workflow

With all the building blocks in place, let's go through what would look like an AI-powered vibration diagnostics interaction.

At some point during factory IT startup procedure, the LLM establishes a connection with our MCP server by sending a POST request:

```
POST /mcp
{
    "jsonrpc": "2.0",
    "method": "initialize",
    "params": {
        "protocolVersion": "2025-03-26",
        "capabilities": {},
        "clientInfo": {
            "name": "Super Smart Factory AI Assistant",
            "version": "1.0.0"
        }
    },
    "id": 1
}
```

Our MCP server replies with the following:

```
{
    "jsonrpc": "2.0",
    "id": 1,
```

```
    "result": {
        "protocolVersion": "2025-03-26",
        "capabilities": {
            "tools": {}
        },
        "serverInfo": {
            "name": "ACME-CNC3-M01 Predictive Maintenance Gateway",
            "version": "1.1.0"
        },
        "instructions": " This MCP endpoint exposes vibration,
        acoustic, ..."
    }
}
```

The next step is the agent discovering the available tools. It sends this request:

```
POST /mcp
{
    "jsonrpc": "2.0",
    "method": "tools/list",
    "id": 2
}
```

Our server responds with a list of the tools along with the descriptions provided. These are the relevant parts of it for illustration purposes:

```
{
  "jsonrpc": "2.0",
  "id": 1,
  "result": {
    "server": "ACME-CNC3-M01 Predictive Maintenance Gateway",
    "instructions": "This MCP endpoint exposes vibration...",
    "tools": [
      {
        "name": "read_time_domain",
        "description": "Read time-domain vibration data and RMS values.",
        "inputSchema": { "type": "object", "properties": {} }
```

```
    },
    {
      "name": "read_frequency_domain",
      ...
    },
    {
      ...
    },
    {
      ...
    },
    {
      "name": "configure_pm",
      "description": "Configure predictive maintenance, sensor, FFT, and
      accelerometer settings.",
      "inputSchema": {
        "type": "object",
        "properties": {
          "Accelerometer": {
            "type": "object",
            "properties": {
              "FullScaleG": { "type": "integer", "description":
              "Accelerometer full-scale range in g (2,4,8,16)." },
              "HighPassFilterDivider": { "type": "integer",
              "description": "Accelerometer high-pass filter divider
              setting." }
            },
            "required": [ "FullScaleG", "HighPassFilterDivider" ]
          },
          "MotionSp": {
            "type": "object",
            "properties": {
              "FftSize": { "type": "integer", "description": "FFT size
              (256,512,1024,2048)." },
```

```
                "FftOverlapPercent": { "type": "integer", "description":
                "FFT overlap percentage (5-75)." },
                "FftWindow": { "type": "string", "description": "FFT window
                type (Rectangular, Hanning, Hamming, FlatTop)." },
                "TimeDomainType": { "type": "string", "description": "Time-
                domain type (SpeedRMSOnly, AccelRMSOnly,
                SpeedAndAccelRMS)." },
                "SubrangeCount": { "type": "integer", "description":
                "Number of frequency subranges." },
                "RmsTauMs": { "type": "integer", "description": "RMS
                integration time constant (ms)." }
              },
              "required": [ "FftSize", "FftOverlapPercent", "FftWindow",
              "TimeDomainType", "SubrangeCount", "RmsTauMs" ]
            }
          },
          "required": [ "Accelerometer", "MotionSp" ]
        }
      }
    ]
  }
}
```

Ideally the client would try to discover if there are any prompts available from the MCP server with this request:

```
POST /mcp
{
    "jsonrpc": "2.0",
    "method": "prompts/list",
    "id": 3
}
```

The server will respond with a list of the prompts, if available, along with the descriptions provided and any parameters that are accepted. Again, the complete listing would be rather long, so here are the important parts:

```
{
  "jsonrpc": "2.0",
  "id": 3,
  "result": {
    "prompts": [
      {
        "name": "diagnose_motor_bearing",
        "description": "Evaluate motor bearing health using vibration RMS
        and FFT data, and recommend maintenance actions.",
        "arguments": []
      },
      {
                ...
      },
      {
        "name": "dynamic_diagnose_with_threshold",
        "description": "Assess motor bearing health with a user-defined RMS
        threshold.",
        "arguments": [
          {
            "name": "rmsThreshold",
            "description": "Speed RMS (mm/s) value to consider as vibration
            fault threshold.",
            "required": true,
            "type": "number"
          }
        ]
      },
      {
                ...
      }
    ]
  }
}
```

This completes the ceremony that's required for the LLM to connect and understand what our MCP server is and what it has to offer.

At some point during the day, the LLM is prompted to start the workflow described in `diagnose_motor_bearing`. It starts by fetching this prompt:


```
{
  "jsonrpc": "2.0",
  "id": 2,
  "method": "prompts/get",
  "params": {
    "name": "multi_step_motor_diagnostics",
    "arguments": {}
  }
}
```


The MCP server replies with this:


```
{
  "jsonrpc": "2.0",
  "id": 2,
  "result": {
    "description": "Run full diagnostics: vibration, environment, and MES
    logging workflow.",
    "messages": [
      ...
    ]
  }
}
```


The LLM now has a clear, multistep workflow, which it will start to execute, starting with a call to `read_time_domain`:


```
{
   "jsonrpc":"2.0",
    "id":3,
    "method":"tools/call",
    "params":{
        "name":"read_time_domain",
```

```
        "arguments":{}
    }
}
```

The LLM gets time-domain vibration data from the server.

```
{
  "jsonrpc":"2.0","id":3,"result":{
    "Timestamp":"2025-07-23T12:00:00Z",
    "SpeedRMS":1.5,
    "AccelerationPeak":15.2
  }
}
```

It moves on to call the `read_frequency_domain` (not shown) and receive the reply:

```
{
  "jsonrpc":"2.0","id":4,"result":{
    "Timestamp":"2025-07-23T12:00:05Z",
    "Spectrum":[0.1,0.5,0.3,0.05, ...],
    "SubrangeMax":[0.5,0.3,0.2]
  }
}
```

The, it proceeds with calls to environment and acoustic (not shown) and receives the respective data.

```
{
  "jsonrpc":"2.0","id":5,"result":{
    "Timestamp":"2025-07-23T12:00:07Z",
    "TemperatureC":45.2,
    "Humidity":72.0,
    "PressurehPa":1012.5
  }
}
```

and:

```
{
  "jsonrpc":"2.0","id":6,"result":{
    "Timestamp":"2025-07-23T12:00:10Z",
    "SoundPressureLevelDb":87.0
  }
}
```

The data indicates high temperature, humidity, and noise—strong context for the LLM.

Armed with numeric data from the readings acquired, the LLM, using the prompt instructions, reasons something similar to this:

- SpeedRMS = 1.5 mm/s—slightly above baseline but not alarming.
- FFT shows a 1× RPM peak of 0.5—suggests imbalance.
- Temperature 45°C > 40°C threshold, Humidity 72% > 70%, SPL 87dB > 85dB—environmental stress.
- Diagnosis: combination of imbalance and environmental strain.
- Critical flag: true (due to multiple anomalies).
- WorkOrderId: "WO-5678" (generated from a request to another tool that manages the work orders)
- SuggestedAction: "Plan bearing rebalancing and environmental control."
- RecommendationId: "rec-20250723-1200" (generated from the client tool to correlate with the internal logs)

The last step from the prompt instructs the LLM to call `log_recommendation` with the `MaintenanceRecommendation` JSON structure:

```
{
    "jsonrpc":"2.0",
    "id":7,
    "method":"tools/call",
    "params":{
        "name":"log_recommendation",
```

```
        "arguments":{
            "TimestampUtc":"2025-07-23T12:00:10Z",
            "SpeedRMS":1.5,
            "FftSubrangeMax":[0.5,0.3,0.2],
            "TemperatureC":45.2,
            "AlarmActive":true,
            "WorkOrderId":"WO-5678",
            "Diagnostic":"imbalance_envStress",
            "SuggestedAction":"Plan bearing rebalancing and environmental
            control.",
            "RecommendationId":"f683b6d4-6a7a-462e-b19a-3ed6c2267e42"
        }
    }
}
```


This will cause the MES to receive the maintenance recommendation posted by the MCP server after filling in the details about the machine. The implementation of the MCP tool to handle this was not part of the class listed before, so let's add it for completeness:

```
[McpServerTool("log_recommendation", "Submit a maintenance recommendation
to the MES system.")]
public bool LogRecommendation(MaintenanceRecommendation recommendation)
{
    // This method accepts the recommendation object from an LLM or client
    // and calls the MES logger
    return _mesLogger.LogMaintenanceEvent(new MaintenanceLog
        {
            DeviceId = "ACME-CNC3-M01",
            TimestampUtc = recommendation.TimestampUtc.ToString("o"),
            SpeedRMS = recommendation.SpeedRMS,
            FftSubrangeMax = recommendation.FftSubrangeMax,
            TemperatureC = recommendation.TemperatureC,
            AlarmActive = recommendation.AlarmActive,
            WorkOrderId = recommendation.WorkOrderId,
            Diagnostic = recommendation.Diagnostic,
            SuggestedAction = recommendation.SuggestedAction,
```

```
            // Add LLM message ID for traceability
            RecommendationId = recommendation.RecommendationId
        });
}
```

And that's it! This long workflow step-by-step encapsulates a full edge-to-enterprise diagnostic cycle, from sensor insights to maintenance workflow orchestration. Figure 10-5 summarizes the complete flow.

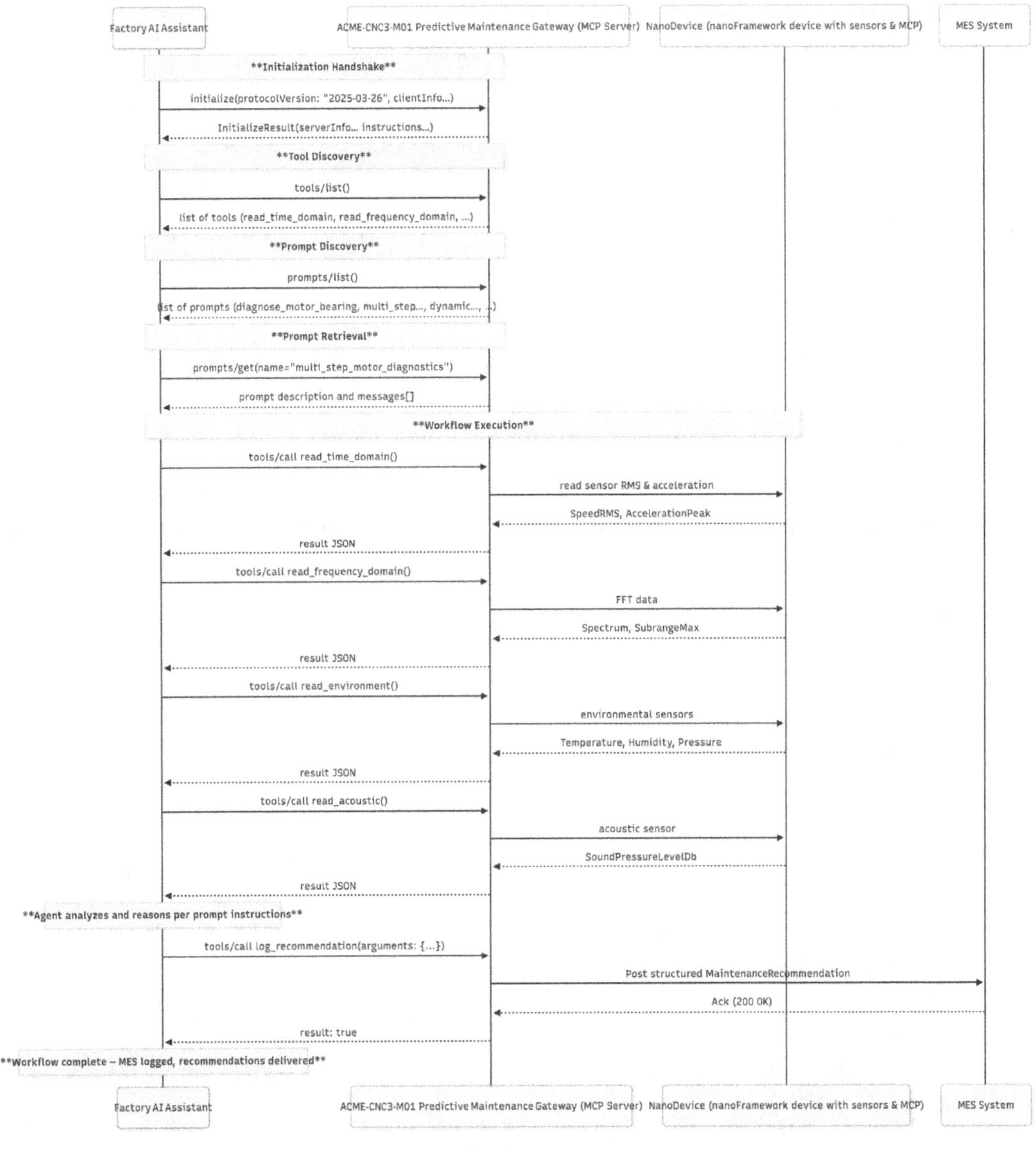

***Figure 10-5.** End-to-end overview of the predictive maintenance workflow*

Summary

This chapter guided you through designing a cutting-edge embedded system: from capturing vibration, acoustic, and environmental data on the STEVAL-BFA001V2B to exposing those sensor capabilities through a nanoFramework MCP server, orchestrating smart LLM-driven diagnostics, and seamlessly logging to an MES. What you're building isn't just functional—it's at the forefront of a powerful wave in industrial IoT.

MCP is redefining how things connect, and it's being fully adopted by major AI players. Unlike traditional IoT that stops at raw data exchange, MCP-based systems enable devices to expose full services—analysis tools, state evaluation, and action triggers—to LLM-driven orchestration. This depth of connectivity marks a true shift: devices can now be orchestrated intelligently, not just pinged for status.

We're only at the beginning of this revolution. While MCP is still novel and early-stage, industrial proof-of-concepts using MCP are emerging. The integration of edge device intelligence and enterprise MES workflows—automatic alerts, structured maintenance logs, traceable, standards-based diagnostics—points to a future-ready model of full automation.

Looking ahead, imagine factories where devices don't just connect. They collaborate with LLM agents, adjust workflows, generate maintenance orders, and feed performance insights into analytics pipelines. That vision is no longer aspirational—it's becoming possible.

This is adding a new I to IoT: we can now have an *Intelligent* Internet of Things. And it's more than just innovation. It's the dawn of orchestrated, intelligent IoT ecosystems. The potential to revolutionize production, accelerate diagnostics, and drive predictive maintenance at scale is here—and it's only getting started.

Additional Resources

You can learn more at the following locations:

MCP official website: `https://modelcontextprotocol.io/introduction`

STEVAL-BFA001V2B sensor: `https://www.st.com/en/evaluation-tools/steval-bfa001v2b.html`

STEVAL-IDP004V2 IO-Link master: `https://www.st.com/en/evaluation-tools/steval-idp004v2.html`

Official C# SDK for MCP: `https://github.com/modelcontextprotocol/csharp-sdk`

Index

J. Simões, *Embedded Systems with .NET nanoFramework*, https://doi.org/10.1007/979-8-8688-2096-0

D

E

F

G

H

I, J, K

L

M

N

O

P

Q

R

S

T

U

V

W, X, Y, Z

GPSR Compliance
The European Union's (EU) General Product Safety Regulation (GPSR) is a set of rules that requires consumer products to be safe and our obligations to ensure this.

If you have any concerns about our products, you can contact us on

ProductSafety@springernature.com

In case Publisher is established outside the EU, the EU authorized representative is:

Springer Nature Customer Service Center GmbH
Europaplatz 3
69115 Heidelberg, Germany

www.ingramcontent.com/pod-product-compliance
Lightning Source LLC
LaVergne TN
LVHW060133080526
838201LV00118B/1731

9798868820953